FRAGILE KINSHIPS

FRAGILE KINSHIPS

Child Welfare and Well-Being in Japan

Kathryn E. Goldfarb

CORNELL UNIVERSITY PRESS   ITHACA AND LONDON

First published 2024 by Cornell University Press

Library of Congress Cataloging-in-Publication Data

Names: Goldfarb, Kathryn E., 1982– author.
Title: Fragile kinships : child welfare and well-being in Japan / Kathryn
  E. Goldfarb.
Description: Ithaca : Cornell University Press, 2024. | Includes
  bibliographical references and index.
Identifiers: LCCN 2024011509 (print) | LCCN 2024011510 (ebook) | ISBN
  9781501778230 (hardcover) | ISBN 9781501778247 (paperback) | ISBN
  9781501778254 (epub) | ISBN 9781501778261 (pdf)
Subjects: LCSH: Child welfare—Japan. | Belonging (Social psychology) in
  children—Japan. | Kinship—Social aspects—Japan.
Classification: LCC HV1312 .G653 2024 (print) | LCC HV1312 (ebook) | DDC
  362.70952—dc23/eng/20240717
LC record available at https://lccn.loc.gov/2024011509
LC ebook record available at https://lccn.loc.gov/2024011510

For Sloan and Evyn

Contents

People and Places

ABE Saori: Adoptive mother concerned with social stigma

AKIYAMA Noriko: Foster daughter of Hosokawa Rie and Masa

Chestnut House: Child welfare institution in the Tokyo metropolitan area

CHIBA Naoki: Tanpopo group member

Edward: Man raised in institutional care

FUJISAKI Hiroko and *Eiji*: Foster parents of Ōta Nozomi

FUKUSHIMA Maiko and *Noriaki*: Siblings in Chestnut House

FUNABASHI Tomomi: Foster mother concerned with social stigma

HAMABATA Toshiko: Adoptive mother concerned with social stigma

HANASHIMA Shin'ichi: Foster parent and child welfare activist raised in institutional care

HARA Kazuko: Foster mother concerned with social stigma

HENNESSY Sumiko (real name): Japanese social worker and expert in attachment disorder, based in the United States

HIRATA Yumi: Experienced foster mother who understood family as a place to return

HOSOKAWA Rie and *Masa*: Foster parents of Akiyama Noriko

ICHIKAWA Reiko: Staff member at a large child welfare institution

IIDA Momoko: Director of Tanpopo

INOUE Yusuke: Child in Chestnut House

ISHIDA Masao: Director of a child welfare institution northeast of the Tokyo area

ISHIZAKA Kumiko and *Kazuo*: Tetsu's parents

ISHIZAKA Tetsu: Former staff member of Chestnut House

KITAHARA Shinobu: First director of Chestnut House

KOJIMA Sachiko: Foster mother concerned with her son's developmental disability

MAEDA Eri: Child in Chestnut House

MATSUMOTO Taichi: Tanpopo group member

MIYAZAKI Yūko: Staff member of Chestnut House

MURAKAMI Takako and *Kunio*: Adoptive parents who understood their children to be connected to them by *en*

NAGAI Miho: Staff member of Chestnut House

NAKAI Mitsuo: Careworker in a group home Northeast of Tokyo

NAKAYAMA Risa: Child in Chestnut House

ŌTA Nozomi: Daughter of foster parents Fujisaki Hiroko and Eiji

OTSUKI Reina and *Akio*: Siblings who grew up in a child welfare institution

OZAWA Noboru: Adoptive father who spoke about the term *violence of blood ties*

SAITO Masahiro: Child in Chestnut House

SAKAI Marina: Staff member of Chestnut House

SHIRAI Chiaki (real name): Japanese family sociologist

TAKADA Hitoshi: Staff member of Chestnut House

TAKAHASHI Sora and *Kenji*: Siblings who grew up in a child welfare institution

TAKANO Saki: Woman pursuing infertility treatment

TANAKA Aoki: Child in Chestnut House

Tanpopo: Tokyo self-support group for alumni of Japanese child welfare institutions

TOKUNAGA Shōko (real name): Life Story Work researcher

TSUZAKI Tetsuo (real name): Retired professor of social welfare and child welfare reform activist; adviser to Kitahara Shinobu for Chestnut House

Wa no Kai (real name): Adoption organization in Japan

YAMANTA Tokuji (real name): Adoption practitioner in Japan

Glossary of Japanese Terms

atotsugi (後継ぎ): Family successor

butsudan (仏壇): Buddhist household altar

en (縁): A divine or ineffable tie or connection

furusato (故郷): Hometown; original home

futsū yōshiengumi (普通養子縁組): Regular adoption in which some legal ties to family of origin remain

ganbaru (頑張る): To struggle on

ichiji hogosho (一時保護所): Temporary care facility

ie (家): Extended Japanese family

jidō sōdanjyo (児童相談所): Child guidance center (CGC), *jisō* for short

jidō yōgo shisetsu (児童養護施設): Child welfare institution for children between the ages of two and eighteen

jiko sekinin (自己責任): Self-responsibility

kakeizu (家系図): Genealogy

kateiteki (家庭的): Household-like

kazoku (家族): Family

ketsuen (血縁): Blood ties

kizuna (絆): A connection, tie, or bond

koseki (戸籍): Japanese family register

mukoyōshi (婿養子): adoption of the husband of a daughter ("son-in-law adoption"), who will take headship of a family line

nihonjinron (日本人論): Discourses of Japaneseness

nyūjiin (乳児院): Child welfare institution for babies

obon (お盆): Celebration for Japanese ancestral spirits; Festival of the Dead

sato oya (里親): Foster parent

shakai fukushi hōjin (社会福祉法人): Social welfare corporation

shakaiteki yōgo (社会的養護): Social care

shinseki (親戚): Kin

tanin (他人): Stranger

tōjisha (当事者): A person directly concerned with a (minority) category

tokubetsu yōshiengumi (特別養子縁組): Special adoption in which legal ties to family of origin are cut

Acknowledgments

In Japanese, I usually write my name in katakana, the syllabary for foreign names and words: ケイト (*kei-to*), a Japanese pronunciation of Kate. But one day, two of my friends and research contacts bequeathed me names in kanji, characters of Chinese origin in which Japanese names are generally written: 恵富, which means "blessed with fortune," and 恵糸, which one might translate as "blessed with connections." (The character 糸 means thread, but it is part of the character for *en* (縁): an ineffable relationship, bond, affinity, or connection.) Connections and human relationships are a large part of one's fortune. I am, indeed, immensely fortunate in my connections.

Gratitude, first, to the many people who shared their lives and experiences with me in Japan. I am thankful for the en of these sustained connections, in many cases over a decade and a half old. This project would not have been possible without the help and continuous engagement of Tsuzaki Tetsuo, who introduced me to the director and staff of the child welfare institution, Chestnut House. The institution's director, whom I call Kitahara Shinobu, passed away shortly after my doctoral fieldwork was completed. I hope my writing does some justice to his energy and generosity of spirit. I thank the child welfare institution's staff for first accepting me as a researcher and in many cases becoming my friends. I will always remember and value the time I spent with the children of Chestnut House. The foster and adoptive families who contributed to my research influenced me profoundly, and I am grateful for their friendship, and for the resources and documents they shared with me. My friends affiliated with two self-support groups for alumni of state care (the Tokyo group I call Tanpopo, and another group in the Kansai region) continue to inspire my efforts as a researcher.

Roger Goodman's scholarship and guidance led me to attend to child welfare concerns in the first place. His generosity enabled me to conduct this research. Conversations with Margaret Lock were instrumental in my preparations for fieldwork, and readers familiar with her work will perceive in this book her profound influence. Junko Kitanaka continues to be an invaluable mentor and friend, pushing my thinking and my courage, sharing her compassion, wisdom, and extensive academic network. I am grateful for the guidance and friendship of Tsuge Azumi, who welcomed me into her medical anthropology seminar and her research group meetings at Meiji Gakuin University. I have benefitted greatly from my collaborations with and assistance from my friend Shirai Chiaki. At Waseda University, where I was affiliated as a Fulbright Scholar, Glenda Roberts welcomed me into her graduate seminar, and I thank her and the other *zemi* members for their thoughtful engagements with my research. Many scholars, practitioners, and activists within the world of child welfare have been generous with their introductions, knowledge, and research materials. In Japan, I thank the foster parents and scholars affiliated with Anne Funds and the Group for Considering Human Rights in Child Welfare Institutions. I also thank in particular Nagano Saki, Nobe Yōko, Murata Kazuki, Tokunaga Shōko, Takanabe Ryūichi, Watanabe Mamoru, Emmanuel Sherwin, Shoji Junichi, Nakamura Midori, Mike Rivera King, Mori Kazuko, Seamus Jennings, Sugiyama Chiharu, Stephen Ucembe, Katsuhide Miyake, Kimu Kayuri, Yokoyama Yūko, Morimoto Shimako, Fujikawa Fumiko, Sakakibara Akemi, Sasaki Masako, Hennessy Sumiko, Terry Levy, Michael Orlans, Kato Shōko, and Irwin Elman. I continue to learn so much from Miho Awazu, Timothy Bell, Chris Chapman and my other fellow International Foster Care Alliance US team board members, and the Japanese team board and youth members.

My research was made possible by the excellent language instruction I received at the University of Chicago, Middlebury's Japanese Language School, Hokkaido International Foundation (HIF), and the Inter-University Center for Japanese Language Studies in Yokohama (IUC). Particular thanks to Noto Hiroshi at the University of Chicago and to Matsumoto Takashi at IUC, whose interest in the early stages of my research was immensely encouraging and helpful. During my time at HIF, Ebina Takeshi and Sachiko, my host parents, assisted me both in language study and in conducting pre-field research.

I am grateful for research fellowships from Fulbright IIE and the Wenner-Gren Foundation and grants from the University of Chicago's Social Science Division and the University of Chicago's Center for East Asian Studies. An International Chapter P.E.O. Sisterhood fellowship and a University of Chicago Toyota Dissertation Fellowship supported the writing of my dissertation. A Post-doctoral Award for Professional Development from Harvard University and the Arts Research Board at McMaster University, the Center to Advance Research in the Social Sciences at the University of Colorado Boulder, and the Northeast Asia Council and Japan-U.S. Friendship Commission have generously supported my more recent research, in addition to faculty research funding at McMaster University and the University of Colorado Boulder.

This book project has had a very long life in manuscript form. I have benefited immensely from the engagement of panelists, discussants, and participants at annual meetings of the Association for Asian Studies, the American Anthropological Association, the Society for Cultural Anthropology, and the Asian Studies Conference Japan, and at the International Foster Care Organization's biennial conference. I am grateful for the engagement of the audiences and participants at many workshops over the years, at the University of Chicago, Brunel University, University of Illinois Urbana-Champaign, University of California Santa Barbara, the City University of New York Graduate Center, the Chinese University of Hong Kong, University of Pittsburgh, Fukuoka University, Indiana University, University of Michigan, and University of Colorado Boulder. Organizers and audience members of colloquium presentations have offered me fantastic food for thought at Harvard University, Tokyo University, University of Toronto, Japan Women's University, Hokkaido University, University of Missouri-St. Louis, Johns Hopkins University, Oxford Brookes University, University of Michigan, Oberlin College, and, over many years, during multiple formative opportunities at Keio University.

Kudō Akiyo has been meticulously transcribing interviews for me for over a decade (!), and I thank her for her friendship and care in this work. I am grateful for research assistance from Omori Hisako, Kelly Zepelin, Matt Zepelin, and Catherine Otachime. Sasha Buckser has beautifully rendered my photographs as illustrations for this book (@sbuckser.illustrations on Instagram) and prepared my field note images for publication. At Cornell University Press, I so appreciate Jim Lance's steadfast support.

The network of people who sustain me in academia is extensive. Sloan Speck is uniquely capable of asking the best questions and offering alternative perspectives on conceptual problems. This ethnography is inextricably shaped by my graduate school writing group: Alex Blanchette, Tatiana Chudakova, Elayne Oliphant, and Carly Schuster. Many others have their fingerprints on this book: Shunsuke Nozawa, Em Cook, Junko Kitanaka, Ender Ricart, Chika Watanabe, Kate McHarry, Joe Hankins, Malavika Reddy, Aaron Seaman, Nick Harkness, Eli Nova Rose, Isono Maho, Nana Okura Gagne, Isaac Gagne, Julia Kowalski, Gabe Tusinski, Rochelle Frounfelker, Andrea Murray, Laura Miller, Anne Aronsson, Gabi Koch, Yulia Frumer, Kristin Roebuck, Hilary Holbrow, Mike Rivera King, Dan White, Elizabeth Fein, Christine El Ouardani, Eric Hirsch, Omori Hisako, Kathryn Tanaka, Hiroko Kumaki, Charlie McClean, Sandra Bamford, Jason Danely, Amy Borovoy, Sabine Frühstück, Hisa Kuriyama, Allison Alexy, Roger Goodman, Dominique Béhague, Mara Buchbinder, Anne Allison, and Jennifer Robertson.

I have had many excellent academic homes, beginning at Rice University with the mentorship of Jim Faubion and Nia Georges. In my graduate studies at the University of Chicago, the members of my dissertation committee—Judy Farquhar, Sue Gal, Danilyn Rutherford, and Michael Fisch—profoundly informed my thinking. I am thankful for conversations with Julie Chu, Kaushik Sunder-Rajan, Joe Masco, Michael Silverstein, Susan Burns, Tomomi Yamaguchi, Jim Ketelaar, Norma Field, and Gina Samuels. Nancy Abelmann and David Plath shared with me the wisdom and generosity for which both remain famous. During my postdoctoral fellowship at Harvard University's Program on U.S.-Japan Relations,

Shin Fujihira, Susan Pharr, Ezra Vogel, Yumi Shimabukuro and my other cohort members, and colleagues in Harvard's Department of Anthropology offered a supportive interdisciplinary environment. In my first faculty position at McMaster University, I was blessed with a wonderful collegial community. Ellen Badone, Andrew Gilbert, Ann Herring, Jasper, Steph Mayell, Tina Moffat, Tracy Prowse, Petra Rethmann, Andy Roddick, Mark Rowe, Daina Stanley, and Meredith Vanstone are among those who made my two years at Mac a pleasure. My colleagues and students at the University of Colorado Boulder have read so many pieces of this book, in some cases many times, and their intellectual influence and friendship cannot be properly accounted. Bert Covert is one in a billion. Carla Jones, Carole McGranahan, Donna Goldstein, Alison Cool, Jen Shannon, Sam Fladd, Kaifa Roland—my friends and companions in anthro-sisterhood—have shaped me as a scholar and a teacher, as have the students I have the pleasure of continuing to learn from and with. Thank you particularly to Kelly Zepelin, Kevin Darcy, Arielle Milkman, Clara Lee, Lucas Rozell, Conor Lanning, Lisa Rhodes, Bailey Duhé, Paige Edmiston, Dawa Lokyitsang, Ayden Parish, Anna Wynfield, Patrick McKenzie, Jessica Misiorek, and all the faculty and student participants in Ethnography in Progress, with special thanks for Dennis McGilvray's steady interest and insights. Audrey Gaudel is both collaborator and heart sister. Sungyun Lim, Marcia Yonemoto, and Scott Skinner-Thompson offer valuable friendship and intellectual community. The structure underlying these networks is held up and cultivated by Diana Wilson, Danielle Rocheleau Salaz, Liza Williams, Alison Davidson, and Renee Kuban. Finally, thanks to the Mansfield Foundation and my incredible colleagues within the U.S.-Japan Network for the Future.

When asked how I became interested in doing research in Japan, I sometimes say, "Yōko Takahashi's *yakisoba*," an answer that, while perhaps incomplete, is not untrue. I thank Yōko and her family. I am grateful for the sustenance of friends so dear they defy categorization: Jessica Kaminsky, Shirin Hakimzadeh, and John Glassmire. For life things in Chicago, Marian Kinney Broderick, Grace Broderick, and Keom Granger; in Hamilton, Anna Dalton Muzzin; in Boulder, Michael Scholl and Linda Asbury. I wish my grandma Barbara Kaufman could hold this book in her hands; she has been so central a part of this journey. My parents, Cyndi and Ron Goldfarb, have read probably everything I've written, and my work is better for it. I am grateful for my sister, Becca Goldfarb Landin, and Kevin, Jacob, and Brian Landin; my second momma, Cindy Alexander; Larry and Stacey Speck; my grandpa Hal Kaufman; my grandma Dorothy and grandpa Harry Goldfarb; Harrison Speck, Amanda Walker, and Elliott and Collin Speck; and the love of my extended family. I am thankful for Harper and Valentine cats, our nonhuman kin who have chosen to love us back. At the heart of it all are Sloan and Evyn Speck. Thank you, Sloan, and thank you, Evyn, for being my people.

Note on Transliteration

All personal and institutional names are pseudonyms unless otherwise noted. Japanese personal names are listed surname first, except in the case of scholars who publish in English. I refer to individuals with either family names or given names based on how I addressed them in interaction, and I include honorific suffixes (-san, -chan, -kun) only in direct quotes. Japanese terms are romanized using the *Monumenta Nipponica* style guide. Macrons have not been used in common geographical names like Tokyo or Osaka. Japanese words are italicized in their first occurrences and not subsequently, unless these words are used as analytical concepts.

FRAGILE KINSHIPS

PRODUCING PEOPLE WHO HAVE NO ONE

Almost all the children at Chestnut House nominally had kin, albeit kin who were unable to care for them. Chestnut House was a child welfare institution (a children's home or orphanage) in a suburban neighborhood outside of Tokyo, Japan. Institutions, rather than family-based foster care, remain the primary child welfare placements for Japanese children who, for some reason or another, cannot be cared for by their parents.[1]

There were only two children at Chestnut House whose parents were both entirely absent, staff member Nagai Miho told me. We were sitting in the Chestnut House library, cups of chilled barley tea and my audio recorder in front of us. At the time, I had been connected to Chestnut House as a researcher for six years, and I knew one of these children well: Maeda Eri was one of the first children to move into the newly constructed institution in 2009, when she was in second grade. She had been removed from the care of her grandmother, who was rapidly declining from Alzheimer's. Eri had been seriously neglected, and her grandmother was emotionally abusive. Eri had told a staff member that her grandmother had told her that when she was a baby, her parents had stopped needing her, so they tossed her into a garbage bin—an injurious chain of secondhand half knowledge to which the staff member had felt unable to respond.

It was actually due to Eri that I had been allowed to focus my research in the house where she lived. Chestnut House was divided into five houses of six children and three staff members each. The head caregiver in Eri's house felt that

1

any social connections for Eri were better than none—hence her welcoming me, a white American anthropologist. Eri's radical disconnection from caring others was a central condition of possibility for my research.

It wasn't Eri whom Nagai wanted to discuss.

"There's one child, a six-year-old," Nagai told me. "The first time I met him, he said, 'I might as well be dead. It doesn't matter [*boku nanka shinda tte ii n da*].'"

Somehow I knew.

"Yusuke-kun?"[2]

"Yes, yes."

My own prescience had startled me. I hadn't previously known anything about this child's background. "He said he might as well be dead?"

"You know there's a road right out front, and the cars come fast around the bend. It was right after I started working here. That child—he's the kind of child who comes right up close, but how do you describe it? . . . He's also, like, ungrounded [*fura fura*]? Sometimes I feel he is really fond of me, and other times I don't. Sometimes he's attached to my hip, and other times he doesn't come near me."

Nagai had been next to the road with Yusuke, who made to run into the street. She called out for him to hold her hand and attempted to stop him, and that was when he said it: "I might as well be dead. It doesn't matter." The words seemed seared into Nagai's memory. She had stuttered a response—"If you weren't here I would be sad"—and the exchange ended.

"For a six-year-old to say that . . ."

"It was painful, painful for me. Like, what can I do?" Nagai laughed shortly. "I feel like crying." She wiped her eyes. Other staff members had also reported that Yusuke said these sorts of things. "I may be overthinking, but it feels like in these instances, a fundamental lack of security rises to the surface."

How did I know it was Yusuke, out of all the other little boys at the institution, who said he might as well be dead? We returned to this question later. He had always seemed untethered to me, as though he was floating along the surface of interactions, but also uncannily observant. He remembered every adult's name, including mine. He had wide, round eyes that sometimes sparkled with intelligence and sometimes seemed odd and vacant.

Yusuke, untethered to parents or ancestors. Untethered laterally to siblings or caregivers who felt deeply for him. His path had taken him through an institution for infants, where he apparently had had a caregiver who was fond of him. But he had been separated from her, moved to Chestnut House because he was too old to stay in the baby home. He was a person without other people to root him to this earth.

Fragile Kinships: Child Welfare and Well-Being in Japan

Policymakers, caregivers, and people with experience in state care endeavor to imagine and implement child welfare systems that support the well-being of those imbricated in them. Yet despite these efforts, social welfare systems too often produce people who have no one.[3] This book takes as a starting point the fragile relationship between the system of child welfare in Japan and the well-being of the children and adults connected to the system.

One might understand Eri and Yusuke to be without people because their parents abandoned them. However, rather than focusing on individual actions, I aim to illustrate how social disconnection is the product of social structures and policy that are shaped by culture, history, and politics. As a cultural anthropologist, I work to denaturalize the conditions of marginalization in which my interlocutors found themselves. In Japan, kinship ties explicitly scaffold one's place in the world, and kin, rather than the state, are expected to provide care for those in need. People disconnected from biogenetic kin tend to be understood as uniquely and profoundly lacking. This ethnography explores how cultural norms surrounding kinship, many deeply connected to national ideologies of Japanese identity, play out when familial realities diverge from normative expectations surrounding nurturance and care. Social policy institutionalizes and enacts these historically specific cultural norms. But there are many ways to ground a person in relationships with others. Although cultural norms are powerful, culture and systems change and are changing.

While describing the specificities of the Japanese system, I emphasize that these systems are not natural or necessary outcomes based in Japanese character. Japanese discourses of self (*nihonjinron*) are often mobilized to explain or support the status quo. Many people, including foster and adoptive parents, told me that because Japanese people value blood ties in families, family-based foster care and adoption will be difficult to popularize in Japan. Yet nihonjinron discourses of self are famous for internal contradictions. For instance, social systems in Japan are often characterized as profoundly relational, but simultaneously, recent discourses have painted Japan as "a society without connections" (NHK 2010; Allison 2013).[4] Rather than confirm this representation, the pages that follow bring particularity to the systemic ways that disconnection is produced through the structures and practices of Japan's welfare system—not through any innate cultural character. Even if dominant narratives focus on social disconnection in Japan, my ethnographic data powerfully show the transformative and creative energy people put into creating new forms of kinship and relatedness.

Although this book is about Japan, my findings are relevant to child welfare settings across the world. My central argument is that well-being is inherently relational and that by centering relationality in our analysis, we can better theorize care and embodied socioemotional well-being. This argument leads to a normative claim: to support the well-being of people in state care, child welfare systems should prioritize the cultivation of diverse interpersonal relationships.

Chestnut House was my first site for participant observation, and what I learned from the children, staff, and director backgrounds this book. Yet this is not a book solely about Chestnut House, and it will tell only a partial account of the institution and people connected to it. Throughout this monograph, I juxtapose stories of those I came to know through two years of initial fieldwork and over twelve more years of longitudinal study. The structure of this ethnography reflects intensely multi-sited fieldwork and a methodology of triangulating ways to understand the stakes of interpersonal relationships for people disconnected from nurturing kinship networks.

Kinship Norms and Japan's Child Welfare System

How and why does the Japanese child welfare system produce relationlessness? Certainly, social disconnection is not a welfare objective. Child welfare workers labor to theorize relationships and enable those that they view as beneficial. Perspectives surrounding kinship, relationality, and belonging orient the pragmatic actions of policymakers, child welfare caseworkers, institutional directors, foster and institutional care workers, and the children and youth within the system.[5]

This book centers the ways interpersonal relationships shape well-being. At the same time, cultural norms shape the types of relationships that people perceive as possible or desirable. Children who become subject to child welfare system intervention in Japan are in a double-bind: while the nuclear and extended family is the culturally normative base for care and the most legible way individuals are identified and known by the state, children end up in the child welfare system precisely because those relationships are perceived as a source of danger. Removed from the care of their families of origin, wards of the state are part of a system of social care (*shakaiteki yōgo*).

By definition, these are children cared for by the state. As of a 2024 report, there were 42,000 children in Japanese state care (about 0.3 percent of the Japanese child population).[6] A total of 23,008 children were placed in child welfare institutions (610 locations); 2,351 infants and babies in baby homes (145 locations); 6,080 children in family-based foster care (4,844 foster families; and 1,718 in family homes run by foster parents and staff (446 locations). Additional placements were children's psychotherapeutic facilities, youth correctional facilities, institutions to support independent living, and institutions for single mothers and children (Kodomo kateichō 2024, 5; for discussion, King 2021, chap. 2).[7] Although child welfare placements are ostensibly temporary, the average placement is almost five years, and around 15 percent of children in institutional care live there for over ten years (Kodomo kateichō 2024, 35). Child guidance centers (CGCs) are in charge of implementing alternative care arrangements for children. Although 40 percent of CGC workers are educated in social welfare, there are no professional social work qualifications in Japan. An additional 20 percent of CGC workers have some sort of human service qualification, but the remaining employees are general administrative officers without training in child welfare who rotate among government placements in departments as diverse as transportation and water sanitation (Bamba and Haight 2011, 181; Goodman 2000, chaps. 3 and 4; Goldfarb 2021; King 2021). The lack of required specialized training for case managers, high caseloads (sometimes more than one hundred individual cases per year), and generally the lack of legal support while making difficult decisions (Goldfarb 2021) are all factors that influence what many critics view as a system that does not support the well-being of children and families. Residential care staff are required to have some kind of educational background relevant to child care work (courses in sociology, psychology, or four-year university training), but these qualifications are generally not specialized or tailored to working with children in state care (Goodman 2000, 76–78). Clinical psychologists began being employed in child welfare institutions only in 1999, with increased public concern about the trauma of child abuse; these positions were made mandatory in 2011. While there is increased attention to the need for children's mental health care and a strategic focus on incorporating clinical work in residential spaces as part of daily life (an approach called *seikatsu rinshō*), clinical staff often lack specialized certifications and clear roles within the institution (Ukai 2010; Aoki 2012; Ide 2012; Narahara and Masuzawa 2012; Watanabe 2016). For their part, when young people age out of care, mental health care support is often discontinued, and psychological counseling is expensive to procure.[8]

Child welfare institutions were initially built to care for children orphaned during World War II, and some continue to be run as family businesses with deep ties to local governments (Goodman 2000). Supporters of the institutional care system highlight insufficient governmental and private support for family-based foster care. On the other hand, the dominance of institutional care placements in Japan is often held up by child welfare reform activists as an aberrance, compared to countries like the United States, Canada, and Australia, which prioritize family-based foster care.[9] Critics of institutional care—most specifically critics of the use of institutions for newborns, infants, and toddlers—argue that social care in institutions is the site of maltreatment and neglect and causes attachment disorders and developmental delays.[10] Japan has received persistent criticism from the United Nations Convention on the Rights of the Child, which it ratified in 1994, on the grounds that all children have the right to be raised in a family. In 2017, the Japanese government put forth a New Vision for Alternative Care where it committed to increase placements in "household-like environments" for preschool-age children to 75 percent by year 2024, where "household-like" includes actual family-based foster care and placement in family homes but also placement in small-scale group care and institutional settings (MHLW 2017; Kodomo kateichō 2024, 3). Yet as of 2020, only 1 percent of localities had reached these goals (Mainichi Shimbun 2020), and as of 2021, the average placement rate for children less than three years old with "foster parents etc." (including placement in "household-like" institutions) was reported at 25.3 percent, with substantial variation across prefectures (Kodomo kateichō 2024, 62).[11] The government also implemented changes to the adoption law in 2020 that enabled older children to be more easily adopted, reinforcing a legal and policy framework for family-based care (MHLW 2019b).[12] Importantly, child welfare institutions in Japan are not adoption agencies. Individuals can adopt children through the child welfare system after registering as foster parents with intent to adopt, a process mediated by the local child guidance center, or through private adoption agencies, of which there were twenty-four registered in 2023 (Kodomo kateichō 2024, 90).

Family-based foster care placement rates in Japan are steadily increasing, from around 9 percent in 2012 to about 19 percent in 2023.[13] When I began this research in 2008, the government's rhetoric and policy persistently focused on the lack of foster families and a perceived cultural prioritization of blood ties that would, so I was told over and over, prohibit the development of a family-based child welfare system. Over the span of my research, I have seen a sea change in governmental approaches to welfare and vastly increased public interest in family-based foster care and adoption (see also Chapman 2024). At the same time, top-down policy directives go only so far to produce practical change, which localities—sometimes under-resourced—are responsible for implementing.

At the root of policy debates are the core questions: What are the relationships that matter most for children and for the parents who are unable to care for them? When benefit to children seems in conflict with benefit to parents, which should take priority? In my research, I found that because family affiliation takes precedence in ensuring a person's social legibility, the Japanese child welfare system is oriented to the goal of keeping children bureaucratically connected to their biological parents (Goldfarb 2021). In most cases, parents have the right to determine their child's residence, and caseworkers negotiate with parents to place the child in out-of-home care. It is rare for parental rights to be terminated in family court.[14] Either because parents explicitly oppose family-based foster care or adoption or because caseworkers anticipate that they will, caseworkers are motivated to place children in institutional care.

Since child welfare placements average many years in Japan, it is understood that family-based foster care, like adoption, has the potential to produce durable affective bonds between the child and caregivers, and those bonds are believed to threaten continued connection between the child and biological parents (Goldfarb 2021). Michael Rivera King (2021) has called the belief that a child can belong to only one family "the single family bond." This cultural ideology is related to what Allison Alexy identifies as a "legal fiction at the heart of the *koseki* household registration system: a person must be in one, but only one, household" (2020, 112).[15] (Dual custody has thus been impossible in the case of divorce. However, as this book was in production, Japan's parliament passed a Civil Code revision allowing divorcing parents to choose either joint or single custody.) Child welfare placement officers must determine which relationships should be prioritized in what they perceive a zero-sum game where the people they are negotiating with—the child's parents—could be the losers. By placing a child in an institution, a professionalized workplace where staff turnover is generally high, the child will likely not develop bonds to caregivers competing with the child's potential connection to biological kin, as attenuated or nonexistent as those connections may be.[16]

What are the opinions of young people who were raised in the system? Careleavers have diverse sentiments. Some interlocutors who grew up in institutions would have preferred to be placed in a family. But for many people, even the relative deprivations and restrictions imposed by institutional care were far better than the family contexts from which they had come. People who were placed into state care as older children often felt no need for a replacement family, and celebrations of family-based care rang hollow. Many people valued long-term lateral connections with friends in the institution and pointed out that institutional care offers multiple options for relationships with staff and other children. A family placement, in contrast, could feel oppressive and even dangerous.

A 2021 national survey of careleavers and caregivers—the first survey of its kind—offers a sobering perspective on outcomes for youth from Japanese state care (MUFG 2021).[17] The survey examined people who had left care between 2015 and 2020. Careleavers reported anxiety about finances and about the future. Many were financially unstable, with 22.9 percent reporting expenditures that exceeded their income (MUFG 2021, 43). Those with the most financial stability were those who worked full-time with no experience in higher education (MUFG 2021, 44).[18] While about 25 percent of respondents reported currently not having substantial worries (MUFG 2021, 96), the free-entry portion of the survey was filled with expressions of anxieties: nothing and no one to fall back on in case of misfortune or ill health, concerns with social stigma against state wards, and, most substantially, feelings of social isolation (MUFG 2021, 87–89, 92–95).

The survey was broken down into child welfare placement categories. To my read, the young people in the most precarious situations were those who had experienced placements in institutions for specialized mental health care and youth correctional facilities. Placements in family homes and family-based foster care were correlated with the most financial stability (MUFG 2021, 45) and better medical security (having insurance, knowing where to go for medical care, having relational support for medical care) (MUFG 2021, 53). These populations also had the most frequent contact with former caregivers (foster parents) (MUFG 2021, 58). These findings align with my own research in both institutional settings and with foster and adoptive families in Japan: when it supports lasting positive relationships between children and caregivers, family-based care can be very beneficial to children.

Violence That Borrows the Shape of Love: Blood Ties in Historical Japanese Context

Ozawa Noboru was the type of person I considered a local philosopher, having developed his own concepts and explanatory frameworks to make sense of cultural norms. The adoptive parents of a little girl, Ozawa and his wife had coined a term that encapsulated what they perceived as the dangerous ways Japanese kinship ideologies operated in everyday life: "the violence of blood ties" (*ketsuen no bōryoku*). In this formulation, blood ties were agentic, merging a biological phenomenon with the cultural weight placed on genetic relationships.

Sociologist Shirai Chiaki (her real name) and I had together interviewed Ozawa's wife, who encouraged us to ask Ozawa about this concept. Shirai readily arranged a group interview. We met in a cacophonous gathering in Shirai's narrow apartment with her three sons, Ozawa, his wife, their daughter, and a friend of Shirai's who was considering adoption. Ozawa's reflections on child welfare, kinship, and family law were continuously interrupted by laughter and howls from the children playing around us. Ozawa did not end up being someone I kept in touch with, but in the long afternoon we spent together, he worked to articulate the violence of blood ties in a way that remains vivid. Like an ethnographer, Ozawa pulled on many forms of story as evidence to paint a picture that, for his family, explained a form of social suffering and evoked the pressure of kinship norms in daily life.

Blood ties became an obsession in Japan during the Meiji era (1868–1912), when the extended family (the *ie*) became the basic, legally recognized unit of society, Ozawa asserted. In historicizing a Japanese focus on blood ties, Ozawa destabilized a claim made by many of my interlocutors: that Japanese child welfare was bound to prioritize parental rights and institutional care, rather than foster and adoptive care, because of inherent Japanese cultural valuation of biological relatedness.

Ozawa's argument aligned with my own understanding of the culturally and historically specific attention to blood ties in contemporary Japan. Previous to the Meiji era, family practices across Japan were diverse; the Meiji Restoration of 1868, which returned the Japanese emperor to power and ended samurai rule, marked a new centralization of government and new ways to track the population, including the family registry system (koseki). These bureaucratic registers institutionalized elite samurai practices in which elder sons inherited family headship. However, these norms did not overdetermine the ways kinship was lived. Both before and after the Meiji Restoration, people commonly used adoption to incorporate non-kin into families for the purposes of upholding the family line: adoptees would inherit property and family businesses, provide elder care, and look after graves. Notably, adoptive kin in these contexts would not have been children from unknown families. They were "extra" children of cousins, children of impoverished families in the community, or, quite often, adults—an unrelated couple, employees, and even servants or slaves. In cases where people did not have male heirs, the husband of a daughter might be adopted to take on family headship (*mukoyōshi*, a type of adoption still used in contemporary Japan). In addition to these adoption practices (which a nineteenth-century legal scholar described as "promiscuous" [Hozumi 2004]), eldest sons were not always the preferred household heads: daughters and younger sons sometimes took this role. While scholars often describe kinship practices in China and Korea as focused on maintaining the patriline, the ie system in Japan was not historically oriented around upholding a literal male bloodline. Indeed, blood ties have not historically been a significant metric for accounting for membership in an ie (Norbeck and Befu 1958; Nakane 1967; Bachnik 1983; Lebra 1993; Paulson 2010; Nobe 2018).[19]

When and how did blood ties become commonly cited as the basis for Japanese kinship? Research on the transformations of Japanese family practices often points to spatial regimes since the mid-1800s, most particularly the increase of nuclear families in the twentieth century. These include the decline of multigeneration households, housing structures with units divided from the surrounding community and further divided into private bedrooms, and a gendered division of labor and availability of household appliances that, for middle-class households, ended the use of outside domestic laborers in the private space of the home (Ochiai 1997; Sand 2003; Ronald and Alexy 2011). In his exploration of the emergence of modern "myths of Japaneseness," Eiji Oguma (2002) argues for the mutual influence of family ideologies and national policies of inclusion and exclusion. Oguma links Japanese openness to non–blood-related ie members with Japanese colonial rhetoric about incorporating and assimilating non-Japanese others into the national body. However, after World War II, Japanese myths of self were reoriented not as inclusive, containing heterogeneous and diverse peoples, but as homogeneous, exclusive, and "mono-ethnic" (Oguma 2002; Dale 1986; Harootunian 1989; Lie 2001; Robertson 2002). These national discourses of self, focused on narrow conceptions of Japanese bloodlines, have likely played a role in shaping contemporary perceptions of Japanese selves as valuing blood ties within families. Further, as Japan's birthrate has declined, there are fewer undesired children in families. While a childless couple might have in the past adopted a child of a sibling or a cousin, decreasing family size makes this practice less pragmatic.

These processes have contributed to changing family ideals, in which the concept of blood ties has new ideological salience. However, rather than indicating exclusively biogenetic relatedness, discourses surrounding blood ties in Japan point to culturally legible ways of articulating intimate connections (Goldfarb 2018). These discourses are part of broader conceptual frameworks through which people understand what it takes to be considered family. For instance, Emiko Ochiai (1997, 76–77) describes the type of contemporary Japanese households viewed as ideal as those in which families are intimate and, by their very intimacy, also exclusive, with their boundaries narrowing to encircle a generally nuclear family separated from public spheres. In such a family, emotion binds members, and kin are separated from non-kin. At the same time, discourses about genetic relatedness have increasingly become relevant in understandings of kinship. Scholars of infertility treatment in Japan have argued that the availability of advanced reproductive technology enabling couples to have their own biological children means that the standard of having a biologically related child has become a coercive norm (Tsuge 1999; Shirai 2010, 2013). Family in Japan has been progressively medicalized and biologized, such that blood ties have increasingly come to refer to narrow concepts of genetic relatedness, even as—at the same time—blood points to the expansive or symbolic interconnectedness that anthropologists of kinship have long examined, focused on affect and intimacy (Schneider 1984; Carsten 2004; Nobe 2018). These transformations have contributed to the contemporary centrality of blood ties in discourses of Japanese family. While blood ties are often described as a characteristic of Japanese national-cultural family values, I see them more appropriately understood as an "invented tradition" (Vlastos 1998). Finally, changing perceptions regarding blood ties speak to broader concerns regarding kinship practices among people who are not socially recognized as family, anxieties about intimacy with unrelated children, and stigma against children of unknown origin. While on the one hand, blood ties themselves are conceptualized as a type of intimacy, discourses surrounding blood ties also reflect fears that intimate ties will fail to generate durable family bonds. Blood ties, in short, point to much more than biological relatedness. Reference to the importance of blood ties in family does a great deal of symbolic and discursive work.

It is this discursive labor that Ozawa Noboru evoked when he described the violence of blood ties. Over the course of our three-hour interview, Ozawa reflected on the symbolic weight of the common-sense belief that family in Japan means "related by blood." This presupposition holds so firm that merely stating the fact that a child is adopted—which Ozawa glossed by saying "there is no blood connection" between parent and child—provokes shocked incredulity. Even as an outspoken adoption advocate, Ozawa said, he had to choose his conversation partners wisely or face the awkwardness of people's lack of comprehension. This is harder still for children. The fact that confessing adoption (both to outsiders and to adopted children themselves) is a fraught topic in Japan was further evidence to Ozawa that the norm of blood ties within families comprised a coercive standard.[20] Yet the concept of blood ties as the basis for kinship contained its own contradiction. "There is a perception in Japanese society that blood ties within families will maintain family solidarity [*rentaikan*]," Ozawa said. Pointing to child abuse cases in the news, increasing divorce, and low marriage rates, Ozawa continued, "But at the same time, families are collapsing in Japan. Even as they are falling apart, blood ties are a device that simulates familial unity [*ittaikan*]."[21]

In Ozawa's hands, the violence of blood ties took many forms. It was the impulse among child welfare protection workers not to separate children from their parents out of a sense that it was improper to pull apart family members, which put the child at risk. It was also the priority the child welfare system placed on relationships between biological kin, at the expense of supporting multiple familial ties for a child. Caseworkers often placed children in institutions in the hope that someday, somehow, they might be able to develop ties to their biological parents. But because the children were cared for in institutions, they often developed relationships with no parent, neither biological nor foster nor adoptive. The violence of blood ties evoked for Ozawa a dual character of intimate kin relations, a character different from love but appealing to its form. "It's a type of violence that emerges precisely because of proximity and intimacy," he said. "It's a violence that borrows the shape of love."

Kinship, Gender, and the Child Welfare System

A major project of this book is to illuminate how the Japanese child welfare system disrupts normative understandings of kinship in Japan. The family in Japan is a highly gendered institution, both at the level of bureaucratic family registry (where it is common for heads of household to be male and spouses cannot have different surnames) and in daily practice (where, for example, women conduct the vast majority of unpaid household labor).[22] If the child welfare system challenges how we think about family, how does it interact with gendered norms?[23]

Gendered expectations inform orientations toward adoption, fostering, and infertility treatment in Japan. Women in particular are sometimes still seen as full-fledged adults only once they have a child. Gendered norms that shape labor and employment practices also powerfully impact family. Women who delayed childbearing to focus on their careers were a common demographic seeking infertility treatment or fostering and adoption, and thus the child welfare system could be viewed as a tool to replicate normative family forms in the face of changing gendered labor patterns. At the same time, both women and men pointed out to me that salarymen generally have little contact with unrelated children and thus do not tend to imagine that other people's children could be lovable—a barrier to adoption or fostering, as both men and women viewed the family as a locus of intimacy. However, the longer couples struggled with infertility, the more likely an unrelated child might become imagined to fit within this intimate sphere (Goldfarb 2018; Nobe 2018).

Child welfare institutions themselves are not significant sites of disruption for normative gender roles. Institutions tend to have more female caregivers than male, a gendered balance that reflects the fact that women are more represented in childcare employment in Japan. Indeed, about one-third of child welfare institution staff members were found to be women in their twenties (Yoshimura and Yoshimura 2022, 3). At Chestnut House, particularly in the early years when the children living in the same residential unit were of mixed genders, each house had two female and one male caregiver. This gender balance reflected an attunement to normative heterosexual households with both female and male parents. While division of labor in institutions among careworkers and among children might be uncommonly equitable across genders, Goodman notes more gendered labor division between management (dominated by men) and careworkers (dominated by women) (2000, 83). Youth who grow up in the system are more likely than the national average to get married at a young age (Futaba Flat Home 2012, 6), and earlier studies note that the parents of children in state care also tended to marry and have children very young (Goodman 2000, 56). In my own observation, many careleavers sought the perceived stability of marriage to establish a household independent of their families of origin or as an agentive way to start fresh.

Engagement with the family-based foster care and adoption systems in Japan in some ways does destabilize normative gendered family structure and practice. Some foster parents I knew had uncommonly equitable divisions of household and childcare labor, especially those who fostered many children over many years. This was likely because people who decided to foster professionally were often more interested in childcare and because older foster parents were already retired. Although same-sex marriage is not yet permitted in Japan, in some municipalities, same-sex couples are approved as foster parents, and same-sex couples could in theory adopt a child with only one partner as the legal parent. The ways in which the child welfare system disrupts or reinforces normative gender norms are ripe for further research.[24]

(Re)Situating Kinship

Anthropologists have long considered kinship a basis for social solidarity. But what about when it is not? Feminist scholars, analyzing kinship ideologies within anthropology itself, have focused on the ways analytical concepts, like gender or family, seemed to be rooted in natural difference, but these assumptions participate in producing and solidifying inequality. For instance, Jane Collier, Michelle Z. Rosaldo, and Sylvia Yanagisako argued that anthropologists have taken for granted the notion of family as a universal human institution, bounded as a group, occupying a distinct physical space, and unified by love (1997 [1982], 73). Arguing that "The Family" is "an ideological construct with moral implications" (79), the authors queried whether American notions about "Family" reflect "real relations between people" or just ideals that shape behavior (77). They argued for a recognition of the "irony that in our society the place where nurturance and noncontingent affection are supposed to be located is simultaneously the place where violence is most tolerated" (78; Kuwajima 2019). If family is by definition understood as being about nurturance, then how do we understand evidence to the contrary?

Also in the mid-1980s, David Schneider recanted his own influential arguments that kinship should be seen as existing on a complex matrix of nature, law, and blood, as he had maintained in his 1968 *American Kinship*. In his *Critique of the Study of Kinship*, Schneider argued that anthropologists (including himself) had naïvely assumed that genealogical relations were the same in all cultures because the facts of biological reproduction were the same across humanity. However, he wrote, these claims were actually a European "ethnoepistemology" that "blood is thicker than water." Anthropologists had taken their own com-mon-sense assumptions about kinship to be universal and applied these sup-posedly universal frameworks to evaluate all other forms of kinship (Schneider 1984, chap. 14).

Schneider's critique ended up revivifying anthropological interest in family practices and brought about diverse publications that can collectively be catego-rized as "new kinship" studies. This scholarship has explored the ways kinship emerges over time through caregiving relationships, biological or not, and has been attuned to the ways people experience kinship through sharing food and bodily substance, residential space, and affect and emotion, and how people discursively articulate relatedness. Embracing the turn away from heteronorma-tive reproduction as the basis for kinship, Marshall Sahlins retained Schneider's 1968 framework of kinship as defined by solidarity in his exhaustive analyses of cross-cultural kinship practices to argue that kinship should be understood as a "mutuality of being" (2011) constructed entirely through cultural practice. Thus, while contemporary kinship scholarship has taken up Schneider's argu-ment that we should not understand kinship as (exclusively) focused on notions of biological relatedness, scholars have done less to respond to feminist cri-tiques of the ways anthropologists tend to naturalize kinship as noncontingent nurturance.

This ethnography intervenes into these depictions of kinship as about soli-darity and mutuality by exploring how kinship is not just about connection and inclusion but is also about disconnection, exclusion, and violence (Franklin and McKinnon 2001; Goldfarb and Schuster 2016; Goldfarb and Bamford, eds., 2024). Kinship relationships that feel positive and good take a lot of social work; there is nothing natural about kinship ties being caring. I take seriously the contingency of kinship relationships (Stasch 2009), the continuous moments of choice that collectively evince kinship ties, and the moments when kinship breaks down, is ignored, or is a source of suffering.

This ethnography embraces the cultural dimensions of kinship creation and argues against heteronormative biological frameworks in which kinship, along with human worth, "always seem[s] to be hanging on the more or less fragile branches of a family tree" (Povinelli 2002, 215). At the same time, this book explores how relationality is the stuff of both culture and biological materiality—which is not the same as biological reproduction. Kinship ties impact well-being and bodily life, and caregiving relationships can potentially have transformative consequences for people's holistic well-being, including bodily existence.

My analysis of bodily life in relational context shows why we should attend to caregiving as a type of transformative investment over time. Kinship ties, whether positive or negative, develop over time, and child welfare policy and practice should cultivate—rather than preclude—possibilities for long-term relationships between children and caregivers. In reflecting on the ways that questions of kinship are essentially questions of time, Danilyn Rutherford notes that we tell ourselves stories about both "blood" and "culture" to "help us respond to the pressing questions at the heart of every encounter: where did you come from, what do we owe each other, and what am I to you?" (2015, 247) Attention to both the contingency of kinship ties and the possibilities for creating new connections should inform the way we imagine and then implement welfare frameworks that nurture diverse relational bonds.

Kinship Technologies When Kinship Is Hard to Recognize

I suggest that we examine kinship as a matter of practice, with cultural and biological presuppositions and future-oriented entailments. By presuppositions, I mean assumptions that shape the ways family relationships are recognized as such. Following from these assumptions are open-ended entailments, outcomes and potentialities that are captured in the ongoing and transformative possibilities implicit in interpersonal ties. But how are family relationships recognized as such, particularly when kinship ties take forms that—as Ozawa Noboru described—provoke shock and surprise? What happens when kinship is difficult to make socially recognizable?

This book tracks various *kinship technologies*, which I define as culturally and historically specific engagements with signs of relatedness that people use to understand kinship (Goldfarb 2016a). Cultural frameworks provide the scaffolding for people to perceive relationships as kinship—or not—and also to engage agentively with the semiotics of family in order to socially situate their own practices. Kinship technologies are conventional, culturally informed ways that people in general labor to construct the feeling of being a family. Some people do this unthinkingly because they have never worried that their families might not be recognized as families. Others have to work harder. In some cases, kinship technologies offer people the tools to inhabit unmarked or normal-seeming family forms, although, as I will show, this process is often aspirational, threatened by social stigma. In other cases, kinship technologies offer people the tools to creatively transform relationships of alterity or otherness into intimate familial ties.

Kinship technologies can be discursive, played out through narrative practices of representing self and other, of telling stories of one's self and one's past, present, and future.[25] They can also be material, like engagements with physical qualities of a household (including architecture design, furniture, and practices within these spaces), and biological, like attention to bodily practices (for example, similar physical mannerisms among family members). Kinship technologies can even speak to the physicality of the body and the entailed interpretations of the body's signs, like the ways that brain scans of maltreated children are used to point to certain kinds of past family relationships (Goldfarb 2015). Kinship technologies are thus paradigmatic examples of "material-semiotic" practices in Donna Haraway's term, in which the interpretation of signs articulate with the physicality of objects, practices, and the networked relationships that connect them.[26]

Normativity plays a defining role in how people engage with kinship technologies. The coerciveness of culturally specific family ideologies orients common desires to inhabit an unmarked subjectivity and to be easily recognized as family. Having a "normal" family and being situated within a lineage was, for many of my interlocutors, a source of aspiration and pleasure. What is the content of that imagined normal—the Japanese family as it appears in the minds of my interlocutors, academic literature, and popular culture and discourse? To scholars, the normal may seem mythlike, an ideological construction. But for my interlocutors in Japan, the normal family was something that seemed to be inhabitable because there seemed to be people who inhabited it. When one is asked about one's family in Japan, a common response is to say that one's family or upbringing was normal or ordinary (*futsū*) and to describe one's partner as an ordinary person (*futsū no hito*). This very ordinariness might be a form of modesty, implying nothing special or distinctive, but for my research interlocutors, this lack of distinctiveness itself was an aspiration.[27] They occasionally summoned the normal family in descriptions of what their families were not and what they imagined their classmates' and others' families to be. Normal families were, most centrally, married parents with children. These parents took care of their children's needs. They allowed children to live at home, obviating concerns about staying housed, and paid for their children's school expenses. More than a functional view, however, most of my interlocutors described normal families, different from their own, as happy (*shiawase*).

Research Sites and Methodologies

This book emerges out of longitudinal research from 2008 to 2024.[28] Many of the people who appear in these pages are dear friends. The stories in this book are snapshots taken years ago of complex lives in motion, and some people might not recognize their present selves in my depictions. I have chosen not to offer the reader updates on individuals for two reasons: first, specifics like that would make many people identifiable. Second, my project is not to depict individuals in all their complexity but rather to produce generalizable and richly contextualized insights from moments in time. Some of the stories that are the most poignant to me—many of which are not stories for me to tell—do not appear here at all, but their spirit underlies and motivates this analysis.

All knowledge is situated (Haraway 1988). I have no personal lived experience of child welfare. I grew up in a privileged middle-class household, with married heterosexual parents and a sister. Not only do we generally get along, but we even like each other! My initial research proposal focused on the ways national-cultural ideologies of Japaneseness were challenged by nonnormative family practices, specifically adoption and the use of reproductive technology. The more I learned about adoption in Japan, the more I became fascinated by Japan's child welfare system. Japanese state wards can be characterized as an "invisible minority" (Goodman 2000; Nishida 2011). Some people spoke with me because they hoped my research would bring attention to intractable systemic and social problems—to increase the visibility of this minority. I do feel significant discomfort in my position as a white foreigner commenting on Japanese welfare policy and practice. There is a long history of Japanese practitioners and scholars seeking Western expertise, and reformers in Japan often lean on outside pressure (*gaiatsu*) to invoke the need for change. Still, I hope to be an ally in these efforts in Japan and beyond.

Another way in which these findings are situated is that race does not figure prominently in my analysis. In part as an accident of geographic location within Japan, race was not a salient marker of social difference to my interlocutors. In North America, racial and ethnic minorities are disproportionately represented in the child welfare system, particularly First Nations children in Canada and Black and brown children in the United States, just as these groups are disproportionately policed and represented in juvenile justice systems. In Japan, the government does not collect statistics on the racial and ethnic breakdown of its child welfare population, nor on the representation of children of Indigenous (Ainu or Okinawan) or *buraku* descent (the formerly "untouchable" class).[29] At Chestnut House, a handful of children have been of mixed or non-Japanese ethnicity, in some cases placed in state care because one parent returned to their home country, leaving the other parent unable to care for the children alone. Had I conducted research in a community with a larger immigrant population or closer to an American military base, there would have been greater numbers of mixed-race children in the institution and—I assume—more discussion of what race and ethnicity mean in the child welfare context.[30]

Child Welfare Institution

Beginning in October 2008, I began attending training sessions for staff who would live at Chestnut House, which was scheduled to open the following June. This opportunity was rare and made possible because of a chain of introductions: Roger Goodman, who wrote the first English-language exploration of Japanese child welfare institutions (Goodman 2000), introduced me to Tsuzaki Tetsuo, a professor of social welfare who was running these training sessions. After getting to know some of the future staff members including the institution's director, I received permission to conduct participant observation at the institution after it opened. Chestnut House was part of a movement to create household-like child welfare institutions, and I was interested in how national-cultural kinship ideologies shaped relationships outside the bounds of a normative family, and how these ideologies informed visions of the role of care in a social welfare context. I was particularly intrigued by the ways indices of family and household would be operationalized in an institutional setting. From July 2009 through December 2010, I visited the institution between three times a week and one time a month. At the start of my fieldwork, which was also the start of the institution, it was wonderful to have a research base. After all, this was no village ethnography, and I was living alone in a Tokyo apartment. I attempted consistent engagement at the institution, although this goal was sometimes difficult to maintain. The children were often sick, and thus so was I, although I avoided the institution during periods of significant illness spread (like when influenza or the mumps were going around).[31] As my fieldwork progressed, I focused less singularly on Chestnut House.

The institution was organized into five houses, and at the start of my research I spent time in each house, as well as with the littlest children in their day care at the institution while the older children were in neighborhood schools. Many of the staff members welcomed me as I played with the children, washed dishes, and assisted with other household chores. Other staff members were less glad for my presence, in part because the institution was a stressful place to work, and they struggled to address the children's needs.

I came to focus on one house where the little girl Eri lived. Unlike the other children, who were visited occasionally by parents or kin, this child was visited only by her caseworker. In the years encompassing my initial fieldwork, I watched as the staff members to whom she had become deeply attached left their jobs. When staff quit, they generally didn't return to visit. Even if they missed the children, they had no proper role at the institution, and it was not seen as appropriate for them to continue these relationships. In my odd positionality as a foreign researcher—a quasi-structural insider at the institution—I have been uniquely able to return. However, twelve years after she arrived at the institution, Eri finally decided to live full-time with a foster parent who had been her weekend foster mother. Once she was no longer at Chestnut House, I was no longer able to see her.

Even though I had received Institutional Review Board permission to conduct interviews with the children, I realized that any direct discussion of their pasts could cause unintended harm. Although my relationships with the children were among the most powerful I built over the course of my fieldwork, I did not pursue interviews with them, and they appear indirectly in this book in chapter 2 through snippets of my own field notes, written from my perspective. At the institution, I conducted in-depth interviews with the director and the staff members with whom I became close. I did not pursue connections with children's families of origin.

The first Chestnut House director always encouraged me to show photographs of the institution when I gave research presentations to illustrate the flavor of the place. In this book, Sasha Buckser has beautifully rendered my photographs as illustrations. The features of the child and adult in figure 5 have been altered and are not identifiable, but the image expresses an affective mood of caring intimacy.

Foster Families

One Chestnut House office staff member was a foster parent who invited me to foster care conferences and introduced me to friends.[32] Some of these people, along with their spouses and children, became of central importance to this project, and with them I attended events and foster parent trainings, visited nonprofit organizations that served former foster youth, and gained a window into the activist projects of a passionate group of foster parents who advocated for child welfare reform. At conferences and events, I met other foster parents. One introduced me to an enormous network of activist lawyers, child welfare institution directors and staff, scholars, child guidance center workers, and politicians, many of whom I was able to interview. I was welcomed into a study group run by lawyers at the Tokyo Bar Foundation that was dedicated to protecting children's rights in institutional care.

I became friends with some of my foster parent friends' older children. Because I had spoken at length with their parents and did not want to compromise the confidentiality of any of my interlocutors, I was uncomfortable pursuing interviews with these youth. In one case, however, I conducted an extended interview with one of these young people a few years after my initial fieldwork, and I interviewed other youth with family-based foster care experience whom I met through different avenues.

Graduates of State Care

At a large symposium in December 2009, I met a set of people whose acquaintance would formatively shape my research: a group of young people who had grown up in child welfare institutions and were involved in self-support organizations. Through this network, I became close to people in other areas of Japan and made regular trips to stay with the friends I call Reina, Sora, Kenji, and Akio. Reina introduced me to the Tokyo-area self-support group Tanpopo.[33] I conducted participant-observation research at Tanpopo from April 2010 to December 2010, attending the dinners that were the centerpiece of the organization's activities. I was sensitive to the ethical problems surrounding my involvement in a group that was already (it turned out) targeted for interviews by reporters and other researchers. I interviewed only a handful of those members with whom I had built friendships, and I remain in contact with many of these people.

Infertility Treatment and Adoption

I was interested in engaging with people who were pursuing infertility treatment and those who were considering adopting or had decided to adopt. Almost all the foster parents I knew had undergone infertility treatment. (A minority of foster parents I spoke with had had their own biological children before fostering.) Tsuge Azumi, a sociologist who conducted research on pregnancy and infertility in Japan, advised my research. My friendship and collaboration with sociologist Shirai Chiaki was an auspicious methodological fluke that deeply shaped my work. We had met a few months into my fieldwork; she had long conducted research on infertility treatment and adoption, and I was by then embedded in the world of child welfare. Shirai and I introduced each other to our respective research contacts and conducted many collaborative interviews. Shirai and Tsuge assisted me in building connections with infertility support groups, and I attended research symposia on infertility and reproduction. I interviewed many people the first time we met; some of those connections grew over time, which helped me put these interviews into perspective. However, one-off interviews were also often productive and lengthy. Although little of my research on infertility appears in this book, it backgrounds the project.

Policymakers, Social Workers, Psychiatrists, Academics . . .

Professionals in various fields—from policy to social work to mental health— have deeply informed this research. I conducted formal interviews with government workers at the Ministry of Health, Labour and Welfare and formal and informal interviews with governmental child guidance center case workers, internationally based social workers and clinicians, and Japanese mental health professionals. Japanese academics have been generous interlocutors.

Institutional Visits

I visited over fifteen child welfare institutions, baby homes, small group homes, independent living homes, and youth correctional facilities, touring the facilities and interviewing the directors and occasionally staff members. I spent the night at one residential correctional facility as well as at a family home. Visits to diverse institutions of different sizes gave me a sense of the broad range of institutional forms that constituted the bulk of Japan's state welfare services. These visits occurred in large cities—Yokohama, Tokyo, Osaka, and Kyoto—and also in rural areas of Kantō, Kansai, and Kyushu, which gave me a sense of geographical diversity.

Recordings, Transcripts, and Documents

I audio recorded almost all of my interviews, the majority of which were transcribed by my meticulous transcriptionist. Altogether, I recorded interviews with over 115 people, in addition to multiple follow-up interviews with close interlocutors. I participated in numerous trainings and symposia, and collected recordings from over 40 such events, some of which were transcribed. Transcripts constitute important documents in my analysis, which I treated according to Briggs' (1986) injunction to attend to the context and temporal flow of the interview. I analyzed them manually as verbal texts, tracing narrative flow, contradictions, and recurrent themes. Readers will note that I often quote people using their actual (translated) words. I supplemented my analysis with extensive field notes and Japanese documents (training materials, symposia records, government white papers, newspaper articles, online weblogs).

Family Diagrams

My research methodologies included the collection of visual depictions of many of my interlocutors' families. Unlike anthropologists of old, I was not interested in collecting objective kinship data. I was more interested in the affective dimensions of relationships that were—or were not—reflected in these documentation practices, the relationships that fell off the "genealogical grid" (Povinelli 2002b), and the types of narratives enabled by giving interlocutors the opportunity to write as they spoke.

In many cases, particularly at the beginning of my research, I asked people to sketch a depiction of what they considered family. To my surprise, most of my interlocutors produced standard-looking genealogies. As my research progressed, I began asking more directly for a genealogy (*kakeizu*), often hedged as a visual depiction of the connections that constituted the interlocutor's family. This process yielded fascinating information. Many people drew timelines, noting with whom they lived during different periods. Other people depicted networks of kin by way of marking the headship of a temple or a family business. One woman drew a spidery network of connections that illuminated the people who mediated her relationships to others (so that she was connected to her ex-husband by way of her daughters), before she noted, with a start, that I probably wanted a standard genealogy, which she then drew (fig. 1). Another woman drew a sketch of the groups of people and organizations she considered her family's supporters, drawing a small circle in the center, comprised of herself, her partner (she had not taken his family name, and thus they were not legally married), and their child, with their foster child at the center of the circle (fig. 2). Some people drew standard genealogies and then marked over them to index affective connections, residential groups, or people they considered really or only kind of

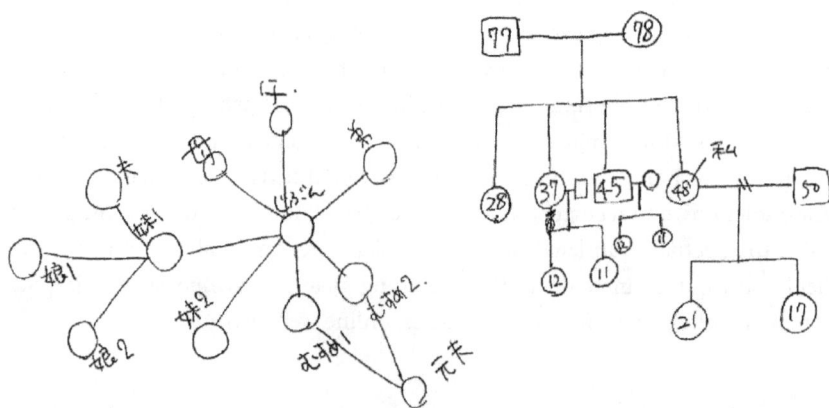

FIGURE 1. Mediated relationships. On the left diagram, the interviewee indicated herself as the central node (じぶん) with lines radiating outward to indicate her younger brother, father, mother, two younger sisters, and two daughters who are connected to her ex-husband (元夫). Branching off from her first younger sister are her sister's husband and each of her sister's daughters so that her nieces are connected to her through her sister, rather than through the union of her sister with her brother-in-law. On the right is a more standard genealogy with the interviewee designated by "私" and her age, forty-eight.

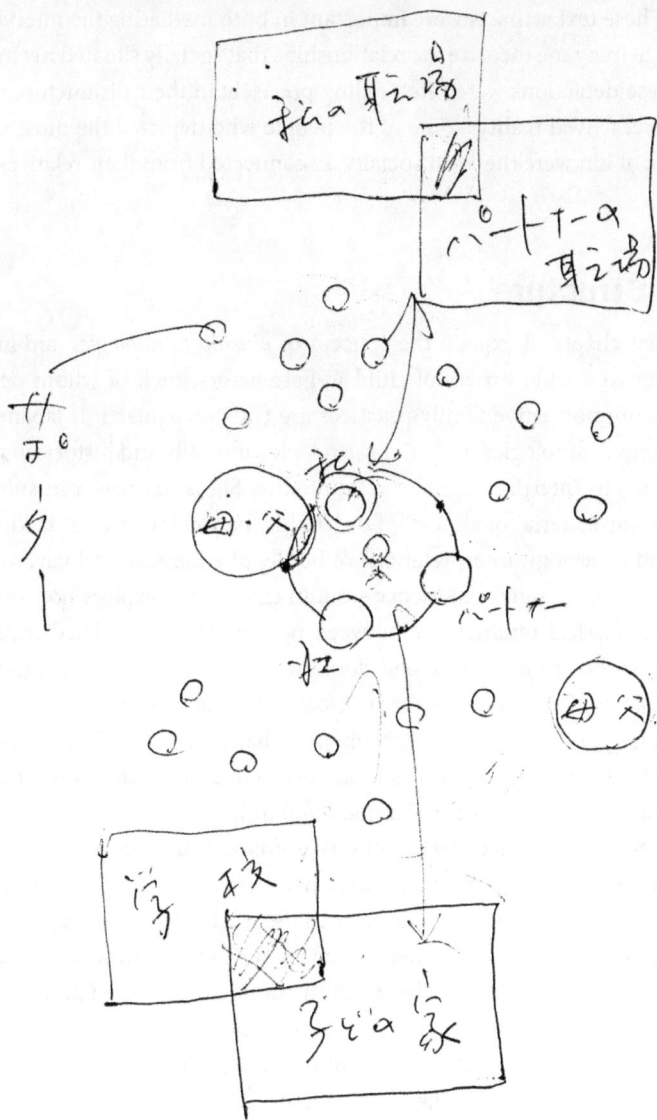

FIGURE 2. "Supporters." This image graphically represents the interviewee's social network with the foster child at the center. The interviewee indicates intimate proximity with her own parents (the small circle between the interviewee [私] and her biological child) and more distance with her partner's parents, indicated in a separate, nonoverlapping circle slightly off to the right, closer to her partner. The small scattered circles indicate supporters. The two rectangles above indicate the interviewee's workplace and her partner's workplace, slightly overlapping. The rectangles below indicate the foster child's school and the institution from which the child came, slightly overlapping.

family. These text artifacts were important in both mediating the interview process and helping me theorize the relationships that socially situated my interlocutors. These depictions were often telling precisely in their disjuncture from my interviewees' lived reality: some of the people who depicted the most extensive networks of kin were the most socially disconnected from their relatives.

Book Structure

In the first chapter, I explain the concept of *kinship technologies* and introduce the reader to a wide variety of child welfare actors, each of whom negotiated the ways nonnormative family practices are (mis)recognized in Japanese society. Kinship technologies offered these people culturally and historically specific frameworks to interpret signs of relationality. Signs discussed in subsequent chapters are material qualities of households, particular ways of talking about blood and genealogy, interpretations of bodily phenomena, and narrative practices regarding personal experience—but in chapter 1, I explore how discourses regarding physical resemblance between non–biologically related parents and children worked to normalize and domesticate the otherwise strange-seeming practice of adoption and foster care in Japan. These actors navigated relationality as both an opportunity and a problem, as a chance to make their interpersonal ties legible as kinship, and also as moments to draw boundaries between those who could and could not be understood as family.

Day-to-day experiences in institutions profoundly diverge from life in a household, and these divergences impact staff members' understandings of their work and residents' perceptions of their place in the world. An interlude, "Bread Days and Rice Days," describes the meal practices at a large child welfare institution, in which a staff member noted the contradictions she perceived between institutional expectations surrounding food and the ways people in the "regular world" perceived meals. How might an institution be less strange, more like a regular home? This is the question taken up in chapter 2, "Approximating a Household," which focuses on the ways the director and staff of Chestnut House attempted to materialize normative signs of a nuclear home, a process that I call *mimetic approximation*. Even as they strove to make Chestnut House as household-like as possible through everything from architectural form to food practices, the likelihood that these mimetic practices would miss their mark was a point of concern for staff members. Although the institution in many ways looked, smelled, and acted like a household, it was an imitation. The children were not siblings, staff were not the children's parents, and the temporariness of these relationships was institutionalized in the very form of state care.

While this ethnography powerfully illustrates the ways that kinship is often "chosen" (Weston 1991) and created through time and effort, the colloquial notion of blood ties remained a powerful draw for many of my interlocutors. An interlude, "Genealogical Returns," introduces the reader to the Fujisaki family, centering the narrative of a foster mother. Even as she and her husband had raised three children since they were small, she was profoundly aware that these created kin ties existed in the shadow of her children's desires to be connected to blood kin, the loss of which must somehow be mourned. Chapter 3, "Normal Aspirations," then examines how the absence of genealogical relationships in Japan is often experienced as a lasting sorrow or lack, which can be remediated through heterosexual marriage and reproduction. The pleasures and compulsions of genealogical ties are exemplified in the account of a man designated the fifth successor in his family line and, in contrast, by the concerns expressed by a couple undertaking infertility treatment, who feared that were they to adopt, they would be unable to love the child of a stranger. Even for people raised in Japanese child welfare institutions, who might seem to be uniquely poised to discard normative models of kinship to create their own chosen families, the possibility to create a nuclear family through heterosexual procreation was a compelling desire. This chapter features three of my interlocutors' kinship diagrams, which highlight the divergences between networks that look like relationships and the actual forms of interdependency and care that constitute families.

An interlude, "Inscriptions," explores a foster mother's concerns about her son, whose past experiences of maltreatment mark his body but cannot be further known or explained. Her concerns about her son's daily struggles with intellectual disability speak to both fears of profound past harms and hope for future healing. This foster mother's interpretive framework is informed by a commonsense notion in Japan that social relationships are reflected in and expressed by the body. Chapter 4, "Materializing Relationships," takes this insight as a starting point to consider the biological materiality of kinship ties and their absence—not through conventional notions of biogenetic relatedness but through the ways that people literally embody their social contexts. This chapter offers central theoretical insights, arguing that kinship scholars and cultural anthropologists more generally should attend to the materiality of the body as co-constituted by a person's relational and cultural surroundings. Some of the accounts that inform these insights are difficult to explain in the context of normative views surrounding human development.

Institutional care is a sharply delimited sphere of experience in which children tend to be offered little freedom. What does it feel like to grow up encircled by cement walls? An interlude, "The End of the World," explores the durable embodied sensation of enclosed space that one man experienced after being raised his whole life in an institution. These experiences become particularly problematic when a person ages out of care and must make their way independently, self-responsible for the first time but with limited social supports. Chapter 5, "The Politics of Chance," features three members of the support group Tanpopo, all alumni of Japan's state care system, who grappled with pasts characterized by constraint and loss and the imperative to be self-sufficient. Their stories articulate a critique of a welfare system in which outcomes are the result of chance encounters and arbitrary child welfare placement decisions. They are an indictment of social norms that require self-responsibility as a response to systematic marginalization and precarity. A subsequent interlude, "Matsumoto's Family Diagrams," presents one Tanpopo member's depictions of his family relationships and a mind map of his life. His kinship diagram depicts an extensive familial network that could not compensate for his parents' financial and health struggles. Upon the death of both parents, Matsumoto and his brother were placed into a child welfare institution. Leaving the institution necessitated that Matsumoto struggle to find the power to live.

Finally, chapter 6, "Knowledge and Narration," asks us to consider how we know who we are if we have no one with whom to remember. Staff turnover is high in child welfare institutions, and children move in and out of state care placements. Many of these children lack consistent relationships with their parents and other kin, including siblings. How are children to keep track of the details of their pasts without other people to help them narrativize and remember? What happens when children do not know empirical details of their pasts, information about why they were placed into the system to begin with, or the cause of embodied memories or physical traces like scars? This chapter explores both the social work practice of Life Story Work and the experiences of two people, Ōta Nozomi and a man called Edward, as they grappled with self-understanding in the face of profound information gaps. The chapter closes by proposing that we consider ourselves collectively responsible for the memories of others as a form of social care.

A conclusion returns to the quandary faced by child welfare systems across the world: the challenge of supporting relationality and belonging for children in the system. A lack of social resources showed itself to be profoundly dangerous in the context of the global COVID-19 pandemic. I close by highlighting key insights from this ethnography for Japanese studies and for anthropology, connecting national-cultural kinship ideologies in Japan with broader arguments about (non)normativity, social transformations in kinship practices, and the embodied stakes of relationality.

This book accounts for relational endeavors in a context where kinship is a source of both suffering and desire, where normative visions of family both repel and are craved. The people who appear in this ethnography each participate in some way in the banal and necessary experiments of care and life that sometimes hew toward normative expectations for relationality and sometimes purposefully diverge. In attending to normativity in this manner, I also show how the normal exists on an ever-receding horizon, a source of aspiration rather than attainment (Berlant 2011).

Most centrally, this book highlights the stakes of relationality for well-being. Child welfare policy and practice systematize particular visions of kinship relationships, with durable effects for the people touched by these systems. Some of these systems cultivate the possibility for supportive and lasting relationships, and some do not. I hope this book offers space for appreciating the creative work of building caregiving ties in and out of kinship constraints and that it illuminates the existential stakes of diverse welfare systems' orientations toward relationality. Relationships can injure and harm, but they can also transform. What are the conditions for a welfare system that nurtures well-being, that produces people who have people?

KINSHIP TECHNOLOGIES

How do people know each other to be family? How might we explain the connections that bind us to one another, that sometimes feel inherent, inevitable, or fated, and sometimes are understood as created consciously and with great effort? What happens when what feels like family to one person is illegible as family to an outside viewer? These are questions about being and belonging, about knowledge, and about the ways we narrate the relations that matter most. Like all cultural practices, they are specific to specific times and places.

With spiky white hair and energetic posture, Yamanta Tokuji embodied the figure of a roguish activist with a well-developed mission.[1] Yamanta had long been one of the most high-profile advocates for infant adoption in Japan, and in his work as a social welfare officer in Aichi Prefecture over the past thirty-plus years, he placed over 170 newborns in adoptive homes, circumventing the conventional practice of placing infants first in institutional care (Yamanta and Yorozuya 2015). I visited the Aichi Prefecture child guidance center where he worked and then later interviewed him and saw him present often at symposia. At one conference, Yamanta participated in a panel focusing on the need for Japanese child welfare officers to find adoptive homes for infants whose parents could not care for them rather than place these babies in institutions. As in my own interactions with him, I was struck by the fervency of his message, as though the speed and force with which he spoke would somehow convert those who opposed his practice. While his work as a child welfare officer had long been seen as maverick within the field, although increasingly more accepted as Japan's national policy moved closer to prioritizing family-based care, Yamanta situated newborn adoption as anything but out of the ordinary: a kinship practice so banal that even outside observers would not notice any divergence from normative family forms.

Yamanta spoke rapidly as he flipped through the images in his Power-Point, which featured photographs of smiling adoptive parents and children and adoptive family support groups. "You see," he told the audience, "support groups are essential because adoptive families are still rare in Japan, and in this country blood ties are considered the most important."[2] He scrolled swiftly through his slides. "The sort of work I do, the goal isn't to give children to couples who *want* children but to choose parents who will be *good* for each child. Here, look at this photograph of an adoptive family—see, look here, over time, their faces come to look alike, don't they? Please look here [*dandan, kao wa nitekurun desu ne, mite kudasai*]." He paused on a photograph of a couple with a young child and then moved onward. "Here's a photograph. What do you think? Don't the parents and children come to look alike, their faces? It's so interesting, isn't it? By living together, they come to look alike. Here's a photograph from a recent sports event. Their faces really look alike. And that's the point [*to iu koto de*]."

Over a period of two minutes, Yamanta enjoined his audience three times to conclude, based on photographic evidence, that despite living in a country where family is understood in terms of blood, even nonbiological kinship ties develop over time and are objectively evident in physical similarity. He made the same arguments in other events where I had heard him speak. Yamanta's focus on material resemblance worked to domesticate what is still seen in Japan as the strange practice of adopting unrelated children, where the intentions and desires of adoptive parents are suspect. In his presentation, onlookers were prompted to see adoptive kinship as materially evident and embodied in the same ways that biological parent-child similarities are often evident.

Yamanta's success as a child welfare reformer depended, in part, on his ability to present adoption as familiar, similar to everyday forms of kinship that do not warrant remark. His engagement with physical similarity is one among many ways that he and other interlocutors of mine interpreted, and discursively represented, the signs that count as relatedness. He skillfully situated his description of adoptive and foster families in cultural and historical Japanese context, obliquely referencing anxieties that adoptive families would be visibly marked as nonnormative. He provided his audience with interpretive tools—a semiotic framework—to self-reflexively interpret particular signs as "kinship."[3] This chapter focuses on these culturally and historically specific engagements with signs of relatedness, which, I argue, people use to understand kinship as such: what I call *kinship technologies*. In chapters that follow, I explore kinship technologies that focus on material qualities of households, discourse surrounding blood ties, physical qualities of children's growth and development that are taken as manifestations of interpersonal relationships, and practices of narrating experience, all of which help people regiment their and others' understandings of what family is and means.

In this chapter, I take up the ways that some people summoned physical similarity as a sign of kinship between nonbiologically related parents and children, often as a way to point to an objective connection in the material world, separate from the caregivers' instrumental desire to create family where there was none before. I place this practice in cultural context by discussing two key terms that people used to conceptualize nonbiological kinship: the Japanese concepts *en* and *kizuna*. I suggest that while *en* is often understood as an ineffable, inherent tie between people organized by similarity, a tie that can be broken but never made from nothing, *kizuna* references new, constructed ties that explicitly span difference. Focusing on the uses of these two terms, I explore the ways durable relational ties are seen to be embodied through physical similarity and caring proximity but at the same time always embrace or are haunted by difference: boundaries between family and nonfamily, and visible markers interpreted as otherness, like ethnicity and race. The discursive regimentation of material similarity points to the changing and often fraught ways relatedness encompasses sameness and difference in Japan, alongside the specter of social stigma.

"You Don't Know from Which Horse the Bone Comes"

My research explores a marginalized and in many ways invisible world of Japanese fostering and adoption. Japan's extensive system of child welfare institutions, augmented by a relatively small family foster care program, is not well understood in Japan. In fact, most people in Japan know little about the 610 child welfare institutions and 145 institutions for babies that extend across the nation, caring for over 25,000 state wards. In general, the adoptive and foster parents I spoke to had come to know about the system only upon investigating the possibility of adoption. About 19 percent of children in the child welfare system are placed in family-based foster care, few of whom are available for adoption, as they have not been formally relinquished by their biological parents (Kodomo kateichō 2024, 5). Many of my foster parent interlocutors had themselves hoped to adopt but were placed with children whose biological parents still retained parental rights. Fostering often ends up being a long-term placement.

Even though in Japan there is a long history of using adoption for the purpose of maintaining a family line, unknown and unrelated children have not been the targets of these adoptions. In traditional adoption, called regular adoption (*futsū yōshiengumi*), adoptees are often children of extended family members or are adults: sons-in-law, cousins' children, employees, or even married couples. This type of adoption is often described as feudal, conducted for the sake or the benefit of the patriarchal family. Adoption in which the legal ties between a child and their biological parents are removed—what most in the contemporary West might think of as adoption—was enacted in Japan only in 1988. This kind of adoption, called special adoption (*tokubetsu yōshiengumi*), was created under the auspices of the child welfare system and is considered for the sake of the child.[4]

Child welfare officials evaluating potential foster and adoptive parents are often concerned with identifying the reasons a couple wants to take in an unrelated child: Is the couple instrumentally hoping to obtain an heir? Are they adopting in exchange for care in their old age? Or are their actions motivated by the desire to love and care for a child without parents? It is for this reason that Yamanta focused on how adoptive placements are done with the child's best interests in mind. A couple expressing too much desire for a nonrelated child is viewed with suspicion. We might consider this tension as an expression of what Viviana Zelizer (2000) calls "hostile worlds": the notion that instrumental (or economically motivated) action cannot also be motivated by emotion. Sylvia Yanagisako (2002) also critiques the ways that instrumentality and emotion are perceived as incompatible forces in conceptualizing kinship. These theoretical frameworks clarify the concern we see in Japan regarding the motivations of an adoptive or foster parent and the emphasis many of my interlocutors placed on distancing their own family practices from their personal desires or the possibility for instrumental gain.[5]

In addition to concerns that their motives might seem overly self-interested, Japanese foster and adoptive parents are aware that taking in an unrelated child is still often thought of as strange or somewhat pitiful (*kawaisō*).[6] My interlocutors located this pathos on two levels: adopted children are considered wretched for having been abandoned by their families, but adoptive parents themselves are also thought to be odd for adopting a child whose origins are unknown and likely unsavory (Bryant 1990). This sentiment is expressed by an adage: you don't know from which horse the bone comes (*doko no uma no hone ka wakaranai*).[7] Children who have been for some reason abandoned by their families are often thought to have "bad blood" (*ketsuen ga kitanai*) and may have difficulty getting married (Goodman 2000; Nishida 2011).

Many foster or adoptive parents grapple with their family practices diverging from an expectation that parents and children should be connected by blood ties. These families generally hope they will not be visibly marked as different: they hope that passersby on the street will not immediately understand that their families are not "normal."[8] Several of my research contacts noted that they would be hesitant to take in a non-Asian child—not because of racism, they were quick to point out, but because a non-Asian child would immediately mark their family as different. Kinship practices in Japan often trace boundaries between self and other that align with persistent notions of Japanese mono-ethnicity. The ways material signs are interpreted in Japan—as in other places—thus articulate with diverse sets of local norms and practices, cultural ideologies that categorize some interpersonal relationships as more desirable than others, national-cultural identities, and boundaries of belonging.

Stigma and Secrecy

Children who are not cared for by kin are often considered pitiful (*kawaisō*), excluded from networks of care that are understood as normative and proper. In an extended interview, two foster mothers, Hara Kazuko and Funabashi Tomomi, elucidated different aspects of stigma against children from state care. Their accounts illuminate the appeal of being unmarked and the reasons some families choose to keep secret the fact of adoption or foster care.[9]

Hara and her husband had two foster sons, and while they had told their family about the children, they represented the boys to their neighbors as children of kin. "If the neighbors looked at the children and thought, 'Ah, they are *that* kind of kid,' it would just be pitiful," Hara said. "Is there less prejudice towards children of kin, then?" I asked. Hara considered. "It's just that '*Those kids were raised in a child welfare institution*,' that kind of, um, it's that—there is no one to take them in [*ukeire ga nai*]. . . . It's different, having people think, '*what kind* of child is that I wonder [*dōiu ko nano ka na tte*],' versus thinking, 'this is the child of kin [*shinseki no ko tte*].'" Hara's comparison of pitiful children, who have no one to take them in, with children living within an extended kinship network, evokes starkly divergent models of family solidarity and care. By representing her foster children as children of kin, the children are socially converted from abandoned with mysterious and unsavory pasts to cared-for and socially legible members of a known family, connected if not through biological reproduction then by extended genealogical lines of sameness. Children raised in child welfare institutions seem to inhabit unincorporable forms of difference.

Funabashi Tomomi, the other foster mother, had herself worked in a child welfare institution and did not feel negatively about children in state care. However, experiences with neighbors and friends had made her aware that her children were perceived negatively. She learned shortly after taking in her first foster son that rumors surrounding the family had been circulating within their housing complex. She had brought her foster son, who was one and a half years old at the time, to play in a nearby park. The little boy was running around and picked up a twig and threw it. A woman Funabashi had never met but who lived in the same complex was watching her own child play. Observing Funabashi's son throw the twig, she commented to Funabashi, "Just as one might think [*yappari*], children raised in that kind of place are violent, aren't they." Funabashi was dismayed by the woman's attitude. Now aware of the rumors circulating, she and her husband decided to move. It wasn't good, she said, for a child so young to be subject to that kind of stigma.

Later on, Funabashi happened to meet a woman who lived in her old housing complex. The woman, referring to Funabashi's foster children, commented, "Wow, in your household you're properly raising them, aren't you?" Funabashi, who is a soft-spoken woman, made clear her indignation as she recounted this story. "It's as if she *wanted* to say, 'Wow, you're not hitting and kicking your children, are you!'" Referring to Hara's account, she noted that because of this sort of prejudice—against both foster parents and children—she understood why it might be preferable to represent one's foster children as children of kin.[10] She and her husband had decided not to tell anyone, including the children themselves, that they are not biologically related.

These logics about *bad blood* and a *pitiful* background constitute what Erving Goffman has called a "stigma theory," an "ideology to explain [a person's] inferiority and account for the danger he represents" (1963, 5). The minor accomplishments of one who experiences stigma, Goffman writes, "may be assessed as signs of remarkable and noteworthy capacities in the circumstances" (1963, 14).[11] For Funabashi, the mere ordinariness of her care for her children provoked wonder and surprise. Despite her children's putative dark pasts, despite the strangeness of fostering and the extension of that strangeness to the foster parents themselves, despite myths that nonrelated parents are more likely to abuse children than biologically related parents—she was "properly" raising her boys.

One adoptive mother named Hamabata Toshiko described how it took her a long time to consider adoption. "It just has a very . . . dark feeling [*kurai kanji*], doesn't it?" she said. "Doesn't it make you feel a little unpleasant [*iwakan*]?" she asked me with a slight laugh. "I've heard people say that," I answered. "It's not the sort of thing you could say easily in public," Hamabata went on, "but . . . it's like, 'pitiful' [*kawaisō*]." When she and her husband finally decided to adopt a small boy from a child welfare institution, she described her surprise at the joy with which the staff sent him off. It was only later, thinking back on our conversation, that I realized her surprise was rooted in the sense that adoption is fundamentally a dark, pitiful practice, connected to the dark past and pitiful experiences of the children in question. This darkness was, for Hamabata, also perhaps related to the pathos of the adopters themselves—often, as was the case of the Hamabatas, people whose inability to bear their own children led them to bring in unknown children from unknown families.

While Hamabata engaged in social welfare volunteer work and had a long-term foster care relationship with a young woman who was now living independently, Hamabata had not told her son that he had been adopted through the foster care system, and she and her husband kept this fact a secret from non–foster parent friends and neighbors. I had met Hamabata through a foster parent research contact, and she agreed to an interview. We decided to meet at a cafe in the area where she lived, a decision we quickly regretted. After peeking into two cafes near the train station, both of which were full, we ended up at a coffee shop where, Hamabata told me in a whisper, the mother of one of her son's schoolmates worked. We conducted our interview in awkward *soto* voice, Hamabata pointing to the word *adoption* (*yōshiengumi*) on my list of interview questions rather than speaking it out loud. She recounted the story of their adoption process and told me how, when the boy first came to their house, they had traveled to a distant hospital to care for him when he got sick, hoping not to run into anyone they knew. After they formally adopted him and changed his name, they switched schools.

At the end of our two-hour interview, after I turned off my audio recorder, Hamabata told me with some concern that as her son grows older, he looks more and more dissimilar to her and her husband. But, she said, his mannerisms (*kuse*) are the same, and his voice on the phone sounds like her husband's. Hamabata noted that this happens with married couples who start to look alike (*nitamono fūfu*)—a natural result, she said, of eating the same food and living together. Troubling physical dissimilarities were thus balanced by slightly less tangible similarities, signs of long affiliation. In addition, Hamabata told me, both her son's and her husband's blood types are B, while she is an O. Since her husband is B, and it was thus biologically possible for their son to also be a B, it's all "okay [*daijyōbu*]"—otherwise, she said, they would certainly have had to confess the truth (*kokuchi suru*) to their son by now.[12]

But this secrecy lived on borrowed time. Irrefutable proof of the Hamabatas' son's origins lay in his household registry, which documented all the addresses where he had lived during his life: a baby home, a foster home, another child welfare institution, and finally the Hamabata household. He had recently taken his household registry with him to apply for his driver's license, and when he returned from that errand, he left the registry unfolded and open on the dining room table. Hamabata knew that he understood the implication of the registry, just as she was aware that he surely remembered something of the time before he came to their household as a five-year-old. ("Do *you* remember anything from when you were five?" she asked me during our interview.) Yet she was sure he could not bring himself to ask her about it, and she could not make herself broach the subject with him. His household registry remained open on the family table, the site of eating and care that had made him come to resemble the Hamabatas to begin with, untouchable proof of that which could not be said.[13]

Abe Saori, an adoptive mother of an eleven-year-old girl, had not told her daughter about the adoption but was generally open with foster parent friends. Although Abe knew that she would need to tell her daughter eventually, there was no necessity (*hitsuyō*) yet. The moment of confession—and the rebellion she imagined from her daughter, upon learning later in life—was constantly deferred to the future. This was because it was not immediately apparent that the Abe parents were not biologically related to their daughter. The teachers at the girl's school, for example, had no idea she was adopted. "And by coincidence," Abe told me in the manner of conveying an improbable tale, "we didn't choose this, you know, but once we had adopted her, we found out—our blood types are the same!" Abe drew out the word *same* (*onaji*) into three slow incredulous syllables, *o-na-ji*. "Truly. And our personalities match too." I asked if they look alike. Whispering, Abe replied, "Well, I guess we don't actually look that much alike now. But at ages two or three, she was my spitting image [*sokkuri*]."

For Abe, the degree to which a family would be forced to confess the fact of adoption was the degree to which it was superficially evident that parent and child were not biologically related. In her own case—since she had become interested in parenthood later in life, after developing her career, and then spent many years doing infertility treatment—her only concerns were the small indicators that something was unusual about their family. "When from the start the faces are different, well, those people talk about the adoption, don't they," she remarked. However, the Abe family's case, she continued, seems to be perfectly normal, except that her more advanced age marks her as being different. Still, the other parents at her daughter's school don't know. "They probably just think, 'That's an old mom.'" Abe's ability to conceal the nonnormativity of her family situation contrasts with transracial adoption, she noted, in which case an onlooker knows immediately that a child has been adopted. The visible evidence would require discursive and communicative clarity; there could be no concealment, a situation that Abe thought might in some ways be easier.[14]

Given the stigma that follows adoptive and foster families in Japan, it should not seem strange that Yamanta Tokuji, introduced at the start of this chapter, repeatedly reinforced to his symposium audience how the adoptive parents and children in his photographs "come to look alike." "Coming to look alike" is a measure of anxieties surrounding the boundaries of sameness and difference, what can be hidden and what is impossible to hide.

When Recognizing Family Takes Work

Certain relationships, in certain places, are more readily understood as kinship than others. This is in part because signs that mediate human relatedness are interpreted in socially and historically specific ways. The concept of kinship technologies situates the production of any kind of kinship as an inherently cultural and historical process, mediated by self-reflexive interpretations of what counts as relatedness. Extending scholarship on assisted reproduction with new reproductive technologies, which examines how novel technologies reconfigure kinship in novel ways (Strathern 1992; Franklin 1997; Lock 1998; Rapp 1999; Thompson 2005; Ivry 2010), I suggest that while specific medical techniques may be new, assistance to reproductive practices is as old as humans have had families. Anthropological studies of reproductive technologies are generally framed around examining new technological assistances that overlay processes of natural biological procreation. In contrast, I suggest that there is no such thing as *non*assisted kinship: the production of kinship relationships is always already assisted by culture and, as I show here, by specific engagements with signs of relatedness. These culturally and historically specific assistances constitute kinship technologies. The artifice implied in the term is intentional: I argue that kinship, even biological kinship, does not emerge naturally without affirmative actions. Contingency and the signs that point back to histories of caregiving are at the heart of kinship (Stasch 2009, chap. 4).

The ways my interlocutors in Japan discursively engaged with signs of physical resemblance point to one way that people organize material qualities as relevant signs of intimate kinship ties. Representations of the body are often used to make certain sorts of claims seem perfectly natural, rooted in material and seemingly objective reality (Goldfarb 2010). For this reason, citing physical resemblance between nonbiological parents and their children might mitigate suspicion that a foster or adoptive parent doesn't have a "real" or socially legitimate connection to a child. Noting physical resemblance—a normative sign of socially recognizable relatedness—may also be a response to common existential anxieties of parents (and children) in general: the desire to interrogate *why* certain relationships exist,

how they came to be, and what the relationships mean. Not all foster and adoptive families in Japan focus on physical similarity as signs of relatedness, although
many do, be it the appearance of a child's face, the way a child moves and speaks,
or the tone of a child's voice. Material similarity constitutes one among many
conventionally understood signs of family in Japan, which additionally include
intellectual ability, personality traits, genetic predispositions and blood type.
These characteristics are all relevant in Japan as indications of relatedness. The
fact that material resemblance, specifically, is commonly mobilized requires
analysis.

Despite Yamanta's claims that parent-child resemblances are self-evident,
Yamanta also had to explain signs of relatedness in conventionally understood
ways. As scholars of representation have shown, representations' persuasive-
ness is often tied to the degree that they seem unmotivated by personal desire,
emanating from a distant source (Keane 1997, 2003; Povinelli 2002a). However,
as Webb Keane has argued, representations are acts in the world, vulnerable to
the same failures as action, contingent on the sign interpreter and giving rise to
and transforming "modalities of action and subjectivity" (2003, 413). Yamanta's
repeated insistence that his audience note the physical similarity between adoptive parents and children highlights how the recognition of material similarity
is itself open to the hazards of (mis)interpretation. Without prompting, others
might not recognize this similarity or see it as an indicator of "true," socially
legitimate kinship.

But similarity is a tricky quality: as Nelson Goodman has pointed out, "Anything is in some way like anything else" (1972, 440). A focus on the semiotics of
material signs reinforces the contingencies of the ways things become taken as
signs and what these signs are taken to mean. These contingencies are in turn
very much shaped by the underlying social context, including power differen-
tials, stigma, and perceived racial and ethnic boundaries.[15]

Here I suggest that kinship technologies are the cultural frameworks through
which people understand the transformation of nonkin into kin—what Signe
Howell calls "kinning" (2006).[16] In Japan, this "kinning" process may be framed
as visible to onlookers, and culturally specific concepts play a role in the ways
a child's future and past trajectory is seen to overlap with that of the adoptive
family. I suggest that in Japan, two concepts organize this future and past trajectory: en (a divine or ineffable tie or connection) and kizuna (a connection, tie,
or bond). Most centrally, my Japanese interlocutors who focused predominantly
on the concept of en in describing a connection to their children portrayed an
adopted child as not a "previously unconnected person" but rather quite the contrary. For these people, their children were always already connected to them in
an obligatory tie of fate and compulsion separate from their own instrumental-

ity or desire. Those who focused more on *kizuna*, however, tended to explicitly recognize their children's pasts as independent of their own and focused on the connections that they created after the child came to live with them. Some people engaged with both concepts at once, negotiating both physical similarity and caring proximity as qualities shaping their family relationships. Both *en* and *kizuna* were often (but not always) understood to be embodied, materialized in tangible evidence of a kinship tie. However, people more concerned with the potential stigma of adoptive or foster relationships were more likely to invoke their children as always already connected to them through an inevitable and ineffable bond, rather than from a connection they built together over time, through effort, and across difference.

En: An Ineffable and Obligatory Tie

En is a Buddhist term for the cause or initial mover precipitating a result, and is commonly used to indicate the grounds for human relationships. *En* is often discussed in an ordered set of three: ties of blood, land or neighborhood ties, and associational ties (including those of a workplace) (*ketsuen*, *chien*, and *shaen*). All three are generally understood as social ties that one does not choose (*erabenai en*) (Ueno 1987).

There is another concept of *en* that has a different logic and speaks to what I call an ineffable bond that operates above individual intention or desire. Referenced simply as *en* without the modifier of blood-*en*, land-*en*, or association-*en*, people describe "having *en*" (*en ga aru*) to refer to a "play of chance and fate" that articulates "an aesthetic of intuition and wonder" (Nozawa 2015, 391). People in Japan use the term, not uncommonly, with relative strangers or foreign anthropologists to place themselves and their conversation partners in a mutual framework organized around similarities that have been retrospectively identified and that, in conversation, generate further open-ended similarities. "Having *en*" with someone means that one is incorporated into some imagination of a relationship that existed prior to its recognition and may guide future intersections of fate.

When my interlocutors in Japan say that *en* brought them together with their adopted or fostered children, they are referring to the ineffable *en* of chance and fate—but at the same time, their use of the term articulates interdiscursively (Bakhtin 1981) with the *en* of blood, community, and association. If *en* binds nonbiologically related parents and children, that is because blood *en* has proven insufficiently durable to connect the child to their biological family. The adoptive bond exists because of the strength of ineffable *en*, which one can neither explain nor seek to understand (Cannell 2013). The inability to know the workings of *en* is a source of *en*'s power: it is a force of divinity or of nature, its very inaccessibility to rational calculation a key factor behind its efficacy. *En* must be made known in what Webb Keane (1997) calls "revealed signs" that are taken to have a meaning rooted in and directly linked to material reality. In the case at hand, indexical factors—qualities that seem to tie two people together through some material causal tie—include blood type, mannerisms, and physical similarity.

A married couple, Murakami Takako and Kunio, elaborated the ways that revealed material signs authorized their parenthood to their adopted sons. The Murakamis framed their seven years of infertility treatment and long path to adoption as a road that led them to the children that Takako, if she had been *able* to give birth, would have biologically conceived and given birth to. The organization through which the Murakamis adopted displayed photographs of available children. When the couple approached the photographs, lined up in a row, they said, they both immediately knew. "My eye fell on one little boy," Kunio said. "This little boy, he looks like I did when I was a child." "And I thought the same thing," said Takako. "That little boy is now our eldest son." "When I think about it now," Kunio said, "I feel that there must have been some connection. I felt compelled [*ki ni natte*]. As soon as I heard about his background, it was like, we have to help him. I had an extremely strong feeling of *en*, a connection." "It was as if there is no child but this child," Takako said. "It was not at all logical; it was intuition [*chyokkan*]." The more they discovered about the boy, the more the sense of ineffable connection increased. It turned out that the boy's biological mother was also named Takako. Later, when they were completing the legal steps for adoption, they saw in the boy's family registry that his mother had given birth to another child after him whom she had also relinquished. The Murakamis were able to adopt him as well. After a year or so, the couple told me, the eldest boy came to strongly resemble not Kunio, as he did initially, but Takako and her father. The younger boy, the couple said, looks like Kunio and Kunio's mother.

The couple's narratives did not focus on a resemblance that emerged over time. Rather, these material ties were always already present. Recognized initially through physical similarity and a sense of compulsion, neither self-centered nor logical, the couple realized in retrospect that *en*, an ineffable connection, tied them and their children. Had Takako given birth, these are the children who would have been born. Notably, Kunio in particular constantly referenced the presence of a blood connection between the brothers and a lack of a blood tie between themselves and the children while simultaneously disavowing the importance of blood as a bond. This constant disavowal (implying the value placed on blood ties) was a pattern for many of my interlocutors; public discourses on adoption and fostering in Japan are similarly often marked by the phrase "transcending blood ties" (*ketsuen o koete*) (Nobe 2018). While the siblings were connected to each other by blood—a bond that Kunio felt should not be broken—the Murakamis sought a way to articulate their own equally compulsory tie to their children, through reference to ties of *en*.[17]

"A 'Blood Relationship' without a Blood Tie"

The sense of compulsion and obligatory ties illustrate the "as if" nature of adoption, as adoptive parents negotiate between the perspective that they are adopting a stranger's child and the perspective that their adoptive child is as naturally tied to them as a biologically related child. One Japanese adoption organization, Wa no Kai, provides an interesting example of this negotiation.[18] Wa no Kai is notable for two major reasons. First, adoptive parents could not specify the type of child they wanted (they could not choose a child). Rather, they had to accept any child regardless of disability or race. If they declined a child that was offered to them, their ties to Wa no Kai would be forever terminated. In this way, adoptive parents were explicitly barred from choice, and the obligatory nature of adoptive kinship was institutionalized within the group's rules and regulations. Second, adoptive parents were enjoined to honor the birth mother and maintain relationships with her, mediated by Wa no Kai.[19] Wa no Kai maintained that the birth mother must remain in the child's life because the child chose to be born to the birth mother. Obligatory relationality was thus situated within the child's own agency.

Wa no Kai made explicit that adoptive relationships should mimic blood ties: the group's objective was to help adoptive parents create a "'blood relationship' without a blood tie" (*ketsuen naki "ketsuen kankei"*). This blood relationship without a blood tie was produced discursively and pragmatically, through training to verbally articulate the sorrows of infertility and social stigma against adoptive families, through the adoptive parents' acceptance of the importance of the child's biological mother, and through recognizing that their own tie to the child was as obligatory as that of the birth mother. Past a certain point, Wa no Kai argued, a pregnant person cannot prevent the birth of a child; nor can the potential adoptive parents pursuing kinship through Wa no Kai. As one of the group's members wrote, "From before birth, you must decide that the child is 'my child'—from before meeting, you must accept the adopted child as your own child and take this fact as predestined [*shukumei*]" (Rakugi 2006, 263). Wa no Kai made clear that neither the birth parent nor the adoptive parent chooses what kind of child will be born—it is the parent's fate to accept the child, no matter what (*unmei toshite ukeire*) (Rakugi 2006, 256). The group argued that understanding that choice inheres in the child, rather than the parent, is the first step in creating a "'blood relationship' without a blood tie." Wa no Kai made explicit the ways biological ties are obligatory precisely because they are distanced from the intent or desire of the parent, a stance that underlay the group's prioritization of the biological mother.[20]

Wa no Kai's objective was to create a world in which non–blood-related parents and children could be recognized and conceptualized as kin within Japanese society. According to the group, this is a process that will require a paradigm shift away from the assumption that parents and children are, de facto, biologically related and will thus look like each other (Rakugi 2006). Creating a "'blood relationship' without a blood tie," in which adoptive parents cannot refuse a child no matter what the child looks like, is also about highlighting the way difference—a lack of physical similarity, or disability, or racial difference—can live within kinship relationships. Wa no Kai's frustration with cultural assumptions of physical similarity expressed how the material semiotics of interpersonal relationships matter precisely because they are vulnerable to outside interpretation. Wa no Kai emphasized the power inherent in a bond not chosen by the parent and in the ineffable tie between parents and children. However, onlookers might find this relationship outside comprehension (*sōteigai*) (Rakugi 2006, 263) or, worse, not kinship at all. No matter where people understand the origin of kinship ties, the possibility of misrecognition remains troubling.

I have illustrated the ways many forms of stigma—anxieties surrounding sameness and difference, concern regarding the confession of adoption, and the question of instrumentality and desire—are negotiated through framing an adoptive relationship as obligatory, specifically through reference to the concept of *en*. Wa no Kai attempted to frame adoptive kinship as obligatory, like biological kinship, but at the same time, the group was frustrated with cultural assumptions that parents and children should naturally look alike. This quandary expresses a dilemma at the heart of kinship relationships in Japan. The following section considers what might happen to people's understandings of relationality if adoptive and foster kinship is explicitly understood as *non*obligatory.

Kizuna: Created and Chosen Ties

I suggest that the concept of *kizuna*, specifically as taken up within the Japanese child welfare community, offers a radical sense of choice inhering within family relationships. *Kizuna*, which is often translated as ties or connections, entails none of the Buddhist connotations of *en*.[21] We might say that the notion of *en* "backforms" the reality of parent-child bonds, mapping these bonds in parallel to a genealogical grid (Povinelli 2002b): *en* reduces potential difference to sameness by uniting a child's past, present, and future with that of the adoptive family (Yngvesson 2010). In contrast, people in Japan often reference *kizuna* to index connections created consciously, through effort over time, and in the face of sometimes very durable alterity.

In popular parlance, *kizuna* implies a connection across distance or difference, an identification of similarity when similarity cannot be taken for granted, and sometimes a unity of hope, will, or effort in the face of calamity. As a concept, *kizuna* has obtained heightened salience in the past thirty years. A search of the archives of a major newspaper, the *Asahi Shimbun*, reveals that occurrences of the term *kizuna* increased markedly in recent years and have been especially high during years of great national misfortune. The trend is striking: there were 8 incidences of the word *kizuna* in *Asahi* archives for 1984; 81 references in 1994 (and 116 in 1995, the year of the Great Hanshin Earthquake in Kobe); and 296 in 2004, tracing a slow increase over two decades. In 2010 there were 636 references. One year later—the year of the earthquake, tsunami, and nuclear disaster in Tōhoku (Northern Japan)—the term appeared 2,531 times in the newspaper. The term was selected in 2011 as the kanji of the year based on a nationwide vote on the Chinese character that seemed to most encapsulate the past year's mood.[22] *Kizuna* became a catchphrase to encompass the putative ties between stranger volunteers from across the country and damaged Tōhoku, which is otherwise perceived as provincial and distanced from the heart of the cosmopolitan nation. Scaling up this logic of connection over geopolitical and affective space, *kizuna* was also mobilized to describe connections between Japan and foreign nations or foreign donors. Additionally, the term was used to reference ties between family members and communities within Tōhoku, who endured with oft-remarked solidarity and without the violence or looting that sometimes follows natural disasters; *kizuna* was mobilized to comment on this unique social cohesion.[23] Other public discourses used the term to describe an upsurge of marriages *and* infidelities as people reevaluated their lives in the wake of the triple disaster.[24] In all cases, *kizuna* traced connections across presumed alterity or social and geopolitical distance.

Kizuna has been used consistently within Japan's foster and adoptive community to reference new and durable ties created out of nothing. The term evokes surprise at the novel and unexpected, the emergent, that which breaks with common assumptions of solidarity. We see engagements with the term in the context of child welfare and the immediate shadow of the March 2011 disasters in a news broadcast a month later featuring several foster parents from the Kantō area who visited Tōhoku to assess the needs of children orphaned by the tsunami. After summarizing these foster parents' investigations, the narrator notes that children are the treasures (*takara*) of the country. From the *kizuna* broken by the tsunami, the national foster parent association will continue to work to build new *kizuna* (*arata na kizuna o tsunagō*).[25] Here, discourses about *kizuna* overtly celebrate adoptive and foster families as a new kind of family (*atarashii kazoku*)—which is, in fact, the name of the journal published by a research group focusing on adoption and fostering. A local program to popularize foster care in a city in southern Japan was called *atarashii kizuna*, or "new ties." The Kizuna Group, an adoptive parent support group that Yamanta Tokuji (introduced above) was affiliated with, published an edited volume entitled *Family Making* (*kazoku zukuri*) (1997). The book of a doctor who, like Yamanta, long operated independently in organizing adoptions references *kizuna* as ties created explicitly through the process of adoption (Samejima 2006). Finally, a book published by the religious group Tenrikyō, whose adherents consider foster care a core religious and ethical practice, proclaims on its slipcover, "Foster parents—*kizuna* created by God" (*sato oya—kamisama ga musunda kizuna*) (2010).

Unlike naturalized ties of blood or ineffable always already present ties of *en*, in the context of adoption and fostering in Japan, *kizuna* are bonds created by doctors, God, or couples working to become parents. Thus, while people in Japan might colloquially say that a married couple decided to make a family by having children, family-making by marriage and sexual reproduction is understood as different in kind from the created families joined by *kizuna*. Many groups supporting adoption and fostering highlight the element of choice, specifically in the face of infertility: the moment at which a couple (almost always heterosexual, almost always married) chooses to welcome (*mukae*) a nonrelated child into the family rather than remaining childless. What binds the parents and child is not blood but love. In fact, as the Kizuna Group's publication notes, "For us parents and children, to the degree that we lack a connection by 'blood,' we believe that we make up for that amount in 'love'" (Kizuna no Kai 1997, iii). Contributors to this edited volume describe how the *kizuna* between parents and child become deeper and deeper over time (for example, "*oyako no kizuna mo dandan fukamari*," Kizuna no Kai 1997, 85). Kinship ties are not assumed to exist already: they must be created over time, compensated in love for what they lack in blood.

A television broadcast from 2010, featuring a foster parent couple caring for six foster children without the intent to adopt, notes repeatedly that these children who seem so much like blood-related siblings are not, in fact, blood-related.[26] Toward the end of the feature, the narrator notes the deepening *kizuna* of the heart or spirit (*kokoro no kizuna*), and the foster father tells the camera, "Eating together, sleeping together, you become parent and child, you become siblings. I always say, even if your last names are different, you're still siblings.

It's interesting; it's fun. That transformation." The narrator closes dramatically: "Even without a blood tie, this big foster family is energetic [*chi no tsunagari nakutemo, sato oya daikazoku, ima mo genki desu*]!" The dramatic tension of the broadcast hinges on the assumption that at first glance, this foster family looks like any large and lively family while the surprising revelation is that the children are not related by blood. The takeaway message is that this family seems outwardly like any normal large family but has come to be that way over time through shared food and contact. The viewer is impressed with possibilities for alternative intimacies.

For many foster parents, difference does not prevent the emergence of chosen and created kinship. This final example articulates with the experiences of many foster families I met in Japan: people I thought of as professional foster parents. These people were not overly burdened by hopes for constituting a normative-seeming family because they took in many children over many years and were active and unapologetic about their activities. Their discursively constructed notions of family were centered on affectively loaded bodily interactions over time. Hirata Yumi was one foster parent who, in her matter-of-fact way, did not belabor her and her husband's kinship with their intellectually disabled adult foster son. In fact, it was a question from her son that prompted her to delineate their family in contrast to culturally standard kinship models. Before her son turned eighteen and would age out of the foster care system, he went through a period of regression, which Hirata realized was connected to anxiety about his future.[27] At one point, crying, he asked her, "What *is* 'family' [*kazoku tte nani*]?" Hirata described her response: "At that moment, I had no idea how to answer him. I thought, 'What is it I wonder,' so I looked it up [in a dictionary]. You know it says a family is a blood tie. . . . But I didn't tell him that definition. I told him that there are lots of different types of family, and even if there isn't a blood tie, if you live together that's 'family.' And then the next question he asked was, 'So "family" is until when [*itsu made kazoku na no*]?' I told him, 'This is *always* "family," even if you leave home in the future, this is "family," so you can come back any time.'"

For Hirata and many foster parents like her, family is most centrally a place to return to (*yoridokoro*), where people who care about each other live. Hirata's statement typifies an attitude shared by many foster parents in which proximity creates kinship. While similarity may indeed emerge through cohabitation, and when remarked upon might in fact bring pleasure to a foster or adoptive parent, a lack of similarity would never undermine the reality of that kinship tie. For these families, relatedness emerges through shared meals, shared baths, shared time, and shared space in which family is chosen rather than prescribed and home is the place to which you can always return.

★ ★ ★

Discourses surrounding adoptive and foster kinship in Japan are exactly the sort of recursive "epistemic device[s]" that Sarah Franklin and Susan McKinnon cite, in which "kinship helps to constitute what it describes" (2001, 2). Much of the "new kinship" literature in anthropology tracks the sorts of processes Yamanta highlights, in which kinship is itself constituted by caring practices instantiated over time. Janet Carsten cites examples of this sort of process from many countries and highlights her own research with Malay people, where foster children are understood to "gradually come to resemble" foster relatives "in appearance and manner." She continues, "If food is gradually transformed into blood in the body, and those who live together come to resemble each other as well as develop emotional closeness, then in the long term this is surely a quite literal process of creating kinship" (2004, 139).

However, an understanding of kinship as emergent over time and visible in bodies requires interactive, iterative labor. In one striking instance, I witnessed a group of foster mothers engage in enthusiastic and almost competitive conversation, in which each woman listed all the ways that the other women and their foster children resembled each other. I understood these foster parents as mirroring to each other the legitimacy of a created kinship bond that was supposedly materially evident and transparent to outside interpretation.

The stigma surrounding adoption and fostering in Japan articulates with specific semiotic frameworks that make adoptive and foster relationships legible or illegible as kinship to onlookers. On the one hand, maintaining a focus on the material body might reinforce biological standards of kinship and what people in Japan call "blood ideology" (*ketsuen shugi*), from which adoptive families are forever excluded. On the other hand, a discursive focus on physical mimesis in adoptive relationships upends narrowly defined concepts of the blood tie as constituting kinship, highlighting ways that blood ties are also often understood as defined by the combination of affective, substantive, and legal ties (Schneider 1968; Nobe 2018). If physical resemblance is evident in adoptive *and* biological kinship, biological descent becomes an arbitrary ground for recognizing family ties.

Yet for many in Japan, bonds within families—*ketsuen*, the ties of blood—should be inviolable, the most obligatory of social bonds. Children in state care scandalously embody a threat to conventional understandings of parent-child relationships as naturally following from the fact of biological procreation and reveal the ways a child must be accepted and welcomed even into its family of origin through caring actions (Stasch 2009, chap. 4). As Kath Weston has illustrated in the case of gay communities in late-twentieth-century United States, the fact that people can be ejected from their birth families both undercuts the presumed strength of biology to make family and reinforces the durability of "families we choose" (1991). The suggestion that parent-child ties might actually be contingent draws into question a foundational myth of human relationality, and kinship more specifically, in Japan.

While scholarship on chosen families generally argues that kinship is, in fact, a product of intimate labor, most deeply a "mutuality of being" (Sahlins 2011, 2013), I close this chapter by highlighting how difference underlies and haunts the pragmatic semiotics of the kinship technologies I have described (Goldfarb and Bamford, eds., 2024).[28] While *en* and *kizuna* may authorize foster and adoptive relationships, the child's own differences from the family can be a constant source of concern from parents who hope to conceal the fact of adoption. In other cases, a child's differences are elided through the notion that the child always already belongs—what Barbara Yngvesson calls a violent transformation of the child's "radical difference" into "sameness" (2010, 45; Eng 2010).

In the case of children who have spent time in neglectful or maltreating families—as many children adopted or fostered in Japan have—troubled pasts may in fact require parents to recognize and accept the child as touched by difference and indeed trauma. In her ethnography of attachment disorder treatment, Rachel Stryker has argued that a major problem for adoptive families in the United States is the desire to adopt a child without a past, a child that is perfectly incorporable into the perfect family (2010). Beyond the specter of disorder, however, Yngvesson speaks for her own family's experience in arguing that "the child had a history already and must have its history the whole time, without my attempting to transform this into our history" (2010, 174). This requires "respecting the differences of the child without insisting on the child's difference, and it means acknowledging our connections to our child without insisting on the child's sameness" (Yngvesson 2010, 174).

Many of the foster and adoptive parents I met in Japan do, to some degree, recognize and respect their children's differences and their connections to other places, other pasts, and even other families. These are the parents who see kinship as emerging most centrally out of material proximity rather than insisting on material similarity. One mother of two adopted children from separate biological families often noted that the four of them are family, "although all with different faces." Yet dominant understandings of kinship in Japan still situate physical similarity as an index of a real family connection. Discourses surrounding physical similarity tether kinship to what Karen Fields calls the "invisible ontology" of "racecraft": a set of understandings about the ways that visible signs reflect invisible qualities of a person. This invisible ontology also has a corollary, which is that inward qualities of sameness or difference require and acquire "anchors in sensible experience" (2001, 295)—in this case, physical resemblance. If a non-biologically related parent and child are said to look alike, it might be assumed that they share an ontological similarity in kind, a connection that transcends differences of origin. Stigma, however, haunts the experiences of families "with different faces."

While the newness of families joined by *kizuna*, rather than blood, might make them stand out as unusual in a Japanese context, discourses surrounding physical similarity mark adoptive and foster ties as comprehensible within a broader ideological framework of Japanese ethno-nationalist identity, an ideological alignment that the notion of *en*, as transcendent tie, reinforces. The ties that bind, in this case, refer in the negative to the ties that as yet remain difficult to imagine in Japan: families that trouble boundaries between putatively visible markers of difference, ethnicity, and race. At the same time—at risk of cliché, in a *kizuna*-saturated contemporary Japan—the prevalence of the notion of new ties created by choice implies the loosening of Japanese kinship relationships from the fated or obligatory, including those presumed by ethno-nationalist frameworks. These new ties, rather, embrace the hard work of intimacy that at first glance may not look like kinship.

BREAD DAYS AND RICE DAYS

Ichikawa Reiko was a staff member at a child welfare institution in the Tokyo metropolitan area that cared for around sixty-five children between the ages of two and eighteen. This institution was divided into two dorm-like buildings that housed fourteen children each and small houses, similar to those at Chestnut House, that served six children each. Ichikawa, who worked in one of the small houses, explained to me that the staff in her house thought carefully about ways to limit the differences between their house and a "regular household" (ippan katei). But with group living (shūdan seikatsu), she said, there were just going to be significant differences—specifically when it came to food.

> ICHIKAWA REIKO: For instance, there are three bread days and four rice days. Tuesday, Thursday, and Saturday are bread, and—
> KATE GOLDFARB: In the morning?
> REIKO: Right, in the morning. And the other days are rice. But normal households aren't like that, you know! Without exception, "It's Tuesday, so, bread." But the nutritionist is thinking about nutrition, and it's convenient that way. . . . A kid who comes here at age two, and Tuesday, Thursday, and Saturday are bread, and four times a week it's rice, that routine becomes engrained within that child. There are kids who like bread and kids who like rice, but without fail three times a week it's bread and four times a week it's rice. And on rice days you always have miso soup and an accompanying dish, and with bread you always have fruit, milk, and an accompanying

dish. . . . Seriously, there's such a difference between the sense [*kankaku*] of an institution and the sense of a household. These totally set things [*kimari kitte shimatta mono*] become a problem, and you know why? It's when one of these kids goes into family-based foster care. Do you get what I mean? It's that, in the morning bread is served, and the kid goes, "Eeeeh, there's no fruit?!" It's rude! And, the thing is, the staff are always telling the kids, "When you eat bread, it's good for your body to eat fruit with it." So for instance, [at the foster parent's house] the kid says something like, "There's milk, but why isn't there fruit? You've got to eat them together." Also, in an institution, there's a rule that any food has to be eaten within four hours of being prepared. You can't eat leftovers the day after.

KATE: What? Why?

REIKO: Huh? Food poisoning. Your stomach will start to hurt.

KATE: Wait, explain this again?

REIKO: If you make food for lunch, you can't eat it for dinner. You throw it out.

KATE: You throw it out!

REIKO: It's about hygiene. At least that's what the nutritionist and the cooks say: you have to eat it within four hours, otherwise bacteria . . . If you don't eat it within four hours, you have to throw it out. I don't know if it's a law or something; it's probably a public health rule.

KATE: Chestnut House is different. They eat leftovers. It's probably because they want to be household-like.

REIKO: That way is more natural [*shizen*], I think, but for a big institution, you have to throw out everything you don't eat in four hours. And the kids grow up hearing this, and then they go to a family foster home, and it's like, "Why is leftover stuff from yesterday being served at breakfast? It's dirty. I can't eat it." That's really rude to say. But the kids think this way naturally. It's the adults who create this sensibility [*kankaku*], saying things like, "If you eat old food, your tummy will hurt, you'll get sick, you shouldn't eat it" and such. Within an institution that sort of talk is correct; it's correct from a public health point of view, but in a regular household, a foster parent will think the kid is really rude. . . . When you take the commonsense of an institution outside into the regular world, the entire thing becomes wrong.

APPROXIMATING A HOUSEHOLD

As Though Siblings

Field notes: July 30, 2009

   Chestnut House has been open for two months. This small-scale child welfare institution is designed to eventually house thirty children. Kitahara Shinobu, the institution's director, hands me a typed report from a group of students who visited Chestnut House to learn about the welfare model embodied in this unique household-like institution. Their interview questions for Kitahara centered on children's rights, changes in institutional practice over time, and the ways that Kitahara had obtained the understanding of local residents, many of whom had opposed the creation of a child welfare institution in their community.

   As I read the report, I am struck by Kitahara's response to one question in particular. The students asked, "How will you prevent violence among the children at the institution?" This question is of central concern to child welfare activists in Japan, pointing to often endemic inter-child violence in institutions. Kitahara had responded by citing a survey showing that 30 percent of children in medium-size (fifty person) institutions had reported experiencing sexual assault.[1] He explained that in larger institutions, in which there is usually only one staff member on duty at night, there is much that staff members are unable to prevent. By contrast, he told the students, at Chestnut House the staff members are residential and responsible for sleeping with the younger children. The children will grow up together, living as though siblings (kyōdai no yō). Kitahara continued to explain that the institution prioritized meal practices, with the staff members cooking all meals, which would in turn support the children in living rich daily lives. These elements would lead to the development of a family-like (kazoku no yō) atmosphere and family-like bonds. These things, he asserted, would help prevent inter-child violence.

In contrast to Kitahara's rosy depiction of family, the families of origin of many of the Chestnut House children had been a source of danger. How did Kitahara imagine that family-like relationships in an institution would be better, safer, more supportive? Although the children would ideally either be reunited with their families of origin or placed in family-based foster or adoptive care, Kitahara described the children as "growing up together," pointing to a characteristic of Japanese child welfare practice. He knew these children would likely be in institutional care for a long time.

Opting Out

Field notes: October 12, 2010

At Tanpopo, the self-support group in Tokyo for young people who have experienced care in child welfare institutions, I am introduced to Naoki. He tells me about his background; I tell him about my research. Chestnut House, the child welfare institution where I have been conducting participant-observation fieldwork for almost a year and a half, is nothing like the large, government-run institution in the northern part of Japan where Naoki grew up. In fact, several of the Tanpopo members seem a bit envious when I describe it, and one Tanpopo friend, Matsumoto, visits Chestnut House with me and pronounces that he'd like to live there.[2] At the same time, I have watched the staff at Chestnut House struggle with the ideal articulated by the institution's director—to create a household-like institution.

Even though the institution is supposed to be like a household, I tell Naoki, in the end it's still an institution. Naoki's gaze is as piercing as his query: What things make Chestnut House, to me, still an institution? Naoki had earlier offered acerbic critiques of the staff members at the institution where he grew up, noting that they were merely working there, that they could quit. I pick up his critique. That is the difference, I tell him. Chestnut House is still an institution, not a household, because one-third of its membership, the staff, are hired. They can quit. Chestnut House is an institution because over one-third of its members can opt out.

Child welfare institution staff do quit, over half within the first three to five years, many working for a shorter time at the institution than the average child will live there (Kameda et al 2014, 149; Kanda et al 2009, 35).[3] Yet not just institutional staff opt out of households and children's lives. People opt out of their families all the time. The children of Chestnut House—like young people in state care across the world—are evidence of the contingency of households and kin groups.

What makes an institution an institution? What makes a household a household? Which social formation is better and safer for children, and under what conditions? In Japan, the majority of children who cannot live with their own parents are placed in child welfare institutions rather than in family-based foster care. The Japanese government is working to increase family-based foster care and adoption, but state actors have found it easier to produce small-scale institutional care that embodies qualities of a household—household-like (*kateiteki*) institutions. These institutions are discursively represented as encompassing all the nice characteristics of a family without any of the dangerous parts that sent children into alternative care in the first place. Nostalgic imaginaries of community-based care and warm, nurturing households orient this vision.

In Japanese, the term *household-like* is a combination of the word *household* (*katei*) and the suffix *teki*, which means "-esque." The suffix *teki* highlights the fact of an approximation toward some objective, just as, one might argue, the Japanese government is approaching but never meeting the benchmarks in the United Nations Convention on the Rights of the Child, which states that children have the right to be raised in a family. A kateiteki institution was not a household, but it aimed to be household-like.[4] I theorize this process as *mimetic approximation*: an engagement with signs conventionally understood to index kinship and family, in a context only intended to approximate, rather than arrive at, the objective of a household. Mimetic approximation is a project of self-reflexive engagement with signs perceived to point to and embody normative qualities of kinship but with the knowledge that this mimesis will always inevitably be a mere approximation, never the thing itself.[5]

In this chapter, I explore efforts to implement qualities of a household within an institutional space. I examine material indices of household-ness—architectural design and furniture, practices surrounding food, and affective, emotive sociality—that seem to entail the interpersonal relationships idealized in Japan as central to a normal household. Staff understood that each child could aspire to a noninstitutional household only at some point in the future, in many cases once they were adults and had families of their own. Living in a household-like institution, caregivers hoped, would guide the children in creating their own households one day. Both children and staff were keenly aware that this household-like institution was not an actual household; the original concept of a household "preserved all its authority" as the real, the archetype, upon which this imitation was modeled (Benjamin 1968, 220).

However, despite the presumed authority of the real household, I suggest that the presence of an imitation and the active process of mimesis highlights the instability of the original itself. The case of Chestnut House asks us to consider how concepts of household and family are in many ways co-constituted in tension with their perceived opposites—in this case, the "institution" (Gal 2002). What *does* make a household? While households might seem to bear normative characteristics that mark them as distinct from other social groupings, I suggest that we consider the concept of a household as ideologically defined, and as context-dependent, as other social phenomena (Collier et al 1997 [1982]).

Further, institutional moments of alignment with qualities that seemed central to a household were matched by moments of disalignment: "mimesis registers both sameness and difference, of being like, and of being Other" (Taussig 1993, 129). Attending to the processes of mimesis, including constitutive moments of alignment and disalignment, tells us something about the ways ideologies surrounding normative families circulate, such that they are literally institutionalized in child welfare contexts outside of kinship settings. This occurs as a matter of both top-down policy and bottom-up practice. This chapter explores the efficacious social labor done in the juxtaposition of institutions and households, both in the realm of policy and in the experiences of those creating and inhabiting such social forms. Most prominently, this chapter asks the reader to center the social stakes for children in care.

Chestnut House was a social experiment attempting to explode the binary categories of household and institution and offer new models for relationality. This project was, in the end, untenable—precisely because the institutional structure persistently undermined the potential for lasting, substantial relationships.[6] There is no imitation for durable positive relationality, the stuff of kinship when kinship goes well.

Social Experiment

"We want the children to feel that Chestnut House is their home, their *furusato*," Kitahara Shinobu, Chestnut House's director, told me. Located in a suburban area outside of Tokyo, this small-scale (*shōshasei*) child welfare institution was opened in 2009 as part of a national initiative to make child welfare institutions as household-like (kateiteki) as possible. The institution was split into five self-contained houses, each with six children and three residential staff members. "We want it to be a place for the children to return for holidays, a place to visit when they are sad or happy or need advice," Kitahara continued. The term *furusato* can be glossed as hometown or original home and in contemporary culture entails a sense of nostalgia, longing, and a desire for a return to one's origins, a project that may be as aspirational as it is unattainable (Robertson 1991; Ivy 1995;

Watanabe 2019). Kitahara, ever a teacher, reached for pen and paper and wrote the character for *sato* (郷), the second character of *furusato*. Below the character, he drew another image (fig. 3).

"In the archaic form of the character," Kitahara said, "you see that on the left, you have a person, and on the right, you also have a person. In the middle is a platform with food placed on it for the gods. But it is also an image of two people eating a meal. You have one table and two people eating the same food together." He wrote as he spoke: *tomo ni shokuji o suru*, eating a meal together. "That is the meaning of this character, *sato*. In each house at Chestnut House, you have the children and the adults sitting at the table eating together." In Kitahara's telling, the character for *sato* itself—a place to return—iconically indexed the prosaic,

FIGURE 3. Kitahara's depiction of the meaning of *sato*.

everyday practices of food production and consumption that he envisioned to be the foundation for a home.[7] Specifically, he emphasized, the dining room table was a site for re-socializing children, for helping them express affect and emotion and to develop reciprocity with staff members. Kitahara had proudly described how he discovered the furniture maker he commissioned to make dining room tables and chairs for Chestnut House. He saw these pieces as the centerpieces of each home, the site for gathering and communal eating, a key element of making these houses home for the children and the institution household-like.

Chestnut House was an unusual institution. Housing a maximum of 30 children, it was in stark contrast to the majority of other child welfare institutions in Japan that housed 50 to over 150 children in dormitory-like buildings.[8] Kitahara had carefully selected the site, a hilltop with a bamboo thicket, across the street from a playground and agricultural land that had been donated to the organization to use as an organic vegetable garden (fig. 4). Chestnut House's two-story homes were oriented around a central courtyard and included a temporary-stay unit for parents visiting their children. A final building housed the main office, a library, a room for the staff psychologist, and upstairs multipurpose rooms.

In Kitahara's vision, the built environment would scaffold interpersonal relations. The houses were much like single-family homes. The ground floor was open-concept, with a kitchen and dining area centrally located and abutting the living room, which boasted a television and shelves holding books and toys. Upstairs there were small individual bedrooms for older children and larger rooms with tatami matting and futon for the younger children to sleep next to staff members who were on night duty, in the manner adults commonly sleep with young children in Japan. The staff members' schedules attempted to avoid the shift system common in institutions. The shift system was often described as a situation in which a child would say goodbye to one staff member in the morning on the way to school and greet a different staff member upon returning home. At Chestnut House, the staff caregivers were residential (*sumikomi*), working for days-long shifts, and the same staff member would ideally be present both morning and evening, providing consistency and relational stability. Siblings lived together in the same household so they would grow up with sibling consciousness (*kyōdai ishiki*). The children in each home were of mixed genders and ages, as in a normal family, in contrast to typical institutions where children in residential groupings are single-gender and the same age.[9]

Finally, the staff were in charge of cooking the household meals. In contrast to conventional child welfare institutions where food is often produced and sometimes eaten in a central cafeteria, Kitahara and many of the staff idealized the notion that the same people caring for the children would also cook for and eat

FIGURE 4. One of the homes within Chestnut House. Illustration by Sasha Buckser, based on photograph by author.

with them. Even as these children were receiving social care by the state and were cared for by a broader network of people than a typical child living in a nuclear family, in at least the production and consumption of food, caregiving roles would not be distributed across a network but instead inhere in the identities of three residential caregivers in each house. As Kitahara often noted, "The food itself conveys the feelings of the person who created it," and the children would "come to understand the feelings of other people" through the food and the process of eating together. In Kitahara's vision, the social relationships that would emerge though the comity of shared food and laughter would in turn produce an affective environment that would nurture children whose experiences in households had thus far been characterized by neglect and maltreatment.

In fact, although the institution would eventually hire a staff psychologist, many of the staff members felt that a good environment would itself be therapeutic and was all that was necessary to rehabilitate and re-socialize the children. In an early Chestnut House newsletter, Kitahara documented the first month of operation. "The first children to move into Chestnut House were two- and three-year-old toddlers," Kitahara wrote. "These children come from baby homes or temporary emergency care at child guidance centers.[10] Up until now they lived in groups of 10 or 20 other babies, so they were not accustomed to living in little homes with specific staff members . . . but within about a week, they have gotten used to the homes and the staff. From now on, they will form attachment relationships with the staff members that will provide a stable foundation for their lives." The terms Kitahara used to describe Chestnut House—*little homes*, *specific staff members*, *attachment relationships*, and *stability*—are central values articulated in Japanese policy documents (for example, MHLW 2019a, 50). Thus, the material structure of the institution, the structure of staff working conditions, and the structure of resident child composition paralleled each other in aspirational attention to what an idealized household would look and feel like.

Origin Story

Like many social experiments, Chestnut House's creation had an oft-told origin story. Working as a staff member in a youth correctional facility for over eight years had taught Kitahara that the young people who were hardest to help had a common quality: "rootlessness."[11] Many of these youth had been wards of the state their entire lives, cared for entirely in institutions, first placed as infants in baby homes (*nyūjiin*) and as toddlers transferred to a child welfare institution for children between the ages of two and eighteen (*jidō yōgo shisetsu*). But then, because of antisocial behavior like stealing and setting fires, and sometimes more serious crimes like homicide, they ended up in correctional facilities, institutions for children who were too young to be emancipated from the child welfare system or placed in juvenile detention centers or prison. Kitahara's job was to support these young people in finding employment. Many of these children would graduate from middle school, completing their compulsory education but nothing more, and at age fifteen would be on their own. They were deeply in trouble (*komatteiru*).

What should one do to prevent others from being rootless? His time working in the correctional facility oriented Kitahara's subsequent work in social welfare. At the time I knew him, between 2008 and 2012, Kitahara was a director in a social welfare corporation—an umbrella organization that contained multiple social welfare organizations—and his vision drove the creation of day-care institutions for elderly people and people with disabilities. Those who received services at Kitahara's institutions took part in rich community networks of reciprocity, running a small café and shop that sold delicious homemade noodles, bread, house-roasted coffee, homemade tofu and other soy products, and organic vegetables, served on handmade pottery also shaped and fired there. The pottery, along with woven products like scarves, were sold in the community. The servers at the café were mostly people with developmental or intellectual disabilities, supported by staff members and volunteers. Although disability is far from normalized in Japan (Lock 1998), I was always struck by the absence of places like this in the United States. This space felt deeply inclusive and infused with the pleasure people take in making, selling, and consuming delicious and beautiful goods that are valued by others.

Relational interconnectedness was a central part of Kitahara's formulation of the meaning of social welfare. Social welfare should "create happiness," he told me, by supporting people together as a community (kyōdō de sasaeru). His institutions were designed to be deeply situated within communities, bringing volunteers into the institutions and producing goods that could be sold and enjoyed within the community.[12] He wanted local residents to understand that the children and adults his institutions cared for were part of the community, that they could contribute positively and productively. More than anyone, these people needed relational ties.

This was the context in which Kitahara was approached by the local government with the proposal that he create a new child welfare institution as part of his welfare corporation, the institution that would become Chestnut House.[13] Kitahara consulted with his friend, Tsuzaki Tetsuo (his real name), then a professor of social welfare at Kyoto Prefectural University. Tsuzaki was famous—and also infamous—for his scathing critiques of Japan's reliance on institutional care rather than family-based foster care and adoption, reserving his most fiery rhetoric for institutions for babies. When Kitahara asked Tsuzaki what he thought about the idea of building a new child welfare institution, Tsuzaki responded, "Why would you build a new institution when we need to be moving toward family-based foster care?" But at the time the government was not putting energy into family-based care, and institutions were full. Kitahara decided to accept the challenge, and Tsuzaki agreed to work with him as an adviser and staff trainer. Kitahara's goal was to create an institution as household-like as possible.

Thus, Kitahara held an overarching vision of Chestnut House as an institution, yes, but an institution that could provide roots—a furusato, a place to return—to children who so often lacked these connections and for whom this lack proved an ever-present source of suffering and trouble as they got older. Welfare services were in turn rooted in the local community, in which relationships and enjoyment were paramount. Some members of Kitahara's social welfare organization saw him as a naïve idealist and criticized his vision for Chestnut House as unsustainable and extravagant, excessive (*yokei*). While Kitahara may have been a bit naïve, he was also a visionary with a richly developed ethos that oriented everything he did as a practitioner. He understood the problems of children in state care as inherently social problems with social solutions.

House Number 3

Despite Kitahara's goals to create stable relationships among residents, the membership of House Number 3, where I focused my research, was continually in flux. As I reread my field notes on Chestnut House, 110 pages of typed, single-spaced notes spanning ten years, I attempt to track the exit and entry of staff members and children, first as staff members were hired and then quit, and then as the management attempted to mitigate personality and behavioral conflicts among the staff and among the children, moving residents into different houses within the institution.

The four children and three staff members who most centrally shaped my time at Chestnut House were members of House Number 3 for an uncommonly stable period of six months during my primary fieldwork. The fragmented stories below offer a glimpse into the prosaic world of this house, a small taste of the personalities of the people whose friendship shaped my research most powerfully.

One of the first children to join the newly opened Chestnut House was Nakayama Risa, three years old when she arrived in June 2009 directly from a baby home, with parents who cared about her but could not care for her. Then Maeda Eri, eight years old when she arrived at the beginning of July 2009, with no kin to speak of. Two boys joined the house over the summer: three-year-old Tanaka Aoki, who had been in temporary care and before that a baby home, and ten-year-old Saito Masahiro, who had lived with his mother in a series of institutions for single women and their children, child welfare institutions, and temporary care institutions before his mother was, once again, hospitalized for mental illness. Miyazaki Yūko and Sakai Marina were two staff members who had been at the institution from the start. Miyazaki was an experienced caregiver in her midforties, the mother of three children, and a registered nurse. Sakai was single and in her early thirties. A male caregiver worked in House Number 3 for the first four and a half months and then quit; he was replaced in House Number 3 by Ishizaka Tetsu, a man in his late twenties who had worked at the institution from the start in a different house. Tetsu and his wife, newlyweds, had recently moved to the area, and his wife was pregnant during the time he switched to House Number 3. This household membership stayed the same until two new children, siblings Fukushima Maiko and Noriaki, joined five months later. A month after that, Tetsu left the institution, and Sakai left her role as a primary caregiver but stayed on as office staff; Miyazaki remained at the institution for another year and a half before leaving her job at Chestnut House.

Acts of Care

Field notes: December 8, 2009

Much praise tonight for the kids' studying. Eri studied for a long time this evening; she also wrote a letter to her caseworker. Miyazaki and I went up to Masahiro's room, and we listened to him read aloud. His reading has really improved, and he was proud of having been complimented by his sensei. Masahiro gets lonely when he is by himself, and I stayed with him when Miyazaki went downstairs to cook. He decides how long he's going to study each night and tells the staff, and then he enforces his own decision; he set an alarm for twenty minutes to finish kanji practice.

After dinner, I took over the dishes as soon as I could, and Sakai ceded her apron to me. Risa brought me her dishes one at a time, depositing each with a loud expression of thanks: "Arigatō!"

Aoki emerged naked from the bath and was told to bring me his cup. He handed it to me and then stood behind me trying to close one of the apron buttons. He's always so aware of other people, worried about their happiness somehow.

I chased Aoki upstairs to the little kids' bedroom. I hadn't ever seen it when the futon were all laid out for the night, one next to the other. It was very sweet, the kids and Sakai all in pajamas. Risa and Aoki had each picked out a book to have read.

Ritual and Research

Field notes: December 15, 2009

Today was Aoki's fourth birthday and the last day I would visit Chestnut House before Christmas. I came carrying a lot of stuff—six little apple cakes with cream cheese frosting, one for each house and the office, two beers to contribute to dinner, and Christmas presents for House Number 3 (pistachios, a chocolate orange, and

Celestial Seasonings tea). As I was heading up the steep hill from the bus stop to Chestnut House, I heard Aoki's voice and saw Tetsu in the garden. They were picking vegetables for dinner. We walked back to House Number 3 together. Eri helped me frost the cakes, and the kids ate the rest of the frosting.

Aoki was very cute today, full of energy but better behaved than normal. He was very aware that he was turning four that day! The kids had made paper chains to decorate the dining room. Aoki was making a fuss about having a special birthday seat, the middle of his side of the table. There was consternation about where others would sit, and Masahiro was thrilled because Aoki wanted to sit next to him.

Dinner was fun, lots of laughter and hilarity. Risa was pretty quiet as always, sitting in her high chair at the end of the table farthest from Aoki. Amidst a particularly boisterous moment, she suddenly burst out with a stern recrimination, "This is not a laughing matter! [Warau bai jya nai yo!]" The staff members and I burst out laughing.

Aoki had requested a Baskin Robbins ice cream cake with Snoopy on it. There were little sugar decorations on the cake, and the kids were gnawing at them and crunching into each other's faces. They kept handing sticky, half-sucked candies to me, Miyazaki, and Tetsu to eat; the staff accommodatingly consumed them. Then Eri and Masahiro both attacked Tetsu at once and were on top of him, and it was as though he was being tickled, he was laughing so hard.

The kids were all over the place, ran upstairs without being excused from dinner. I started doing the dishes while Tetsu cleaned the floor, which was a mess. He suddenly said, "Kate-san, don't worry about the dishes, I'll do them." I said, "No, I'm doing them!" and Miyazaki came in and said, "Kate-san always does the dishes." This is the first night I've been there when Tetsu was on duty.

Aoki had run upstairs without having opened his birthday present. This struck us as funny and then kind of poignant. I asked if he had ever received a present before, and Tetsu didn't know. Miyazaki commented that she tells her own children on their birthdays that they should be grateful to their mothers, who suffered on that day. She thinks it's funny that parents have to give their kids presents and not the other way around! Then she laughed her characteristic Miyazaki laugh. She had told Eri on her birthday that she should think of her mother and be grateful. I told Miyazaki about a social worker I know who says that kids should feel okay about having gratitude even to horrible parents. Loyalty conflicts can be painful, and these words had struck me as wise rather than cruel.

They called Aoki downstairs, and he opened his present, which was a big album like Eri has, full of photos of him. Miyazaki got out red ink and paper and had him mark a handprint. We all put our hands on his and pressed, which blurred the imprint but was cute. Miyazaki got out the paper where they had done Risa's hand on her birthday. They had written things like, "Risa-chan can say 'no,'" etc.—milestones. The staff member who had been in the house before Tetsu appeared in some of the photos in Aoki's album. Masahiro really fixates on the fact that he left. He quizzed Aoki to see if Aoki remembered him.

After the kids got out of the bath, Aoki stood naked in the living room while Tetsu slathered him with lotion for his eczema. Tetsu laughed as he told me that earlier, as soon as Aoki got into the shower area with his clothes off, he peed directly into the shower, and then Tetsu realized that Aoki had pooped a little, and it was poking out. He didn't know what to do, so he wiped Aoki with his hand! He and Miyazaki started laughing. Yuck! So many layers of intimacy.

Miyazaki said how helpful it is to have me there, which was nice. I told her that I'm grateful to them for making my research possible. She replied, "I'm sorry, this won't really yield research for you [Gomen, kenkyū ni naranai]." I demurred, and Miyazaki suggested we make time to talk over beer.

Tetsu was mopping the floor and listening to us. "It's warm here [koko wa atatakai yo]," he said. In so many ways, I thought.

Contagion

Field notes: January 19, 2010

Yesterday Sakai told me that Aoki had been sick but was now better. I called right before I left for Chestnut House today to see if Aoki was okay, and Sakai said he was "totally energetic [zenzen genki]." When I got to Chestnut House, I learned that kids in every house have the flu. And Tetsu was really sick yesterday from a stomach virus. Sakai told me Tetsu would need extra help today because she was helping in another house. Tetsu really didn't look so good when I got there. It was actually a great day for talking with him; I'd never been there just with him (Sakai was in and out, mostly out). When I arrived, Aoki, Risa, and Eri were also there, with Eri's caseworker, whom she seems to be close to. The caseworker hung out while the kids had snacks, and then she and Eri went somewhere together.

I folded laundry while Tetsu and the little kids took a bath. Tetsu then got out Aoki's eczema lotion. Such an intimate process. Tetsu rubbed it all over Aoki's little body, up around his bottom.

Tetsu had done most of the cooking for dinner in advance, but he asked me if I knew how to make kara-age. I never had—but he really didn't want to make it. Masahiro made the first batch, and I made the rest. It was fun—buri (yellowtail tuna) or something, coated with egg and ginger and soy sauce, plus katakuriko (potato starch), dropped into a pot of boiling oil. Tetsu ate a lot at dinner so seemed to be feeling fine. Dinner puts everyone in a good mood.

After dinner Sakai came in wearing a mask and said she felt feverish. She took her temperature: low-grade. "Risa-chan, shall we go to bed? [Issho ni nemashō ka?]" *she asked, and Risa responded, "Poop!" as she stood oddly with her legs apart and arms slightly out. It was too funny. At least no midnight accident. After cleaning up, Sakai and Risa headed upstairs. Sakai had been saying how yucky* (iya) *it would be if she had caught the flu from Aoki. After she went to bed, Tetsu put on a mask, saying he didn't want to catch what Sakai had. The intimacies here are thick and sometimes unwanted.*

Tetsu was worried about when I needed to leave—I hadn't stayed in the evening before while he was on duty. I told him I was fine until the 8:17 bus. He said, "Oh, good, it's lonely here." The work at Chestnut House seems to weigh on him.

Twice today Sakai and Tetsu joked with me about taking Aoki home with me. He really is a bundle of trouble, but I love that kid.

Risa is crazy sometimes. This afternoon, she suddenly decided to move a bunch of chairs (her high chair, two short chairs) into the bathroom and sink area. I followed her in there and saw her move the sink stool into the little corner of chairs that she had created. She then went and got a book, and when Tetsu asked where she was, she was sitting in a chair surrounded by other chairs, next to the sink, reading.

Silly

Field notes: February 9, 2010

This month, a bunch of new kids have come to Chestnut House. No new kids in House Number 3. There was much craziness; I went out into the courtyard, and Miyazaki was walking around on stilts!

Miyazaki and Tetsu and all have such fun together. Tonight at bath time, Tetsu had apparently told Aoki that I would go in the bath with him—so Aoki came up and said, "Want to take a bath? Together?" Thanks, Tetsu. Then later, Masahiro went in after Tetsu and the little kids, and suddenly he tore out of the bathroom holding one of the water pitchers, yelling, "Poop!" He found what looked like a little flake of something in the bath water—maybe poop!—and everyone gathered around to see. Much hilarity and grossed-out-ness.

I had brought two beers, both of which were big hits with the staff, plus some quick bread. As always, lots of laughing at dinner. Risa slid down from her high chair, saying she was done, and Miyazaki wiped a piece of rice off Risa's cheek and absently ate it.

After the little kids went to bed, Eri, Masahiro, Miyazaki, Tetsu, and I played a card game. We were laughing so much, I can't believe they were able to sleep upstairs. The winner got to pang the loser with a plastic inflatable gavel that made a squeak upon impact. Tetsu very theatrically got on all fours and stuck his butt out so Masahiro could pummel him, and then I got to hit Masahiro. Once Eri lost and Masahiro got to hit her, and she acted like she might cry—but then she held out her hand to be banged there and burst out laughing. I'm always amazed by how the staff use their bodies. Tetsu and Miyazaki do a fair amount of rolling around on the ground.

Fortune Teller

Field notes: March 3, 2010

Today I finally told Tetsu that I had heard he would be leaving Chestnut House. His wife was going to be giving birth soon, and they were moving back to their hometown. He hadn't told the kids yet. While Eri and Masahiro were watching TV, Tetsu and Sakai and I stood in the kitchen and talked about what it means to become the "sacrifice" somehow, either at work or at home, and what it takes to have a happy life. Sakai is also unsure how long she'll be able to continue at Chestnut House. In part this is because the institution is still in its beginning stages; its form isn't yet stabilized. Tetsu had told me earlier that Chestnut House was an ideal institution for the children but brutal for the staff.

The kids were kind of rough today; it was super cold out, everyone was cooped up. Miyazaki had made both girls dresses for the Girls' Day (hina matsuri) (fig. 5). *Lots*

FIGURE 5. Girls' Day dress. Illustration by Sasha Buckser, based on photograph by author. Personal features have been altered.

of playing and twirling. When Tetsu told me that Miyazaki had made the dresses, I expressed admiration. He responded with something like, "It's because she has love." I wondered if he meant to imply that Miyazaki loves them but he doesn't, or that he doesn't have enough dedication. I think he feels pretty bad about leaving.

Eri kept wanting to have me or Tetsu hold her in her princess dress, like she'd been swept up. I taught her how to waltz and then got Tetsu dancing with her. While Tetsu was in the bath with the little kids, Eri and I played "fortune teller" with her wearing Risa's pink princess skirt over her head. She read my palm. One of her fortunes was, "You will live to 105," and another was, "You eat only vegetables." Ha. When I read her palm, I told her something like, "You have a long life line. Your heart is very good, and you will have a lot of friends, and you are very smart." She seemed impressed.

Friend

Field notes: October 13, 2010

Today I was walking with Aoki in the park across from Chestnut House, and a little boy who had come to the institution at the beginning of September approached us. "Are you someone's mom?" he asked me. I said no, and he asked, "Aoki-kun's mom?" "No. Do we look alike?" He considered for a moment. "Well, you do look alike."

Field notes: October 18, 2010

Went to the park for a while with the kids. The same little boy we saw before asked me again who I am in relation to Aoki. "Are you his elder sister?" "I'm his friend," I said, which was an answer both boys seemed to accept.

Outsiders, Inside

Kitahara's vision of a household open to the community starkly differed from the normative Japanese household. The typical view in Japan was that families are private, and households are bounded units separate from the outside.[14] Like all stereotypes, this generalization's power is rooted in its social relevance, although these views are not specific to Japan; kinship theorists Jane Collier, Michelle Rosaldo, and Sylvia Yanagisako note that a core quality of "modern bounded Families" is that they "try to keep their neighbors out" (1997 [1982], 76; capitalization in original). If Chestnut House was both a household and open to the community, it was a strange household indeed. By that token, Chestnut House was also a strange institution. Child welfare institutions in Japan are seen as isolationist (*heisateki*), and many people expressed surprise that I was able to conduct research in one.

The cultural understanding that families are private deeply infuses child welfare policy and practice in Japan, highlighting what Allison Alexy describes as the "contradictory pulls embedded within Japanese family law": pressures to adjudicate family matters outside of official legal frameworks, even as families in Japan have long been a site for enforcement of state ideologies (2020, 87; Garon 1997; Frühstück 2003; Garon 2010). By definition, child welfare work entails state actors intervening into family matters. However, child welfare officers in Japan often hesitate to intrude into family problems, although they have legal standing to make forceful entries into homes and to take cases to family court. Tragedies that ensue from such reticence, like cases of children dying because caseworkers did not intervene, regularly become news stories. Normative family ideologies—specifically, cultural orientations toward the inside (uchi) and outside (soto) of Japanese families—powerfully structure child welfare policy and practice in Japan, even that which occurs outside familial spaces.

Kitahara may have been asking staff to work toward a paradoxical goal: to create a context where children were connected to multiple caregivers and community support networks and were also cared for in a setting as close to an actual household as possible. This social experiment demanded a household far more inclusive than the homes the staff themselves likely grew up in or cultivated outside work. Kitahara's project continuously bumped up against these tensions at the level of both national policy and intimate daily practice.

To maintain the affective and emotionally laden dinner table so central to Kitahara's vision, many of the careworkers felt strongly that the household staff themselves must prepare the food and eat together, such that food preparation and dining practices mapped out the boundaries of the household (Carsten 1995, 2004, chap. 2). However, the constraints of the institutional form often conflicted with these ideals. At any given time, there were fifteen residential staff, and within a year of opening in June 2009, seven original staff members had quit with new members replacing them. The requirement to live on-site during their shifts was hard.[15] Some staff members who had moved from out of town to take the job at Chestnut House had no other housing, so even when they were off duty they were still on-site, sometimes doing small tasks. One staff member told me that he could still hear the "crying voices" of the children from his bedroom, even when he wasn't supposed to be working.[16]

Kitahara and the other administrators made two significant concessions to decrease the burden on staff. They created work schedules more aligned with the shift schedules they had so eschewed at the start, and they hired part-time workers to prepare evening meals on weekdays.[17] Despite the significance he attached to food practices, Kitahara pointed out that the most important thing was for the children and staff to eat together: the staff did not have to be the ones preparing the meal. Further, the staff could spend more time with the children, particularly helping them study, if they were not responsible for food preparation. The staff members were still expected to make rice and miso soup for dinner, and they still made breakfast and prepared lunchboxes (fig. 6). By the time of this change, Tetsu (himself an excellent cook) had left Chestnut House; two new children—Maiko and her little brother, Noriaki—had joined House 3.

While I never heard anyone complain about the shift to more regular labor hours, the cooking change was not popular. As Miyazaki said to me with a wrinkled brow, "What kind of household doesn't cook?" (From Miyazaki's perspective, the kinds of households that did not cook were also the kinds of households from which the children originally came.) Other staff members expressed gratitude for the release from an additional daily obligation. In these diverging perspectives, age was a more significant factor than gender, as staff members who focused on the benefits of food preparation tended to be older. Enjoyment played a role as well. Both Miyazaki and Sakai found cooking to offer relief from the pressure of constantly interacting with the children, a chance to relax

FIGURE 6. Preparing for dinner at House Number 3. Illustration by Sasha Buckser, based on photograph by author.

and reflect on the day. They would have rather had outside volunteers help the children with studying. For his part, Kitahara, as stubborn as he was idealistic, did not inquire deeply into the staff members' preferences. He often made top-down decisions that aligned with gender norms (claiming, for instance, that the male staff members did not like to cook), and he would hear none of these complaints.[18]

A week after the part-time cooks began preparing evening meals, I conducted a formal interview with Miyazaki and asked her how she felt about the change. She replied, "It's like the kids feel there is no connection between them and the meal anymore. We're just pretending to make food; we just dump it onto a plate. When you're actually cooking, the kids come up and say, 'I want to do it!' and such, which is communication. Then, when we're eating that food at the table, they say, 'Mmm, yummy,' or, 'We put in too much sugar, didn't we' or something, and that kind of conversation at the table is fun. It's just, I don't know, if the person who made the food isn't there at the table, it feels weird to talk about the food that way. Well, we're all eating the same food at the same table, so there's meaning in that, but . . . there's no smell or noise of food preparation, there's no sense of anticipation for the food, and then none of that communication, the kids wanting to help." For Miyazaki, if the food was not made by a house resident who also took part in the meal, there was no point in commenting on it. There was no real exchange of time and labor for emotion.

In a separate interview, Sakai told me that having an outsider do the cooking seemed strange because Chestnut House was supposed to be a home, and preparing food while watching the kids is normal in a normal household. The children were initially confused by the change and would say, "Why is this person coming to cook here?" and "I don't want to eat it—it's not made by one of the adults who belong here [uchi no otona ga tsukuttenai kara iya da]." Sakai noted that Noriaki would always ask, "Who made breakfast today?" and she would say, "I made it today," which would prompt a happy, "Mmmm, Mari-chan's breakfast is yummy!" Sakai told me, "I know he'd say the same thing if I said that today Miyazaki-san made breakfast. . . . I don't know, I think there's meaning in it being someone who lives with you, who spends time with you, who cooks the food." Sakai sensed that there were boundaries between people who belonged inside the house and people who did not and that her understanding of those boundaries was the same as that of the children. Further, if Chestnut House was to be experienced as a home like any other home, it too should draw clear distinctions between interior and exterior.

Miyazaki and Sakai's sentiments, that the affect associated with meals changed after the meal policies changed, accorded with my own experiences eating dinner at Chestnut House. When the staff were still cooking for the children, dinner conversations were lively with discussion of each dish's qualities, joking about dishes that did not turn out so well, and loud expressions of appreciation from the children. I myself always made sure to thank the staff member who cooked that night. After the part-time workers started preparing the food, however, meals were often served lukewarm, and conversation about the food all but stopped. The children came to be familiar with the part-time cooking staff, but the children in House 3 were uninvolved in food preparation, and the cooks departed as soon as they prepared the meal.

Miyazaki described the changes as "a little lonely these days." She reminded me of an event that had occurred one time when I was there. Maiko, Noriaki's older sister, threw a tantrum about where I was going to sit as we were setting the table for dinner. She had been positioning everyone's chopsticks at their places when she realized I was not going to be sitting next to her. She began screaming, threw all the chopsticks on the floor, and then sank to the floor herself, her legs splayed indignantly as she grabbed the dinner table and pushed it away from her, sloshing the bowls of broth on the table. Miyazaki picked her up and carried her upstairs, and we could hear Maiko's screaming until it was finally quiet. After twenty minutes or so, the two returned to the table to eat after everyone else had finished. We were having udon noodles that had been prepared in advance and delivered by the cook.

Miyazaki recalled, "I took her upstairs until she stopped crying, and then once she was quiet, we talked. I said, 'You know, it was really a shame tonight that dinner became not delicious anymore. Because you had a tantrum, it made us all feel really bad, even though we had yummy udon to eat.' Then Maiko-chan said, 'There's not any udon. There's no smoke.'"

Miyazaki paused and looked at me significantly.

"Then I said, 'But the soup looked really yummy, didn't it?' and Maiko-chan said, 'It doesn't smell like anything! There's no smoke.' And that's when I thought, wow, the kids really get it, don't they? Because when you boil udon, when you prepare the broth, if maybe the kids are fighting and everyone's kind of mad or something, if they're in a bad mood, the kids still come up and say, 'What are we having today?' The fact that there isn't food preparation right before their eyes anymore, it's incomplete, isn't it? . . . It's just . . . There's no fire in the kitchen; you don't feel any warmth. The kitchen isn't living. It's that kind of loneliness."

There were several significant moments in Miyazaki's recollection of this incident. It was actually an isolated event—it was not as though Maiko was constantly complaining that the food lacked a smell or was not delicious. However, for Miyazaki, it held meaning. When Miyazaki reproachfully told the little girl that her behavior had made the food less delicious for everyone else, Maiko was able to refute Miyazaki's argument by claiming that the food wasn't delicious to begin with. If communication and mutual understanding of another's emotions emerged through the process of cooking and eating together, Maiko seemed to be saying that food brought in from the outside cannot function as this medium. Her statements struck Miyazaki, who appeared to agree, as poignant.

Miyazaki elaborated on her own sense of loneliness associated with a fireless kitchen. When she was a child, her mother was hospitalized for a long period of time, and there were many days when no cooking was done, and her family brought in food from the outside. "That feeling of the mother being in the hospital, the mother being out of the house, that lack of warmth—and then the image of no fire in the kitchen, somehow they're connected in my mind. Meals are just really important. . . . It's not like we make anything so gorgeous when we cook!" she said, laughing.

Takada Hitoshi, a forty-year-old male staff member in a different house, told me that the main reason Kitahara had hired the cooks was precisely to open up the houses, which had become overly isolationist. Takada had felt frustrated many times when he offered to help other staff members by watching children from another household, only to be declined. There was the sense at Chestnut House, he said, that the staff from one house would take care of only that house's children. Similarly, many staff members were reluctant for non–house staff members to enter the houses. This isolationist perspective stood in stark contrast to Takada's ideal image that he shared with Kitahara, in which children were raised by a community. Chestnut House would never be truly household-like unless it embraced this precept, Takada maintained. "When I was growing up," he told me, "you'd go to the next house and ask to borrow some soy sauce. No matter who was around, they would look after you, they would scold you. If we don't return in some way to that era, nothing about institutional care will change." Kitahara had hoped that bringing in outside cooks might give staff more time to play outside with the children from all of the houses, to create a community out of the internally isolated residences. In Takada's opinion, the staff members' resistance to opening their kitchens to outside workers was a manifestation of these tendencies to self-isolate, despite Kitahara's community-building efforts.

The tensions surrounding food preparation at Chestnut House were expressions of the ways the staff members conceptualized *household*. Takada's own welcoming of the cooks meant that they became one more node in a network of individuals who were helping to care for the children, one more resource for the children and one more opportunity for an affective relationship. A particular ideology of a proper household, in which the caregiver prepares food that is eaten at the same time in the same place as other household members, is an ideology of boundary production and maintenance. These boundary lines shift as *household* is continuously redefined (Irvine and Gal 2000). Indeed, my own involvement with Chestnut House was possible precisely because of the inherent flexibility of these boundaries.

Work Relationship

I kept in touch with Tetsu after he left Chestnut House. In June 2010, three months after he and his wife moved back to their hometown and shortly after their son was born, a research opportunity brought me to Tetsu's hometown, and I stayed with his parents. Everyone doted on the baby. My field notes from this time are full of country-style recipes that his parents taught me. Like House Number 3, Tetsu's own home was warm.

I missed Tetsu at Chestnut House, and his leaving felt like a palpable loss for the children. My own mobility—I was able to visit Tetsu and his family multiple times that year—stood in stark contrast to the Chestnut House children, who were stuck in place.

During that first visit, I conducted a recorded interview with Tetsu. Relistening to our conversation so many years later, I am struck by how evidently painful I found his leaving Chestnut House and how he knew it. But secure in himself, and also a good enough friend to me, he was honest.

> KATE GOLDFARB: What was your relationship like with the children at Chestnut House?
>
> ISHIZAKA TETSU: Well, honestly, it was a work relationship.
>
> KATE: A work—ah, yes. Of course.
>
> TETSU: There's nothing to be done about that.
>
> KATE: Did you, well, did love enter in somehow?
>
> TETSU: Yeah, love is there. But it's a different kind of love from the kind you have for your own child.
>
> KATE: Um hmm.
>
> TETSU: With your own children, you've got to try 100 percent to raise them well, but the children in an institution, it's not like raising them is your particular responsibility, you know? There is that. But in the end, they are also strangers, unrelated [tanin].
>
> KATE: [Laughing, unpleasantly taken aback.]
>
> TETSU: You are raising them for your work, and you receive money for it. That's all.
>
> KATE: Ah!
>
> TETSU: And as part of that, as a professional, there are certain things you have to do. You do your best in the amount of time you have while you are working. That's just the reality.

KATE: Mmm hmmm.
TETSU: Is that sad? To hear that?
KATE: Well, I mean, I knew that . . .
TETSU: Hmm?
KATE: I knew that reality.
TETSU: Right.

Tetsu continued to think and worry about the children to whom he had become closest. But he said that over time those feelings of connection would fade, just as the children's own sense of connection to him would fade. The relationship would be over when they had both forgotten each other. There might be one or two children who, far into the future, he continued to think about. He knew this to be true from his work at a previous institution, where he had been a staff member for four years. Even as he sometimes wished he could contact the children and check in on them, he knew this would be perceived as inappropriate, as his connection to the institution was terminated, and he was now a structural outsider.[19]

TETSU: That's just how it is [*sonna kanji ka na*].
KATE: Mmmm.
TETSU: Is that odd [*okashii*]?
KATE: Hmm?
TETSU: Is that bad [*dame*]?
KATE: No, no [iya] . . . [laughing uncomfortably]
TETSU: That's just how it is.

The truth was, I had been naïve. Tetsu knew when he moved to the Tokyo area that he wouldn't be there forever, for his family, with its land and graves, were back in his hometown. More broadly, the staff knew from the beginning that their engagements with the children were temporary, knew that their responsibility began and ended at the institution's front door, even if their affection and care for the children lingered after the fact.

Intimate Danger

In November 2012, Kitahara Shinobu passed away after a rapid decline in health. Multiple institutional directors followed in the wake of his death. And as time passed, Kitahara's visions for the institution began to show some wear. The social experiment he had begun—the dream of an institution that was also a household—in many ways faded into pragmatic and bureaucratized management schemes, its idyllic visions seen by administrators as excessive. Further, while

Kitahara had envisioned household intimacy as producing positive affect and durable relationality, intimacy had also emerged as a source of danger.

A couple years after Kitahara's death, Takada Hitoshi, the staff member who had championed many of Kitahara's initiatives, reflected on the goal of making the institution as household-like as possible. Takada had long before told me that the strangest aspect of working at Chestnut House was that the staff members were raising children together even though they were, in the end, strangers (tanin) to each other; staff members were not intimate with each other in the way that cohabiting and coparenting adults would normally be. Yet at the same time, they were attempting to raise the children as if the children were actually siblings to each other.

It had taken the staff too long to realize that no matter how they cultivated a household-like atmosphere, the children were ultimately strangers to each other as well. Takada explained how the staff had had the innocent view of the children as children always, as siblings, even as they grew up and entered puberty. In this, Takada felt, the staff had failed to recognize the children as fellow humans with human curiosity and desire. There had been incidents with children shutting themselves up together in closets, some showing, some touching. The involved children had been separated into different houses, and sexual education was implemented for both children and staff. Takada described these incidents as moments of reckoning. Imagining the children as siblings had produced a naïve and harmful view: staff had been unable to protect the girls who were targets of attention, but they had also been unable to protect one of the boys, who had to leave Chestnut House, where he had lived since he was a toddler. At the same time, the Chestnut House staff had become increasingly attuned to the danger posed by some children's families of origin. Some of the children who had spent years at Chestnut House were eventually reunited with their biological kin, after which it was discovered that they had been maltreated once more. Staff members felt unable to keep the children safe, inside or outside the institution. The intimate and isolated household, either mimetic or actual, had confirmed itself as a threat to well-being.

In addition to sexual education, the staff had begun trainings in Life Story Work (see chap. 6) and were newly aware of the importance of children knowing about their families of origin even if these truths caused distress. To Takada, this also meant helping the children understand the difference between siblings and others (tanin). Raising them in an *as-if* world—as if the institution were a household, as if the other children were their siblings—was ultimately a disservice hindering the children's understanding of reality. Socializing the children properly thus hung on reasserting normative boundaries between family and nonfamily— this time, with the recognition that only children with biological siblings at

Chestnut House had family within the institution. The children needed to see themselves as unrelated individuals sharing a house or apartment building. They were strangers to each other; there was no incest taboo, Takada noted.

For some of the administrators within the social welfare corporation, these incidents confirmed their initial beliefs that Kitahara's vision was flawed from the start. Over the coming years, the children would be grouped based on biological sex, splitting sisters and brothers into different houses. Staff labor hours would be further regularized. Discussion of making the institution household-like was undertaken only in initial staff orientations. When I visited Chestnut House in the summer of 2019, I was told that the children were doing quite well in this new structure. Staffing had also been more stable, and no one had quit in months. It was not as household-like, but everyone seemed to be doing okay.

Was the initial instantiation of Chestnut House better for the children? Or did this new, more standardly institutional form offer better care? I liked knowing that working conditions for the staff facilitated longer tenures. However, the administration at the time enforced stricter professional boundaries between staff and children, which seemed to constrain their relationships. In that iteration of the institution, it did not seem to me that Chestnut House functioned as a furusato, a place to return, for children who had aged out. It was, rather, a place for the children to live when they had nowhere else to be.

Yet the institutional form, as with individual lives, continues to evolve. In the summer of 2023, after Japan's COVID-19 pandemic entry restrictions eased, I was able to visit Chestnut House once more. There were a handful of staff who had been working at the institution for more than ten years, and these staff members were now in leadership positions, doing their best to support Chestnut House alumni after they left the institution. The children who had been three years old when I'd begun fieldwork were teenagers and close to aging out.[20] Many of the older children were gone. Eri had left the institution to live with her foster mother, and Masahiro aged out and was living in a group home intended to help him transition to independence. A couple alumni, like Masahiro, continued to visit. Most of the young people who had aged out struggled to live independently, and the staff continuously faced the limits of their capacity to help.

In tracking the birth and dénouement of the social experiment to produce a family-like institution, I have worked to conceptualize a key modality by which people in Japan experience and perceive kinship and belonging: in many cases as a form of "aspirational normalcy" (Berlant 2011), a set of interpersonal projects oriented asymptotically toward normative goals that can never quite be realized. This aspirational, nostalgic, and perhaps even utopic project to create a furusato for children aligns with broader ethical visions of community, even as realization is ever deferred into the future (Watanabe 2019). Staff members' efforts to construct a household for institutionalized children poignantly rested on practices of substitution and temporal deferral, as idealized relational qualities of a household were approached and approximated but never actualized. These mimetic approximations, in which material objects, practices, and interpersonal relationships never quite coalesced into an actual household, were in many ways the most—although never quite enough—that staff members could provide the children.

I started writing about Chestnut House almost fifteen years ago, and I am completing this book chapter last. How could I possibly do justice to this place, the people in it, Kitahara's vision? I have been reading D. W. Winnicott (1992). His concept of the "good enough mother"—let us say "good enough parent"—is a figure of sufficiency, not perfection. In the eyes of the state, most of the children at Chestnut House did not have good enough parents. But for some of them, the children who had relationships with their parents that did not feel mostly bad, those relationships may have been good enough in at least some ways. The staff members were, I know, haunted by a sense of insufficiency, if only in their awareness of how much the children needed and how limited their capacity was to give and keep on giving. But many of the staff members at Chestnut House were and are good enough, including those who loved the children and, in the end, left. Staff member Sakai Marina often said she hoped to maintain a connection to the children that was "long and thin" (*nagakute hosoi*), being to them like the neighborhood auntie who nags about whether they are keeping their rooms clean. I honor the staff members' work and care.

In this context, what does it mean to write a good enough account, to be a good enough anthropologist? It seems fitting to close this chapter firmly in my own shoes, attuned to the partialness of my perspective that is, after all, long and thin, attenuated by time and space.

I want to tell the Chestnut House children: *I remember the day I met you. I wrote about it.*

GENEALOGICAL RETURNS

Fujisaki Hiroko and Eiji began fostering because they were unable to have children of their own. They were active in the local and national Japanese foster parent communities and had fostered more than twenty children over the years, but they had raised Yuka, Jun, and Nozomi from the time the children were small. When I met the Fujisaki family, Yuka, at twenty-six, had moved out of the home; Jun and Nozomi, both twenty-two, still lived with Hiroko and Eiji. The family welcomed me into their home and lives, and I spent many nights there, at first sleeping on a futon in the nicest room of the house and later sharing Nozomi's room or sleeping in her bed when she was away.

Late in my initial fieldwork, both Jun and Nozomi experienced their own sort of homecoming, as Hiroko described it to me. Jun had been placed in a child welfare institution and then family-based foster care as a toddler because his natal mother had been physically abusive, but he had many older brothers and sisters he had never met. As Jun grew older, his siblings contacted him every so often, and upon his graduation from college, they decided it was time for him to re-meet his biological mother. So before he left the area for a job in a different prefecture, Jun met his mother for the first time since he was a baby. More than a relationship with his biological mother, however, Jun began building ties with his siblings. As Hiroko told me, Jun realized that he was part of a large network of kin who cared about him and welcomed him into the fold.

Nozomi's homecoming was of a very different nature. She had never known her biological parents. One day, around the time Jun reconnected with his family, Nozomi's mother's brother contacted the Fujisaki family to tell them that

Nozomi's mother had died. According to Hiroko, Nozomi went with her boy-friend to her mother's grave and stood before it. It was a silent and still day, without wind. But as she stood there, the wooden tablets behind her mother's grave suddenly began to clatter against one another. As Hiroko recounted it to me, it was at her mother's grave that Nozomi and her mother finally met. Also at that moment, Nozomi realized herself to be truly alone.[1]

For Hiroko, these two homecomings connected uncannily to her own family's history. Hiroko's father had been the second to last of twelve children, and he was a twin. When Hiroko's grandfather suddenly died, Hiroko's father was sent away as an adoptive son to a couple who had been unable to bear children. He was unhappy there, and when he went to college, he moved far away from his adoptive parents and sought out connections to the family of his birth. He became close to them, and Hiroko herself grew up considering these people her extended family. Although as an adoptee he had taken his adoptive parents' name and was their heir, it was his natal family with whom he felt kinship.

"One day I realized," Hiroko told me, "that what I'm doing"—raising unrelated children—"is the same thing that the couple who raised my father did. But the people my father felt a connection to, in the end, were his original family, the people he was connected to by blood. That family of twelve siblings. Now there are lots of them, all together thirty-three children and cousins. The couple who took him in and raised him—that connection [en] is cut." However, some traces remained. Hiroko's own unmarried name was the name of her father, which was the name of the couple who adopted him. The couple's graves also remained, and Hiroko's father and mother were buried with those adoptive parents. They died long ago. "One feels like apologizing to them [mōshi wakenakute ne]," Hiroko said with a small smile. "That couple who adopted my father, that did the favor of raising him [sodatete kureta]." For despite the favor of having raised her father, and despite having taken their name, Hiroko's father did not feel an affiliation to them. Hiroko seemed lonely on their behalf.

Musing on the broken connections between her father and the couple who raised him, Hiroko noted, "And, well, recently my son Jun, he's become connected to his biological siblings, right? And in the end, from now on . . . Well, he will always consider our family important, but probably his relations with his siblings will increase over time. He's already making a fuss over his little nephews. That's just how things are. That's where things are for me." She paused. "There are many things I wish I could have asked my father. Because it's as though I, my father's youngest daughter . . . I am somehow living my father's destiny, his life over again."

Perhaps Hiroko's father might have been able to tell her something about her own foster children, something about the sorrow of separation and the pleasures of reconnection, the durability of blood. Perhaps he could have also told her about the bonds that connect a child to the family who did the favor of providing care.

Hiroko was unsure how to understand her relationship with Nozomi, who, she felt, pushed her away. I pointed out that Nozomi's behavior was typical of a young woman her age. But I also suspected that Nozomi was unsure how or if ever she would be able to reciprocate care for the parents who raised her. She had decided she did not want to be adopted. At the same time, with the new knowledge that her biological mother had died, she seemed shaken by the foreclosed possibility of reconnection. Eiji had told me over lunch one day that, after the death of her biological mother, Nozomi suddenly asked whether she could remain with the Fujisaki family (*Koko ni ite ii?* she had asked). Of course she could remain, they told her.[2]

In her intimation of the loss of Jun, Hiroko felt a new sense of connection to the couple who had raised her father, to whom she was not related by blood but whose name she had shared before her marriage to Eiji. She imagined that she was somehow reliving the life of the people who had raised her father. Jun's biological siblings, she felt, would inexorably draw him away from the Fujisaki family. At the same time, Nozomi's realization that the absent family of the past would remain the absent family of the future was a moment in which expectations of long-term interdependencies were refigured. Nozomi's question, whether she could remain in the Fujisaki household, reflected both the ways she might have imagined a future separate from the Fujisakis and the ways her status as a foster child was always a source of insecurity, regardless of the intimacies that were apparent in their household.

It was at the Fujisaki home that I was most viscerally aware of how kinship emerged in daily practice: the ways the family shared food, drank out of each other's cups and ate off each other's plates, laughed and teased. The house was filled with material evidence—photographs, mementos, personal belongings—of how Yuka, Jun, and Nozomi's steady presence in the household, in contrast to the many temporary foster children, constituted a stable family unit. Yet the moment Jun found his birth family and Nozomi lost hers threw into relief the fact that the kinship ties that had emerged over almost twenty years were, in some ways, still experienced as fragile to the Fujisaki family.

NORMAL ASPIRATIONS

Hanashima Shin'ichi had not planned to marry, a fact that had somehow escaped the woman he was dating. A mutual friend dropped the hint that his girlfriend was waiting to be asked. Surprised, Hanashima took the young woman aside. "I can't get married," he told her. "Marriage is between two households, and I have none." Hanashima had spent his entire childhood in a Japanese child welfare institution and lacked a relationship with either his mother, who was in a psychiatric hospital, or his father, of whom he knew nothing. Hanashima's girlfriend scoffed. "What old-fashioned thinking," she told him. "Marriage doesn't have to be between two households these days. It is a contract between two people." And that is how Hanashima and his wife decided to get married.

The couple seemed to have quite different understandings of how marriage and genealogy operate in contemporary Japan. The young woman argued that marriage is a contract between individuals, separable from extended networks of kin. Rather than marriage pointing toward the continuity of a preexisting family line, the marriage contract operates as a beginning for two individuals facing the future together. Hanashima, on the other hand, had never imagined himself as able to enter into a marriage precisely because he lacked the kinship network that would enable a union of families. Unmoored from ancestors, he was equally unmoored from the future generations entailed in his imagination of marriage. In contrast to his partner, Hanashima took kinship in Japan as normatively a process of replacement regulated by death (Weiner 1980).[1] However, he lacked a family to replace.

Arguments like that of Hanashima's soon-to-be wife, maintaining that a genealogically oriented mentality is old-fashioned, seem to imply that contemporary kinship logics have escaped from genealogical bondage. However, genealogical replacement preoccupied many of my interlocutors, and a lack of ancestors to replace was a source of lasting sorrow. Although some people expressed a desire for alternative kinship forms, the ability to reconcile a lack of genealogy largely depended upon heterosexual procreation within the confines of marriage. The imperative to create one's own small genealogy looking forward, toward the coming generations, if not backward toward one's ancestors, was challenged by the specter of infertility and normative prescriptions surrounding marriage.

Traces That Look Like Belonging

For people who lack family in Japan, it is a liberating notion that one can independently enter into marriage contracts and seemingly escape the kinship logics that have long structured the ways people are identified vis-à-vis each other and vis-à-vis the state. However, normative family forms remain a source of aspiration and desire, even among people who might gain the most by destabilizing or overturning these norms (Berlant 2011). These normative aspirations were materially evident when I collected depictions of families during interviews. Initially, I was careful not to ask for genealogies (kakeizu), keeping in mind the (hetero) normative constraints of genealogical reckoning. Further, I was not interested in gathering objective data that mapped my interlocutors as parts of family systems. However, with only a few exceptions, my interlocutors produced something resembling a genealogy, characterized by horizontal lines indicating marriage and vertical lines for descent.[2] In many cases, people depicted extensive networks of kin and either verbally or visually noted the deviations between what looked like family on paper and what they perceived as family. The genealogical model was thus a compelling heuristic even for those whose lives were least amenable to being slotted into normative kinship frameworks.

These diagramming practices, in the context of interviews focusing on complicated and conflicted sensibilities about kinship, literally illustrated how, for many people, the desire to situate oneself within a lineage existed in tension with the perspective that an individual theoretically should be able to self-determine through chosen intimate relationships (Weston 1991). These tensions are exemplified by Elizabeth Povinelli's (2006) discussion of two models of selfhood that are coproduced in liberal discourses. Povinelli terms these models the "genealogical society" and the "intimate event," respectively. The "genealogical society" refers to how people are most socially recognizable if situated in family networks, specifically ones characterized by heterosexual biological procreation, in which worth and status are shaped by the long shadow of origin and lineage. Povinelli's concept of the "intimate event," in contrast, refers to the notion that one can self-create through intimate mutual recognition with a lover and that human worth is not bound by kinship or genealogical ties. Despite the power of this nonheteronormative vision, Povinelli shows how even societies that most stridently embrace the concept of self-determination remain, in the end, normatively genealogical, viewing citizenship rights and responsibilities as rooted in heterosexual family forms.

Although Hanashima and his wife married with the understanding that they were forging a contract between themselves as individuals, Hanashima's depiction of his and his wife's families in a kinship diagram looked very much like the joining of two households (fig. 7). He drew this diagram for me during the first of two four-hour interviews (conducted jointly with Shirai Chiaki). I had met Hanashima the previous month at a conference, and I liked him immediately. His insights appear throughout this manuscript, and I owe much to his friendship.

When I note that Hanashima's kinship diagram resembles the joining of two households, I refer to the Japanese ie, a patrilineal line that perdures over time. Between the Meiji Restoration of imperial rule in 1868 and the end of World War II, the ie was the legal entity that anchored individuals into networks of kin and made those networks of kin legible to the state. In postwar Japan, American occupiers ordered the ie system officially abolished: the ie was thought to sup-

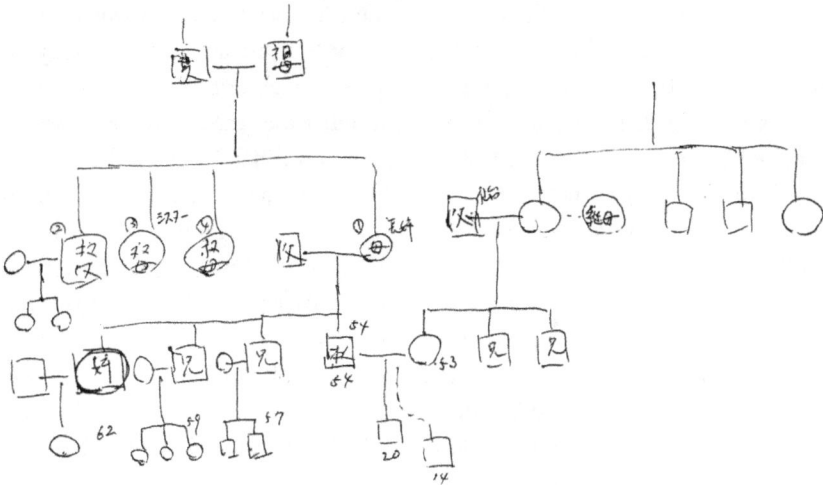

FIGURE 7. Hanashima's family diagram. Hanashima indicated himself as the square in the center marked with his age, fifty-four. His wife's family extends to the right, and his son is depicted below him and his wife. Their foster son is connected to the family with a dotted line.

port the power of the imperial system, which figured individual households as part of the larger family-nation (*kokka*) with the emperor as paternal head. In the postwar system, rather than individuals remaining in extensive family registries, when a couple married, both exited the registries of their parents and started a new registry of their own (Paulson 2010; Holloway 2011; Krogness 2011; White 2018). At the level of legal category and procedure, the American occupation ushered Japan from a genealogical society model into one that valorized the individual who constituted themself through marriage. This was consistent with the broader American project to press Japan to engage Western notions of individual rights and self-determination. The abolition of the ie was an attempt to deny a genealogical form of belonging that was seen to undercut liberal sensibilities. This is still the context within which marriage is legally and bureaucratically experienced in Japan. According to legal procedure, then, at the time of marriage, Hanashima and his wife both exited their family registries and created a new register under Hanashima's name.

Yet the American occupation's attempt to excise genealogical thinking through new registry practices did not eliminate it from people's everyday sensibilities. Family registries are bureaucratized representations of nuclear families: individuals with their spouses and children.[3] But this atomized individual view falls away when people are asked to diagram their families. On paper, the genealogy of Hanashima, who said he had no household, looks similar to the genealogy of a person who has maintained a household across generations, passing on family names, property, family businesses, and responsibilities of ancestor worship.

The traces of genealogical documentation or bureaucratic family registry do not transparently reveal the degree to which kinship ties exist at the level of affective experience. This divergence brings into relief the reasons why Hanashima said he had no household. The family registry into which Hanashima had been listed until marriage was that of his mother—a mother who had never raised him. And the extensive kinship network he depicted during our interview makes all the more poignant the fact that Hanashima lived in institutional care for the first fifteen years of his life, until he became independent. When Hanashima was small, living in a child welfare institution, he and his siblings occasionally visited the home of his mother's brother. One day he managed to escape the child welfare institution and traveled by himself to his uncle's house. His uncle promptly sent him back to the institution, which, he told the boy, was his home. At that moment, Hanashima learned in no uncertain terms that although these people may be kin, where they lived was not where he belonged. The household Hanashima retrospectively documented for my purposes was neither the household that cared for all of its members nor a household whose members would care whom he married. Finally, in everyday life, Hanashima's family was constituted by himself, his wife, his son, and his foster son. However, Hanashima connected the latter to his genealogy with a dotted line, highlighting a divergence from standard genealogical relatedness in spite of the tight-knit family unit that existed in practice.

When he was younger, Hanashima could not imagine himself situated within a lineage in which he replaced his ancestors and his own children would replace him. The absence of death as a regulatory force in kinship was a source of distress. Hanashima recalled, "When I was young, I always imagined that I would die before I reached thirty. I just couldn't imagine living longer than that. The idea that people get older, get married, have children, become grandparents, and then die . . . I just didn't have that image. Growing up in a child welfare institution, you don't know what a life path looks like. You never see old people." Hanashima's own life had been unimaginable as extending through time precisely because he had no way to situate himself temporally, as the replacement of those who had come before.

As Hanashima noted, the fact that people are born, grow older, have children, die, and become ancestors, like their parents' parents, is not usually a familiar concept to children who grew up in institutional care. "Living my entire childhood in an institution," Hanashima once told me, "I had never seen the *obon* dances" (which are performed in community festivals for the annual celebration of dead ancestors) "and I didn't know obon rituals or their meaning. There was never any discussion about ancestors. I had never thought about where I had come from or where I was going." "Descent—and the relations with the dead that it entails" could not give Hanashima a "taste of transcendence" (Rutherford 2013, 276). The sense of being disconnected from vertical relationships, among parents, grandparents, and both dead family members and family members who are yet to be born, mirrored his sense of disconnection from lateral relationships—an isolation from peers, friends, and siblings by virtue of his experience of being raised in institutional care. Growing up meant an increased awareness of the network of kin that had abandoned him, which he could now conceptualize academically in a kinship chart. Growing up also meant the realization that with marriage and procreation, his own life could extend forward, his line continuing with the birth of a son.

The Fifth and Sixth Successors

Families with long histories to maintain are often intensely concerned with couples' procreative relationships. Scholars of Japanese kinship practices have noted—sometimes with consternation—that Japanese kinship tends to privilege lines of descent while simultaneously exemplifying "promiscuous" adoption (for discussion, see Lebra 1993, 107). Takie Lebra has called adoption, using a blood metaphor, a "cultural transfusion" into families anemic with lack of an heir (1993, 16). While in the past, both servants and employees were commonly adopted as heirs (Paulson 1984; Bryant 1990), over the past century, families have become more nuclear and less likely to incorporate servants and employees into the intimate circle of kin. Celebrations of a private home (*mai ho-mu*), a boom in women becoming housewives during Japan's post–World War II period of rapid economic growth, and decreasing numbers of multigenerational households encouraged a narrower definition of family borders (Ochiai 1997; Sand 2003; Holloway 2010; Ronald and Alexy 2011). Further, as Japan's birthrate has declined, there are fewer undesired children in families. While a childless couple might have in the past adopted a child of a sibling or a cousin, decreasing family size makes this practice less pragmatic. Finally, scholars of reproduction and infertility in Japan note that with the development of advanced reproductive technologies, definitions of family have become more firmly rooted in biological descent (Tsuge 1999; Shirai 2010). Thus, just as with couples without long histories to maintain—but who find opportunity in the possibility to bear children and begin their own small genealogy—families concerned with the maintenance of a patriarchal line are focused on biological procreation more in contemporary Japan than in the past.

I was often told that if I really wanted to know about traditional Japanese families, I ought to talk to people from the countryside, the supposed bastion of feudal thought in Japan where the extended household still holds sway. The notion that the countryside is the site of Japanese tradition or originary identity motivated Yanagita Kunio, Japan's most famous nativist ethnologist, to focus his studies of Japanese tradition in rural areas, where his accounts offered a return to a timeless Japanese past-in-present (Ivy 1995). The perception that rural people maintain traditions lost to city dwellers is common and is part of nihonjinron discourses on Japaneseness. These discourses reify Japanese culture and tradition and simultaneously shape Japanese people's sensibilities about what it means to be Japanese.

There is some truth in the characterization opposing rural and urban kinship ideologies: the countryside is where families are better able to maintain houses and land passed down through the generations. My interviews of people in both rural and urban areas of Japan indicated exceptional diversity, which belies any easy statements that urbanites (or rural-urban migrants) have lost awareness of traditional family continuity, or that rural families are feudal in nature. Perhaps more salient factors shaping people's perceptions of lineage are gender and whether that person belongs to the main branch (*honke*) of an ie or a tertiary branch (*bunke*).

For an eldest son in the main branch of a family with a long history, property, and responsibilities for maintaining ancestor worship, genealogical continuity remains very salient. Such was the case of the Ishizaka family, who lived in a rural town in southern Japan. The Ishizaka family's conceptualization of kinship was guided by the notion of death and the replacement of father with son over time.

Ishizaka Kazuo and Kumiko were always willing to indulge my curiosity about kinship practices. "Marriage is between two families," Kumiko told me with her hands on the wheel of her car, as she maneuvered along narrow roads between rice paddies and houses built right up against the road. She had been born into the main branch (honke) of an old family and married the eldest son of the Ishizaka household, which was also a honke. She and her husband had three children, first a boy and then two girls. Their son was my friend Tetsu, formerly staff at Chestnut House (see chap. 2). Tetsu had married a woman named Harue the year before. Although they moved to the Tokyo area for Tetsu to work at Chestnut House, they returned to their hometown before Harue gave birth. This was the first of many visits that I stayed with the Ishizakas, and Tetsu and Harue's baby had just been born. It was a boy.

There is nothing quite like the birth of the family's successor to make a grandparent proud, Kazuo told me with a broad smile. Tetsu and Harue's son, Hiroaki, was not their first grandchild; Tetsu's younger sister, Chizuko, had married first and already had two boys. But these were children of another household, Kumiko told me. Chizuko's eldest son would succeed Chizuko's husband's family's line. "Of course we were excited and proud when Chizuko's sons were born," Kumiko said. "But we were more excited when Hiroaki was born."

Kazuo was the fourth in a line of successors, which made Tetsu the fifth and Hiroaki the sixth. The family successor (atotsugi) played an important role in the Ishizaka family. Beyond inheriting name, land, and property, the successor was responsible for smoothing relationships within extended family and providing a home for other family members to return to for the new year and obon, when the spirits of ancestors are celebrated. The Ishizaka land contained two houses: an old house built in a traditional style with heavy ceramic roof shingles, tatami floor matting, and an old-fashioned kitchen with a cement floor and a new, modern house that was built when Tetsu was a teenager (fig. 8). The old house was where the family altar (butusdan) remained, and at obon the family gathered there. In years to come, the family would renovate the old house for Tetsu and his wife and children to inhabit.

"What would happen if Tetsu and Harue hadn't had a son or hadn't been able to have children?" I asked Kumiko.

She frowned. "Well, we would have tried to do mukoyōshi," she said: the adoption of a daughter's husband who takes the daughter's family name and acts as

FIGURE 8. Two houses, new and old. Illustration by Sasha Buckser, based on photograph by author.

the family's successor. Tetsu's youngest sister, Emi, might have married a man willing to leave his family line and join the Ishizaka line. "If mukoyōshi didn't work," Kumiko continued, "well—that's the end, then [*owari*]." The end of the Ishizaka family line.

Tetsu described his place in the family, and the importance of bearing a male child, in much the same way. "I grew up being told, 'You're the fifth successor, you're the fifth successor [*go dai me, go dai me*]." He paused. "I'm not sure what the basis was for the start of the family, the first generation, come to think of it . . . but anyway, I'm the fifth.[4] My father was the fourth. And Hiroaki is the sixth. Since the time I was little, my father was always telling me, 'You're going to succeed the Ishizaka family line. All of this is your land, money, property . . . this will all be yours.'"[5] Tetsu's description of his position as the fifth in a line, the basis of which he did not fully understand, speaks to the highly affective compulsion to participate in the system in which he had been raised as his father's replacement.

"What did your sisters think of that, do you know?" I asked.

"My sisters? They thought that was ordinary and obvious [*futsū de atari mae*], I think. . . . Anyway, they don't complain. They grew up hearing my father telling me that I would be the successor. They think it's obvious. And then my firstborn was a son. I have to say, I was relieved."

"Were you worried?" I asked.

"I wasn't worried . . . but if it had been a girl, we would have kept having to have kids until we had a boy! It's a lot of pressure, bearing the weight of all this history."

This pressure also weighed on his wife. Harue had once told Tetsu that if for some reason she couldn't have children, he was free to remarry. (In a separate conversation, Harue told me the same story and said that Tetsu had likely forgotten this exchange. They both seemed to feel this was a nonissue now that they had a son.) That sort of thinking, Tetsu continued, may seem old-fashioned, but the possibility of not being able to have a child was something that he truly hadn't been able to even consider. Harue's own family was the main branch, and she understood this burden well.

"So if you couldn't have had children," I asked, "would you have thought about adopting?"

Tetsu coughed. "Well, but then the family line [ie] would be cut, in the end."

Given that there is a long history of adoption in Japan, specifically when a family lacks an heir, this response may seem counterintuitive. However, it is important to recall that the process of regular adoption (*futsū yōshiengumi*) is understood as a process distinct from special adoption (*tokubetsu yōshiengumi*). Special adoption was enacted in 1988 and allows a child to be entered as the natural child into the adoptive family's registry, cutting legal ties to the natal family. This type of adoption is understood as a child welfare intervention and is for the sake of a child who needs a family. Under regular adoption, by contrast, the main requirement is that the adopter be older than the adoptee. The adoptee remains legally linked to both the adoptive and the natal families, bearing the right to inherit from—and obligation to care for—both. Although regular adoption is still undertaken for many reasons, including to create a legal link between same-sex partners or extramarital lovers (Bryant 1990), regular adoption has long been used as a way to incorporate a child from a known family that has "extra" children, with the purpose of this child carrying on the family line. Mukoyōshi, son-in-law adoption, is also regular adoption. Regular adoption of a child, rather than an adult, used to be more common when more people had children "to spare." The practice of regular adoption has thus changed as Japan's birth rate has decreased, and now the adoption of the children of kin is less frequent. These two types of adoption fulfill very different social purposes.

As it turned out, the third son in the Ishizaka family line (Tetsu's father's father) had actually been adopted as a child through regular adoption. Tetsu drew a diagram (fig. 9) tracing what he knew about his lineage. The second successor in the family line had not had a son himself, and so he and his wife adopted one of his sibling's sons. This boy—Tetsu's grandfather—became the new successor. "He was called over from somewhere nearby, somewhere quite close, one

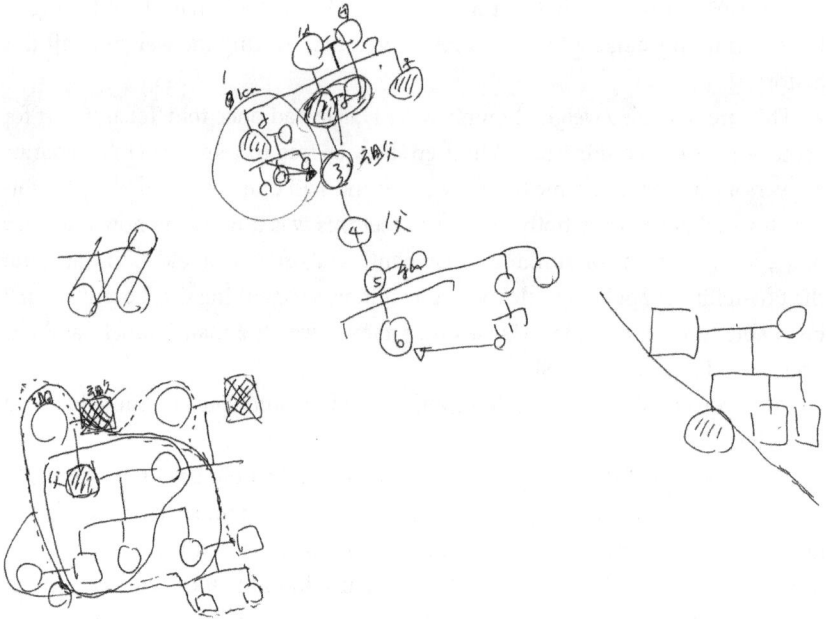

FIGURE 9. Tetsu's family diagram. The figure to the left shows Tetsu's nuclear family with circles indicating affective identification, in one case including his grandmother and in another case excluding his sister who married out to enter her husband's family registry. The center figure shows the six generations in his family, and the man who was adopted to become the third successor is marked by "1km" to show geographic proximity. The figure to the right depicts Harue's family. Tetsu drew a diagonal line to show that Harue was part of his family, but her kin were not.

kilometer, three kilometers away," Tetsu said. "He kept saying that he didn't want to be part of this family, but—'You're this family's child now,' he was told. And so he became this family's child, the third in the line of successors." If this practice had still been common, Tetsu said, were Tetsu and Harue unable to have children, perhaps his sister Chizuko's second son might have been recruited to be the Ishizaka successor.

Tetsu's emphasis on the fact that his grandfather had been adopted from somewhere "quite close" reinforces how the boy had been both geographically and affectively close and was indeed part of the same family line, sharing blood with the Ishizaki family. In contrast, the notion of special adoption—the adoption of an unrelated child with (often) unknown family—was unthinkable to Tetsu or his parents. The incorporation of nonfamily as successor would mean that the family line would be cut. As Tetsu's mother told me, if a male heir had not been born, and mukoyōshi was not possible, the Ishizaka family line would simply end. Adopting a nonrelated child into the family would not solve the problem of succession.

A text written by legal scholar Baron Nobushige Hozumi at the end of the nineteenth century echoes these sentiments with precision. Although mukoyōshi would mean that the family's blood line would be continued through the daughter, the adoption of an entirely unrelated child would cut the family line (Hozumi 2004, 155). Noting historical fluctuations in the ways adoption was viewed (sometimes permitting and sometimes prohibiting the adoption of individuals from other clans), Hozumi cites eighth-century law (the *Taihō* code): "That the object of adoption was the perpetuation of Ancestor-worship may also be inferred from the old strict rule that *only a kinsman could be adopted as a son*. The Taihō code limited it to within the kindred of the *fourth degree*." Violators would be punished. These prohibitions were motivated, Hozumi writes, by the Confucian precept that "'spirits do not accept sacrifices from strangers; people do not offer sacrifices to strangers' spirits'" (2004, 151, italics in original). While other scholars have noted that the readiness to adopt in Japan seems to contradict these same Confucian ethics, Hozumi's text illustrates the ways these questions were recapitulated and reformulated in different legal treatments throughout Japan's history. Even in contemporary Japan, if genealogical extension is about replacement and the care of ancestors, adopting a child foreign to the lineage defeats the purpose.

"I can't imagine adopting a stranger's child," Tetsu said. "That's just . . . I can't stand the thought of it. I don't know how to explain it. But you want my honest opinion, right? It's just that—it's not my own family, right? It's a stranger (tanin), right? . . . You know, one's own child is the best, in the end. A child related to you by blood." Tetsu's aversion to adoption did not contradict the imperative to continue the family line because adoption would introduce unmitigated foreignness. Although marriage involves the incorporation of others through alliance, for Tetsu's family, descent was limited to the biological and procreative.

Loving the Child of a Stranger

In order to imagine the adoption of a child in contemporary Japan, many of my interlocutors felt that adoptive parents must be able to be willing to perceive that child as a possible replacement within a lineage and conceptualize the child of another person as loveable. Tetsu framed his aversion to adoption in terms of the former, but he had no trouble loving other people's children. When Tetsu was a staff member at Chestnut House, he often talked about how love for the children grew out of the intimacies of everyday life. He had been affectionate, playful, and joyous with the children, and they adored him.

Tetsu's mother and sister Emi also worked in the social welfare field, and this work was a calling for him as it was for them. Before working at Chestnut House, he had worked at a child welfare institution near his hometown, and he often told stories about the young people he had come to know there and how they would visit his parents' house during holidays, likely staying in the spare room where I myself stayed when I visited. He imagined opening a family home in the future, working with Harue as a couple to foster up to six children. For Tetsu, the ability to care for a child—caring emotionally and also the physical processes of caregiving—had little to do with the presence or absence of a blood tie.[6]

For many, however, the uncertainty that one could love the child of a stranger (*tanin no ko ga aeseru ka dō ka*) was the most common reason people cited to explain their hesitance to adopt or foster. The focus on love as a criterion for incorporation into the family is arguably new, articulating with liberal ideas of love marriages that emerged postwar, along with contemporary notions of families as characterized by intimacy (Goldfarb 2018).

The term *child of a stranger* requires explanation. My interlocutors generally used two phrases to point to a dubiously lovable non–biologically related child: "*tanin no ko* (他人の子)" and "*hito no ko* (人の子)." *Tanin* can be translated as an outsider, a stranger, someone unrelated and other; *ko* means child. Thus *tanin no ko* could mean "the child of a stranger" or "an other person's child." Similarly, *hito no ko* can be translated as "other people's children" or "an other person's child" and even carries the nuance of "a child of humanity." In all these interpretations, these phrases evoke alterity and difference specifically by engaging a sense of universal strangeness or generality, rather than the particular intimacy of one's own child. The child of a stranger is both the child of another and the child of an other.

In discussions about parenthood, people often distinguished between giving birth to a child and raising a child. Those who thought raising a child was the most important (for whatever reason) were generally more positively oriented toward fostering and adoption. But no matter what a person's position on this topic, many people referenced the social standard that a person—particularly a woman—is not a full-fledged adult (*hitori mae*) until becoming a parent. Further, although perhaps times are changing, marriage is often seen as a necessary prerequisite for childbearing. The rate of childbearing outside marriage in Japan is very low: only around 2 percent of children are born outside of wedlock in Japan, a rate that has remained stable over the past two decades, compared to 43 percent in both the United States and United Kingdom (Hertog 2009, 2).[7] Ekaterina Hertog (2009) explores the reasons why many women believe it would be better for the child for a woman to have an abortion, rather than bear a child illegitimately. Although most literature on the topic indicates that economic and legal circumstances or social stigma make single motherhood undesirable, Hertog argues that the most significant reason women avoid single motherhood is the guilt associated with perceptions of single mothers as damaging their children and common beliefs that single mothers are selfish and egoistic to bring a child into the world without a father.

In this logic, becoming a parent, preferably by conceiving and giving birth to one's own biological child within a heterosexual marriage, takes on performative power to constitute the individual as a self-governing and mature subject. The intimacy and affect ascribed to blood ties in contemporary Japan, within the circumscribed sphere of the nuclear household, articulate with liberal notions of the self that emerges through chosen intimacies. This process may seem particularly enchanting for those who hope for a chance to start over, to reconcile with past loss, or to ameliorate the deprivations experienced because of having lacked family in the past. Yet this dream may be constrained by uncontrollable conditions, like infertility.

Takano Saki had been attempting to have a child with her husband for the past seven years. At thirty-five years of age, Saki felt that she had done nothing with her life so far other than throw money into ever more discouraging infertility treatments, which increased in technological sophistication as she became more and more desperate. Saki had gotten married at age twenty-eight and hoped to become pregnant right away, and so, like many women in Japan, she quit her job after her wedding. She did not become pregnant, however, so she began doing temporary accounting work. After two years, she decided to seek medical treatment. The subsequent five years of treatment involved extensive tracking of her ovulation cycles, multiple tries of artificial insemination at two different clinics, and a short pregnancy that ended in miscarriage. In 2007, Saki began cycles of in vitro fertilization, one of which again resulted in a brief pregnancy. At the time of our second extensive interview in October 2010, Saki had done in vitro fertilization seven times and described the process as physically and mentally exhausting. In January the coming year, she said, she decided to seriously begin thinking about adoption. Although she had been researching adoption, the moment at which she would begin seriously thinking about it was as yet deferred into the future.

Adoption was, somehow, beside the point for Saki. It wasn't so much that she wanted a child because she liked children—she didn't, particularly—and it wasn't that she wanted her husband's child, either. For Saki, having children was part of married life. She wanted more than anything to have children in a normal way (*futsū ni*), to do things in the proper order. To her that meant to date someone, get married, live together, and have children. Her younger brother had a *dekichatta kekkon*: he got married because his girlfriend became pregnant. Saki's parents, before, had also had a dekichatta kekkon, which ended in divorce. After Saki's parents got divorced when Saki was in sixth grade, her mother took Saki's brother and left. The fact that Saki's own childhood was not "normal" was a central factor in her desire to bear and raise a child in a normal way.

Despite her focus on conceiving and bearing her and her husband's biological child, Saki repeatedly emphasized that more than giving birth, raising a child was the most crucial. But this claim came not from a desire to celebrate nurture rather than nature, as so often appears in adoption and fostering literature in Japan and elsewhere (Modell 1994; Murata 2005). Raising a child was the most important, Saki asserted, because babies are conceived and birthed by accident all the time. Just look at her own parents and her brother's family. Raising a child, on the other hand, was clearly not something Saki's own mother had been able to do, she said. "She gave birth to me, but why did she suddenly give up partway through?" Saki asked rhetorically. "She left all the responsibility to my father. To give birth—as if *that's* so special [*erai mitai*]. . . . It's raising a child that's hard. It was my *father* who raised me. That's pretty rough, right? I didn't have a grandmother or anyone helping out, and suddenly he was left with a sixth-grade girl. . . . It was like, 'What the hell are you doing, Mother' [*nani o yatten da yo, haha oya*]? This was something I absolutely didn't want to inflict on a child. But . . . now I can't have a child." Saki wanted to be able to prove to her mother that she, Saki, was different—but she could not enact this proof without having a child herself.

For Saki, who dated her lover, got married, and then started living together, having a child would have been both the proper way to constitute a family and the only way to show her mother that there was a better way to care, a right way to nurture a child. Tellingly, Saki's inability to conceive had been tentatively diagnosed as *fuikushō* (不育症), a medical term indicating that a person is unable to bear a pregnancy full term. The word interdiscursively (Bakhtin 1981) indexes conventional ways of speaking about pregnancy as to "raise" a child in one's womb (Ivry 2010). On many levels, pregnancy was conflated with childrearing, both dependent on each other and both necessary in order for Saki to remediate the loss of her own mother as a caregiver when she was a child.

During this interview, I was sitting in Saki's living room with Shirai Chiaki, my Japanese collaborator. This was a follow-up interview for me and Shirai's first interview of Saki. Shirai was intrigued by the ways that Saki angrily described her relationship with her mother, whom Saki said had become a stranger (tanin) to Saki and her father and, by virtue of taking Saki's brother with her when she left, had also made the brother a tanin. Recall that the term *tanin* was often used to index the concern that a person could not love a stranger's child.

"Were your mother and brother really tanin," Shirai asked, "or perhaps half tanin? But, like, half 'we have a blood connection,' did you feel?"

Saki shrugged. "Like, they're just relatives." Saki had been unable to become close to her brother, having missed the opportunity to build that relationship when they were young.

"But isn't there something about blood, like—'thicker than water,' or 'just the same as water'?"

Saki considered. "I don't know . . . but I've definitely thought that it would have been better if I had not been connected to my mother by blood."

"Really?"

"Come on, it's *because* we're connected by blood that my mother preoccupies me [*ki ni naru*]. I mean, she's all alone now, and she's getting older," Saki responded.

Saki's narrative was replete with examples of the reasons why blood connections did not necessarily lead to positive affect but rather could make someone who was otherwise a tanin into a source of preoccupation and worry. But the otherness of tanin was hard to transcend. She explained, "My husband says about a kid in a child welfare institution, 'I don't know what *sort* of kid that is.' But I'm like, 'What about you, have you had such a fabulous life, are you so good yourself?' And the same is true for me too, you know. But he'll say, 'I don't know *whose* child that is.' But, like, 'C'mon, it could be *your* child in the institution, and someone else would say the same thing!'" Saki saw no difference in this perspective from the one that some people articulated when they did in vitro fertilization and worried that somehow gametes were mixed up, making the child not actually their child, or the worries that parents might have about a baby being born with a disability.

Saki's dismissal of her husband's concerns was self-deprecatory and focused on the contingent nature of conception and childbirth under any circumstance. Her own experience with her mother illustrated how conceiving and bearing a child does not mean that a parent will love that child. Yet the concern whether she and her husband would be able to love the child of another person was persistent, a constant worry that belied any "ontological choreography" (Thompson 2005) that might frame an adopted child as one's own. She explained, "The ability to . . . come to . . . love the child, well, that's obviously the best, isn't it? But not being able to love . . . Like, what about when there is trouble, or when the kid is rebelling, the sort of thing that happens with one's own child anyway—the idea of thinking, despite oneself, 'It's because the child was adopted.' In order to adopt . . . you have to be *absolutely* certain you won't do that." This insecurity was the breaking point for Saki. Her husband's persistent lack of certitude augmented her own fear that the alterity of a nonbiological child would emerge in moments of family tension.

The possibility of conceiving, giving birth, and raising her own child would provide Saki the opportunity for remediations of many sorts, most particularly as a form of proof to her mother, an illustration of how one properly raises a child. But bearing a child with her husband offered to Saki more than that: having a child with him offered her the opportunity to remake herself as someone with a normal family, someone who does things "properly" (Berlant 2011). In the act of beginning her own small lineage, Saki would no longer be defined by the lineage from which she came, in which marriages occurred to prevent out-of-wedlock births, in which mothers abandoned their daughters and blood relations became strangers. But unless infertility treatment finally allowed her to conceive and bear a child, she would be denied the opportunity to inhabit the normal and the proper, the tantalizing status of the unmarked.

Two Ways of Choosing Family

The first time I visited the Otsuki and Takahashi household, we spent the entire weekend eating. The household was comprised of two sibling sets: Otsuki Reina and her younger brother, Akio; and Takahashi Sora and her younger brother, Kenji. The four of them had grown up in the same child welfare institution in the Kansai area. Both brothers, Akio and Kenji, had intellectual disabilities, and at the time it seemed unlikely they could live independently. I had recently met Reina at a symposium in Tokyo featuring the perspectives of youth who had spent time in the Japanese child welfare system; Reina had been one of the presenters. The symposium fell in December 2009, the fourth month of my doctoral research, and my acquaintance with Reina was a key turning point in my fieldwork. When I expressed interest in talking to her more about the self-support organization she had started as a recent graduate of the child welfare system, Reina immediately invited me to visit and said I could stay at her house, where she lived with the people she described as her family. I visited the next month, shortly after the new year.

I was charmed by the easy invitation and the practiced way Reina offered me her own bedroom; she would sleep on a futon in her brother's room. This was a household whose borders seemed unusually porous, open and accepting of outsiders, an eminently "chosen family" (Weston 1991) where people uncared for by biological family had come together to make something beautifully nonnormative. The first evening I was there, Reina playfully indicated stacks of boxes and bags in their main room: "All donations!" Apples and bags of rice, plus lots of treats, from people fond of the siblings who were looking out for them in the new year. The next morning after I woke up, I joined Reina, Akio, and Kenji at the *kotatsu*, the low table with a heating element, covered with a quilt to contain the warmth. Reina indicated the bag of rice crackers they had already begun to dig into, and I offered to peel one of the apples. We were munching contentedly when Sora entered the room. "Oooh, snacks already?" she exclaimed, highlighting the incongruity of the day's morning meal, even as she sat down with us and took a piece of apple. My visit, the proximity to the new year and plethora of unasked for treats, and Kenji's upcoming birthday early in January contributed to a slightly subversive festival atmosphere.

My visit to the Otsuki-Takahashi household would be one of many over many years. Staying in their home was my favorite way to begin a research trip to Japan. Jetlagged and bleary, I would make my way to the siblings' household, stopping along the way for groceries, beer, and *chū-hai* (a canned highball drink) for Akio, and we would sit up late talking. We were all within a year or two of each other's ages, and their friends became my friends. They were convivial hosts, their house open and welcoming. They were people who surrounded themselves with good people.

During the time of my doctoral fieldwork, Reina, Akio, Sora, and Kenji had been living together for a couple years, an arrangement motivated by Akio and Kenji's aging out of the child welfare institution where they had all been raised. Initially, both young men had been sent to a residential facility for adults with disabilities, where they lived until their sisters decided to get a house for the four of them. Reina and Akio actually had six other siblings. Their immediately elder brother lived in a company dorm and came around the house every so often. They were not in touch with the other five, whose age differences meant that they had had little opportunity to interact in the child welfare institution. Sora and Kenji had a younger sister, whom I discuss below.[8]

One morning, Reina and I were eating breakfast and drinking coffee in the kitchen of their house. The doorbell rang, and Reina went to answer. I could hear low voices for a few minutes, and then she returned to the kitchen, shaking her head in frustration. "It was a guy wanting to sell us fire alarms. When I answered the door, he said, 'Are you the mistress of the house?'" Literally, in Japanese, "Are you the wife?" (*Okusan desu ka?*) Reina had said no, and he paused, flustered. "Oh, then, are you the elder sister?" (*Onēsan desu ka?*) She explained, now herself flustered, that she lived there with her housemates, and that they would have to discuss whether they wanted to install new fire alarms. She told me, laughing but irritated, "Do I have to be either the wife or the elder sister? This is so typical." Unrelated people do not generally live together in a house in Japan, and even unrelated roommates in apartments are rare. Further, it is common for one stranger to address another with kin terms (*okusan, onēsan*), which situates an individual within a network of recognizable social relationships. The fact that Reina could not be situated in these terms confused the salesman and reiterated the fact that a family or household composed of siblings and friends is not a social grouping that is easily recognized in Japan. Small moments like these were, for Reina, reminders that deviations from normative social expectations were received with shock and, tiresomely, must be explained.

Perhaps in rebellion against these normative perceptions of family, Reina commonly asserted that she, Akio, Sora, and Kenji were family. If family is constituted by caregiving relationships and embodied intimacies, there were certainly these in abundance. In order to live together, there was even a legal tie binding them, as Reina's older brother was the guarantor for all four of their rental agreements. For Reina, calling this household *family* might have been an expression of hope in the creative power of language to perform relationality and the capacity to choose and make a family that is both separate from one's biological family and independent of marriage and biological reproduction.

Although Reina spoke more than once about how she imagined raising children in the future, she also expressed doubt that she would ever be able to marry. She was, she told me, doubly tainted. Having grown up in a child welfare institution meant, to those judging her, that her blood and family stock were of poor quality. Her parents would be viewed as worthless, unable to care for their own. Further, the fact that Akio was intellectually disabled would be perceived as evidence of the low quality of her family line. Potential marriage partners would be concerned that Akio's disability was heritable, just as the quality of Reina's blood was likewise perceived as something passed from parent to child. Reina's embrace of a nonnormative family might be thus understood as highly pragmatic. But she was also intensely aware of the stubborn inequalities underlying beliefs regarding family origin. In the past, she had worked at an organization whose objective was to raise awareness of discrimination toward buraku people, who had historically been considered an untouchable class and still often face social stigma for "unclean" origins (Hankins 2014). Although perhaps pragmatic, I felt that Reina's representation of family was also political.

While Reina's rejection of normative kinship forms was something she signaled in her spoken representations of family and the very openness of her household to strangers, I learned rather long into my friendship with the siblings that Sora felt differently. For Sora, a normative family was an intense object of yearning and offered the possibility of satisfying dreams that had long been unattainable.

In an extended audio-recorded interview, during which she produced a visual depiction of her family relationships in a series of kinship diagrams, Sora explained her family context (fig. 10). In the smaller genealogy on the left, Sora is the furthermost left circle, labeled with her age at the time of our interview, "26." Kenji, who was 25, is marked next to her, and further right is her sister, who was 23 years old. Sora's mother was with another man, with whom she had a daughter,

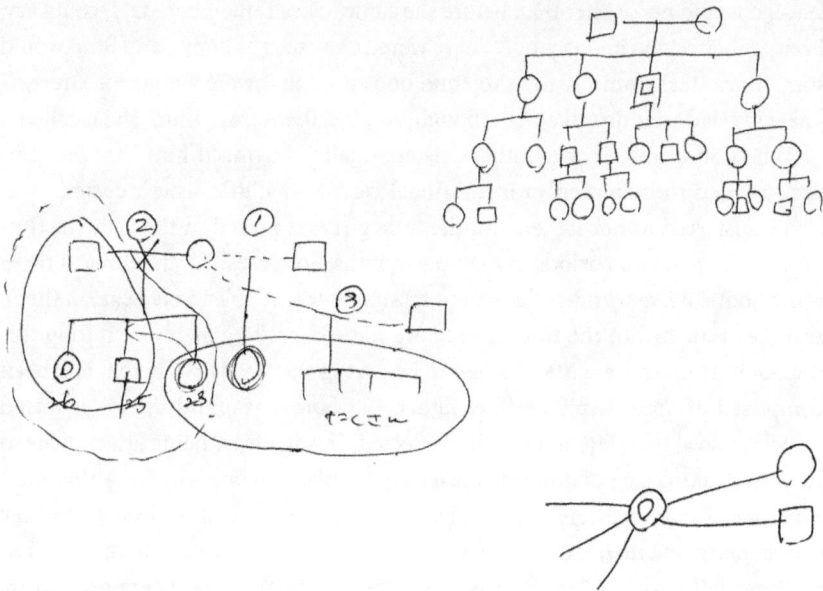

FIGURE 10.   Sora's family diagram. The diagram on the bottom left depicts Sora's immediate kin group and her mother's remarriages. The bottom right diagram shows Sora's social network (names have been erased). The image to the top right is of her father's extended kin; her father is marked by a square within a square.

before she married Sora's father; this union is marked with a 1. Sora's mother's marriage to her father is marked by a 2. After her parents split up, her mother married a third man, with whom she had, Sora told me, many children, although Sora wasn't sure how many; she wrote "many" (*takusan*) below these unknown half siblings. Sora's drawings documented layers of complicated intimacy as she depicted living arrangements at different periods of time by circling residential groups in the diagram on the left and in her social network diagram, with herself at the center, on the bottom right.

Sora's parents split up when she was three or four years old, and the family court gave custody of Sora and Kenji to their father; their mother was given custody of Sora's little sister, who was an infant at the time, and Sora's half sister. Her father left her and three-year-old Kenji in the house alone every day while he worked building scaffolding at construction sites. Each morning, he would make rice balls for the children and leave the house at seven o'clock, returning twelve or thirteen hours later. His sisters occasionally had Sora and Kenji come over, and once in a while an aunt would look in on them at home. "But after the aunt would leave, it would be lonelier than before she came," Sora remembered. "I would cry, I remember crying and crying." There weren't any toys at home, and Sora would sometimes steal from the toy shop and bookstore that were across the street. "I knew my dad wouldn't like that, though, so I hid them from him," she recalled.

When Sora was six, her father's sisters finally convinced him that the children needed to be placed in institutional care. Sora's little sister's custody was also transferred to her father, and the little girl was placed in the same institution. For one or two periods of a couple months, Sora recalled, the three of them came home to live with her father, but he simply wasn't able to take care of them, and they returned to the institution. Sora remembered being aware during this time of how much her sister wanted to be part of the family circle that had been comprised of Sora, Kenji, and her father. But Sora was afraid the sister would somehow steal their father away. She reflected, "I was always being affectionate to Kenji and taking care of him. She must have felt like, 'No one is looking after me.'" The exclusiveness of family networks was viscerally evident to Sora when they occasionally saw their extended family, which was not able to take the children in. Sora's father died when he was fifty-seven, when Sora was twenty-one years old. His family members asked Sora to reach out if they needed anything, but she found this difficult. "The thing is," she explained, "I have my own network, my own friends. I made my own group of people who I can depend on. The idea of depending on kin . . . well, it just won't happen."[9]

Sora had been totally alone when she graduated from the child welfare institution and her nursing certification program. Her connections now were mostly through the support group Reina started. She thoughtfully took up a pen and drew a circle, indicating herself, and lines extending outward like a spider, pointing to the people she consulted when she was in trouble, the people she depended on: Reina, her boyfriend, a few others. (Their names have been erased from the figure.)

"You and Reina and your brothers, the four of you talk about being family, right?" I said. Sora made a noncommittal agreement noise. "When did you really start feeling as though you are family?" I asked.

Laughing, Sora took a breath. "Um, well—never!"

"Never?"

"Never!" Sora said emphatically. I quote Sora's response at length:

> I should say, well, I've always had such yearning [akogare] for family, but . . . before the four of us started to live together, I had been so lonely I wanted to die. I realized things had to change, and I asked Reina if she would live with me, and we started living together. And then my brother . . . It wasn't so much that I wanted to live with him, it's that I wanted to help him get out of institutional care, so for a while—let's all

live together, you know, and certainly yeah, we say "family," but . . . inside of me . . . "What is family?" is something I just don't really understand. But at this moment, if I were to explain "family," there's my boyfriend, the guy I'm dating, and I get married to him, and then after a child is born—it's that image of blood relationship that I just always return to. . . . After I graduated from the child welfare institution, I kept wanting to live all together, my brother, sister, and my dad. . . . Like, "Can't we live together? I'll take care of everything. . . ." That's why . . . one day there will be a family that my partner and I can make together, it's that image of a dad, a mom. . . . Because I really have this like, aspiration [akogare] for "mother." Because it was always me and my brother, and it was like, "I want to become Mother," or something.

Even as a child, Sora felt that she should be able to take care of the house in the manner of a mother, and she remembers folding Kenji's clothing in the institution. "I was like six years old, but I guess I was like a grown-up child." After her sister graduated from the institution, Sora also offered to help out "as though I'm your mother," but her sister asked for too much assistance with money, and their relationship ended up strained. They weren't in contact any longer. Sora had spent her childhood play-acting as Kenji's mother, although she was only a year older, but mimicking the real thing went only so far. This sense of failure perhaps informed a perception that although she, Reina, Akio, and Kenji were play-acting at being family, this project too could not satisfy. In the end, it was to the absent presence of a mother, father, and child, a family unit tied by blood, that she returned. Although she currently lived in a chosen family, it was the family made through intimate heterosexual reproduction that offered promise.

At the start of my fieldwork, as I attended carefully to nonnormative family forms—from the Otsuki-Takahashi household, to foster and adoptive families, to institutions working to create households for children without kin—I had imagined that these would be spaces in which typically recognizable kinship would be exploded, something new and different created, in the face of intense, normalizing social pressure. But that is simply not what I found.[10] Many of my interlocutors yearned, like Sora, to be recognizable, unmarked, unremarkable. Sora's keen sensibilities about inside (uchi) and outside (soto) status mapped graphically in her kinship diagram were reaffirmed in everyday assumptions about kinship in Japanese culture. The performance of chosen kinship failed, for Sora, time and time again.

Two women, both part of the same infertility support group where I conducted some participant observation, expressed in different contexts that their desire to have children was motivated by the hope that familial loss might be remediated through their own childbearing. Both women had lost brothers when they were young, and both independently expressed hope that their own child would somehow give life once more to a brother who had died too soon. The yearning that Sora expressed for mother—to be mother, to have mother—is motivated by the ways heterosexual reproduction is perceived to have the creative power to bind people to one another in the face of past loss, even across the boundary of death. For many of my interlocutors, a felicitous remediation of familial losses remained the birth of a child out of the intimacy of marriage. The inability to remediate these losses, whether because of infertility or because of the constraints surrounding heterosexual marriage, generated new forms of "ambiguous loss"—loss that is unmournable, that "breeds ghosts and births a kind of haunting" (Mariner 2020, 21).

Imagining oneself as the replacement for ancestors, and one's child as the replacement for oneself, affords both pleasures and pressures. Not being situated within the temporal extension of a kinship network can be a source of suffering that many found to be remediable by having one's own child. The concept of a reproductive system, as Annette Weiner (1980) puts it, describes the ways investments in one's children are returned upon one's own death. Weiner argues that by embedding wealth in their children, people are able to replace themselves. Intimations of this coming replacement may be, in part, some of the hope Saki felt when dreaming about the moment she would have her own child and be able to constitute herself, through her partner and child, anew. Tetsu, the fifth in his family line, similarly knew his own role as replacement in his family and was reminded of this fact by the material forms that indexed this obligation: the two family houses, ancestral graves, land, name. Hanashima felt the lack of a genealogy as a lingering loss. The intersection of a genealogical sensibility and the simultaneous understanding that one can create one's own forward-looking kinship trajectory creates the conditions for a particular sort of subject formation, so often aspiring to the normal and the unmarked.

Interlude

INSCRIPTIONS

Kojima Sachiko and I had been talking about her son, Ken, who had recently been asked to leave his job as a sacker at a supermarket. Now he was having trouble maintaining a work schedule at the bookstore affiliated with the community center he attended, which was dedicated to helping youth obtain independent living skills. At twenty-one, Ken seemed young for his age. But Ken had always seemed young for his age, had always needed help with schoolwork. He had never, Sachiko admitted, been able to do much by himself. Sachiko sighed and looked away. Although her twenty-year-old daughter, Airi, caused her concern as well, worries about Ken's future were a major source of Sachiko's stress. Sachiko and her husband, Fumio, had raised Ken and Airi since they were five and four years old but had never adopted them, wanting to leave this major decision to the children when they became old enough to choose.

When Ken was very small, he had been maltreated by his biological father and, after moving between the houses of kin and temporary emergency care, ended up being placed in a child welfare institution. Shortly after Ken's biological sister, Airi, was born, she was placed in a baby home, and then as a toddler she was transferred to Ken's child welfare institution. Sachiko felt that Airi had been lucky to have been removed from her family of origin so quickly. Although Ken surely could not remember the abuse he had endured, it was, in some indelible and ultimately unknowable way, inscribed on his being. "Have you noticed," she asked me once, rather abruptly, "the top of Ken's nose?" I hadn't. She tapped her index finger lightly on her own nose, right below the eyebrow ridge. The cartilage on Ken's nose appeared to have been damaged when he was a young child, leaving a strange indentation. The physical evidence of some long-gone moment of violence.

Sachiko had undergone extensive training to certify as a specialized foster parent (senmon sato oya) and was qualified to care for children with special needs. I was always struck by her motivation to attend professionalization events, and she had jumped at the opportunity to join me at the trainings held at Chestnut House, where scholars of child abuse and welfare presented their research and answered staff and audience questions. But despite her impressive qualifications, Sachiko was not interested in fostering other children long-term. The trainings offered her opportunities to work toward an understanding of her own position as a foster care giver—a devoted parent of over fifteen years who raised two children to whom she had no legal claim—as well as conceptual tools that might help her comprehend her children's pasts and the possible implications for their futures.

Like many of the caregivers to whom I became close, Sachiko sought a framework within which to situate her knowledge and imaginings of her son's early experiences of maltreatment. It was impossible to know if Ken's difficulty concentrating, troubles articulating his feelings, or problems studying were caused by an inborn intellectual disability or were a result of postnatal social causes, like physical trauma or separation from caregivers at an early age. Or maybe it was a combination of these factors. The inscriptions on his body provided only one form of evidence. Sachiko's quest for information expressed an unspoken question that was itself an inarticulable and tenuous hope. Was the harm that might have been done to Ken somehow reversible?

MATERIALIZING RELATIONSHIPS

It was lunchtime at Chestnut House, a small-scale child welfare institution out-side of Tokyo. The older children were in school in the community; the littlest children, ages two and three, had pulled up diminutive chairs to child-size tables and were unpacking their bento boxes. A staff member sat down beside me on the floor. With a thoughtful smile, she watched one of the boys devouring his rice ball. "You know," she said, "I've often noticed that there is a disproportionate number of kids in child welfare institutions who are left-handed. Just as they were when they were born [*umareta mama*]." These children remained as they were at the time of birth because no caregiver had intervened to teach the child to use the right hand instead of the left, as many parents do in Japan. This staff member saw the children of Chestnut House as unchanged by caring intervention.

Caregivers in Japan often understood children's bodies to express accumu-lated histories of both nurturance and neglect. While maltreatment is often understood to have concrete bodily effects, my interlocutors saw the absence of contact as having equally bodily, and perhaps more durable, impact on children. Attention to physical manifestations of a child's past was a characteristic of obser-vations made by nonspecialists as well. For instance, a Japanese woman who had grown up near a child welfare institution once asserted to me that the commu-nity members could tell which children were from the institution. "Their bodies were smaller than normal," she said. "You know, because they were neglected or abused, and that affects physical development."[1] Foster parents and institutional staff members, too, paid close attention to a child's size, noting sudden growth when a child became more secure.

Left- or right-handedness, bodily and affective transformations: these are emblematic examples of "local biologies," the outcome of continuously changing dynamics across domains of biology and culture (Lock 1993). They exemplify the ways that physical characteristics should be understood not as solely biological phenomena but also as results of social and cultural dynamics, just as physical characteristics are interpreted and given meaning through social and cultural lenses.[2]

In this chapter, I follow my interlocutors in understanding intimate relational and caregiving ties—including the absence of these ties—as an embodied presence. People attended to children's changing bodily manifestations as indications of deeper psychological processes. This was in part because caregivers, like Kojima Sachiko in the previous interlude, often sought ways to understand and evaluate the behavior of children and to better grasp how children's past experiences inflected their present lives. In Japan, a culture that is often understood by Japanese people themselves as hyper-relational, my research contacts were very likely to see bodily characteristics as meaning-bearing signs pointing to interactional and social phenomena, even if bodily signs did not always have clear referents. In other words, habits, scars, or body size were taken as signs of *something*, and often something social, but the attribution of meaning was variable and open-ended. Finally, because caregivers were often so desperate for a better understanding of their charges, they tended to objectify and scrutinize children's bodies for signs revealing internal affective states. Observations about embodied life are often very normative, pointing to the ways a child should ideally be cared for and socialized, and children's bodily signs were easily pathologized as indications of disorder. This easy slippage into pathologization illuminates the connections between the disciplinary and normalizing domains of family, public health, and medicine and the academic sciences of child development and neuroscience (Foucault 1995). However, these caregivers did not understand bodily signs as determinative indications of permanent damage: bodies equally indexed ongoing and future-oriented transformations.

I make two significant claims by focusing first on the material embodiment of interpersonal relationships and, second, arguing that these are a core aspect of kinship. Anthropologists often juxtapose biology (supposedly universal and acultural) with embodiment (understood as culturally specific biological processes, often described as "the way culture gets under the skin"). Tim Ingold has pointed out that in popular discourse, "Whatever humans have in common is [commonly] attributed to biology, whereas their differences are attributed to culture" (1990, 210). Rather than understanding biology as a constant base across human populations and culturally particular embodiment as a superficial and changeable layer on top of this base, I propose that biology and its cultural instantiations should not be treated as conceptually distinct phenomena. Biology and culture inseparably and constantly shape each other.

I bring this orientation to theorizations of kinship and interpersonal relationships. I neither ask whether kinship is biological *or* cultural (c.f. Sahlins 2013) nor pose kinship and embodied relationality as biological *and* cultural, a framing that supposes these categories to be independent (Keller 2010). Rather, I assume the fundamental "intra-action" of biology and culture in which biology and culture "do not precede, but rather emerge" through "mutual entanglement" (Barad 2010, 267 and 2007). The materiality of bodily life and the embeddedness of bodies in social and cultural milieu do not interact to shape one another but are intrinsically entangled modes of being.[3]

The following ethnographic accounts prompt us to consider the materiality of human social interactions—including the biology of the body—in the holistic ways we have long considered culture. After a brief discussion of the use of biology within cultural anthropology, I show how child welfare caregivers interpret children's bodily signs to guide their own understandings of the types of care a child is seen to have received in the past. As scholars of semiotic ideologies have shown, the interpretive frameworks that identify one thing as a sign of something else are cultural and often politically inflected (Kroskrity 2000). I suggest that bodies signify through the active attribution of meaning to particular phenomena, a process open to historical shifts and local interpretive differences (Kuriyama 2002). I then explore how contemporary understandings of attachment, neuroscience, and trauma might influence kinship theory within anthropology, directing cultural anthropologists to take biology as seriously as our interlocutors do in their efforts to understand the ways social ties shape lived experience.

In Theory: Biology, Kinship, Embodiment

The social history of the concepts of nature and biology background this discussion. Anthropological kinship studies, paralleling trends in popular discourse, often see nature or biology as applying only to heterosexual reproductive relationships (including genetic heritage), focusing on the moment of birth as the dividing line between that which is innate and that which develops during life. However, many have pointed out the oddness of reducing kinship to conception, gestation, and birth, with little attention to what follows, including death. Other scholars, engaging with anthropological interest in daily life and practice, have shown how kinship processually emerges throughout life, illustrating how bodily similarity is understood to emerge through caregiving relationships and particularly the sharing of food.[4] We thus might see the nature vs. nurture, biology vs. culture polarity as a Western conceptual preoccupation that, as such, is a misleading and ultimately unhelpful framework for understanding human relationships across cultures (McKinnon and Silverman 2005).

With the exception of explicitly biosocial approaches to medical anthropology, studies of both embodiment and kinship generally remain conceptually situated within the cultural domain of nurture, which is seen as open to meaning-making and contestation, rather than nature or biology, which social scientists often perceive as deterministic, the idea "that 'biology is destiny'" (McKinnon and Silverman 2005, 2). Life scientists themselves would find this an oddly limited understanding of biology. Indeed, the notion that biology is predestined and deterministic is historically more an aberrant perspective than recent calls to embrace concepts of plasticity (Meloni 2019). Recall that one of Darwin's central insights focused on the inherent malleability of biology! Biologist Steven Rose refers to the juxtaposition of nature and nurture as a "spurious dichotomy" (1998, 142), a "nothing but" view of human reproduction that might posit kinship as *either* biological *or* cultural (1998, 6, 295). Among the majority of culturally oriented social scientists, however, the content of biology remains either black-boxed or assumed to mean something specifically related to heterosexual reproduction (Lock 2015, 2018). This narrow view of biology shapes a limited theorization of embodiment and inhibits our understanding of the complex ways interpersonal relationships articulate with bodily life.

Cultural anthropology's aversion to biology has a long and well-justified history. Biological evidence has been (mis)used to rank human "races" in a "great chain of being" and to develop eugenic social policies, and biological sex difference continues to be used to justify the subjugation of women and gender minorities. This social history of biology traces a process by which present-day inequalities have been naturalized by reference to supposedly inherent genetic predilections (Gould 1977; Ehrenreich and McIntosh 1997; Rose 1998; Oyama 2000; Meloni 2014; Graves 2015; Lock and Palsson 2016). It's no wonder, then, that scholarship in the service of progressive social change would embrace social factors, like culture, as a better explanation for human differences and societal inequalities. However, there is no necessary reason why biology must be the enemy of progressive and transgressive thought.[5] In my approach to anthropological kinship studies, I take cues from scholars of science like Tim Ingold, who proposes that cultural analysists take "the social life of persons as an aspect of organic life in general" (1990, 208), and feminist theorist Elizabeth Wilson, who argues that "biology is more naturally eccentric, more intrinsically preternatural than we usually allow" (2004, 12). I suggest directions for exploring human relationality through the lens of embodied processes that cannot be parsed as biological or cultural but rather illustrate how bodies and social meaning are co-constituted.

"She Grew Up for Us"

"We are all strangers here; none of us are blood related. But we have decided that we are family, and so we *are*." Hosokawa Rie and Masa, foster parents of first a young man and then, after he left the house, a young woman, recounted that they had welcomed their foster children to the household with these words. These caregivers did not see themselves as substitute parents to the young people in their charge, who, after all, already had parents of their own. They offered, instead, a space of stability. Their account about their foster daughter, Akiyama Noriko, exemplifies the ways that relationality and the affective environment of a home may be a profound aspect of bodily life.

I was at a restaurant with Masa and a few other friends. After a couple rounds of beer, conversation turned to Noriko, who was then in high school. Noriko had been living with Masa and Rie for eighteen months. She had been raised by her mother and had been neglected for most of her life. She had never been placed in alternative care before now.[6]

The first month Noriko spent at their home, she was a "stone," Masa told us. "We asked Noriko to tell us when she liked things, or didn't like things, but she wouldn't respond." Masa wiped tears from his eyes and took a sip of beer. "After the first month, we sat down with her and told her we wanted her to try a little harder. 'If you like something or don't like something, you don't need to say anything,' we told her. 'Just nod or shake your head.'" Masa paused for effect. "And she did! She started responding." That month, Noriko made cookies for him and Rie as a present. "They were terrible, to be honest." Masa laughed. "But we thanked her and thanked her." Then he asked her, "If I just said, 'Thank you,'" his voice flat and his face empty of expression or affect, "'would you believe me?' And she said no." Masa told her that he wanted her to practice something new that month: expressing emotion. When she *felt* something, he told her, he wanted her to try to *express* it. And, Masa said, she did.

In an extended interview, I asked Rie about her experiences fostering Noriko. Rie described an impermeable affectlessness. "When Noriko came, it was like this," she told me, sitting back with her face blank, her eyes slightly unfocused. "Totally no smile or anything. Even if you addressed her directly, 'Nori-chan,' she wouldn't respond. Then if you asked her, 'Would you . . . reply?' she would say, 'Oh, what is it?'" Rie described Noriko's response, "Oh, what is it?" in Japanese as "*Nan desu ka?*"—a formal phrasing at odds in a casual setting. "She would cry really easily, get mad really easily. She would injure herself"—Rie mimicked scratching her wrists with something sharp—"and, like, show it to you. At first it was really, really hard. . . . But now, she's okay. It's okay." Rie had earlier told me that slowly but surely, the atmosphere of the house had become comfortable. "We can finally talk now."

Rie described the changes that Noriko underwent in the months since she had arrived at their house. When Noriko first came, her clothes were unstylish and frumpy (*dasai*), but she started asking Rie to take her shopping. Rie realized that Noriko had been intently watching the way she put on makeup and would imitate her. "She's really, really matured," Rie told me.

Then, as though remembering something crucial, Rie leaned toward me.

"It was incredible. Suddenly she grew up [*kyū ni seichō shita*]!" In an intense whisper: "Her teeth came in!"

"What?!"

Still whispering, Rie explained, "Until last year, her period was also irregular, but now it's started coming regularly, and her teeth came in. She still had five of her baby teeth! They started to get wiggly all of a sudden, and I figured they were cavities. 'You've got cavities!' I told her, and she said, 'I don't ever remember losing them when I was a kid!' Masa and I were like, 'No way, you're kidding, you're kidding!' and we took her to a dentist. They took an X-ray, and lo and behold, her baby teeth were still there, and from behind, her grown-up teeth were coming out—*waaaaa!*—all of a sudden."

"That is so strange!"

"It's totally strange. Around the time when her teeth started wiggling, her period became regular and—suddenly she got—" Rie put her hands over her own breasts and indicated them becoming larger. "And her frame of mind [*kimochi*] became totally adult, she became an adult. It was just when I thought, 'This girl has really grown up . . .' when her teeth started to wiggle. In the end, two baby teeth are still left, but the others all fell out, and one by one the adult teeth suddenly came in [*ikki ni baa! to haittekite*]. She got adult teeth. The dentist was so shocked!"

Later, I commented that Noriko's sudden development might be connected to the good environment Rie and Masa created for her in their home. "Yeah," Rie replied. "She grew up for us." In Japanese, Rie said that Noriko *seichō shite kureta*, which can be translated as Noriko's growing up was done for Rie and Masa, or Rie and Masa benefited from the favor of Noriko's growing up. Rie's description contains an important element of reciprocity: in response to something done for her by Rie and Masa, Noriko returned the favor by growing up.

For Rie, Noriko's unwillingness to talk, and then the emergence of her ability to communicate and to have fun together, was a persistent theme.[7] Masa and Rie had had another foster child, a young man who no longer lived with them, and Rie made many comparisons to his "good character," the ease with which he expressed gratitude (for instance, when he was served a meal), and the enjoyment with which they all talked together. Rie was still struggling with the complexity of the emotions Noriko evoked in her. Because she and Masa had a long-term relationship with their foster son, her fondness for him overpowered any frustration she felt when he caused trouble. "No matter how bad a kid is, if you have love, it's okay," Rie said. But especially at first, she did not feel love for Noriko. "Without love, if she didn't have a really good reaction to something, I couldn't be nice to her. It was really tough; I felt very conflicted. Especially because she's a girl, we're both women, you know? Both of us women, and not mother and child. Girls are just really difficult."

Rie's statement that relationships between women are difficult reflected fraught childhood relationships with her own mother and younger sister, as well as her overall perspectives regarding communication. Rie's mother had not been a safe person for Rie to be around, and she had always needed to be careful around her (ki o tsukau). She had never imagined that mothers and daughters could have a good relationship, that they could speak frankly and honestly to each other. After meeting Masa, who had a very outgoing personality, Rie finally came to respect and express herself, and over time she became able to confront her mother and her sister about some of her past experiences. "For a while, I felt a lot of anger, frustration, toward my mother. I felt a real sense of disadvantage and loss about my childhood," she recounted. "Finally, after my mother was older and had gotten softer seeming [marukunatta], I became able to talk to her, and she could talk to me, and I became stronger. I became able to say, 'This is what I think.'" Within our interview as a whole, for both herself and Noriko, Rie paralleled the process of development with the process of becoming able to communicate one's interior state.

Many months after this initial interview, I raised the topic of Noriko's physical transformations again with Rie. She understood Noriko's growing up as a material expression of her feelings of safety and security (anshin) in her foster home. Before she came to their home, Rie told me, Noriko clearly had not been ready to be an adult. But in the time she spent with them, she finally became emotionally ready, and her body followed suit. "Well," Rie said with a laugh, "you can't see a person's spirit, can you [kokoro wa mienai yo ne]?" In Rie's understanding, the body makes visible and material the status of the spirit, mind, or heart, which otherwise becomes haltingly knowable only as communication skills develop. Rie also made clear that their relationship with Noriko was still sometimes difficult. Although they intended to always be available to Noriko, it wasn't as though their relationship was idyllic or particularly profound. It was just the ordinariness of a stable life, and stable supportive relationships, that provided the space for Noriko's development. Rie did not belabor the significance of Noriko's bodily transformations. As surprising as they were, it seemed clear to Rie that Noriko's body and spirit together expressed the emergent relationships in their home and exemplified the surprising and hopeful capacities of care giving and receiving.

Embedded Bodies

Social relationships are experienced and expressed in the body, which is constantly open to new environmental and social stimuli. Although some might assume that the human body is always animated by internal progressions of growth that fluctuate little across cultures and across populations, many of the foster and institutional caregivers I knew in Japan had experiences, like that of Rie and Masa, that made normal development not a terribly useful heuristic. These findings recall Margaret Lock's theory of local biologies, in which biological processes are "products of an ongoing dialectic between biology and culture in which both are contingent" (Lock 1993, xxi, 2001).[8] Lock and Nguyen call this process "biosocial differentiation," a concept used "to refer to the continual interactions of biological and social processes across time and space that eventually sediment into local biologies" (Lock and Nguyen 2010, 90).[9] The concept of "local biologies" helps explain diverse phenomena. For instance, epidemiological studies correlating the experience of racism with the birth of low birthweight infants is a classic example of "how people, as both biological organisms and social beings, literally embody . . . the dynamic social, material, and ecological contexts into which we are born, develop, interact, and endeavor to live meaningful lives" (Krieger 2006). The lines between biological and social factors are ever blurry.[10]

For example, attention to the ways people use their bodies complicate any supposed divide between biological and social factors, although we see how interpretations of bodily practices are always situated within culturally specific normative social frameworks in which some practices are valorized and some are not (Bourdieu 1977). Marcell Mauss's concept "techniques of the body" offers a tool to explore these ideas. He defines "techniques of the body" as "the ways in which from society to society men [sic] know how to use their bodies" (1973, 70). He notes that differences in styles of swimming, walking, and marching in different cultures are culturally specific "special habits" (72) that "do not just vary with individuals and their imitations, they vary especially between societies, educations, proprieties and fashions, prestiges. In them we should see the techniques and work of collective and individual practical reason rather than, in the ordinary way, merely the soul and its repetitive faculties" (73). Techniques of the body speak to how people learn culturally specific modes of bodily use.

In Japan, techniques of the body, specifically those related to eating, offered many of my interlocutors clues about the backgrounds of children in their care. The way a person holds chopsticks in Japan is sometimes understood as an index of personal histories of care and neglect. This point was forcefully brought home to me when a child welfare officer, Tanabe Nobuko, told me that she attended to the ways her clients ate as a sign of their upbringing. Holding one's chopsticks improperly, in the shape of an X or in a fist, was an important marker of social class and family instability. Adult research contacts who had spent time in child welfare institutions sometimes commented on their own improper way of holding chopsticks, bemoaning the fact that they had never been taught to use them properly. In contrast, highlighting the variations of institutional practices in Japan, chopstick use was a focus of attention at Chestnut House. None of the toddlers who arrived when the institution first opened in 2009 could use chopsticks, but within a few weeks they had all become adept. A lack of caring intervention could have embodied consequences (like the prevalence of institutionalized children who remained left-handed), and the staff were attentive to other bodily practices. For instance, toddlers who came from one particular institution for babies tended to suck their fingers, a practice that was marked as unusual. The staff at that baby home apparently did not remove children's fingers from their mouths as they slept. Lack of caring engagement left embodied traces.

The toddlers who arrived at Chestnut House directly from baby homes had another problem typical of baby homes in general. Many of these children did not know how to chew. Baby homes care for both infants and toddlers, and most of these institutions provide the same food for all children who are no longer drinking formula: rice gruel and very soft pastas and vegetables. The children did not develop jaw strength or the ability to chew and swallow harder foods. A Chestnut House staff member described how one of the little girls put food in her mouth and, uncertain how to chew and swallow, sometimes choked. Those critical of institutions for infants point out that the failure to meet this developmental milestone indicates durable, but less visible, signs of developmental delay caused by insufficient stimulation inherent in the institutional care of infants (Browne et al. 2006). In this sense, staff members understood that bodily capacities opaquely indicated the possibility for (neuro)biological developmental shifts that were perceived as abnormal and potentially long-lasting. Embodied habits traced out histories of care and its normative underpinnings.

Institutional caregivers evaluated the embodied signs of their charges in a manner that might seem eminently cultural, but I return to my argument that it is not useful to define these expressions of embodied relationality as distinct from the biological. Body size, the ability to chew, habituated patterns of chopstick use, and left-handedness are indexes in Japan of absent or improper relationships and expressions of the intra-action of biology and culture. Here, children's bodies are "embedded" bodies, in Jörg Niewöhner's turn of phrase. An "embedded body," Niewöhner writes, is "heavily impregnated by its own past and by the social and material environment within which it dwells. It is a body that is imprinted by evolutionary and transgenerational time, by 'early-life' and a body that is highly susceptible to changes in its social and material environment" (2011, 289–290).[11] Interpersonal histories perdure in these embedded bodies, producing "somatic memory effects" (Niewöhner 2011, 290) that remind both caregivers and children of these pasts. They are traces of these children's "lifelines" (Rose 1998). The experiences of caregivers and children receiving care within the Japanese child welfare system belie the stability of the concept of standard child development across populations and draw into relief the diversity of ways biological processes occur, signify, and are experienced.

The Brain as History

Hennessy Sumiko (her real name) is a Japanese social worker who lives in the United States and has long conducted trainings in Japan on attachment disorder. Hennessy's trainings have highlighted the following core principles about attachment: Healthy attachments are generally understood to form between an infant and caregivers when the baby's needs are consistently met. The expectation that one's needs will be met contributes to the infant's internal working model of self, in which the child grows up believing people to be trustworthy and oneself worthy of care. Disordered attachments often result from separation from primary caregivers, neglect, or maltreatment, all of which lead to profound lack of trust in others, difficulty forming relationships, problems with self-regulation, and antisocial behaviors. Hennessy's trainings are designed for institutional, foster, and adoptive caregivers and rooted in knowledge of interpersonal trauma theory and neuroscience.[12]

Through these training seminars, Hennessy cements a particular set of claims about the neurological basis for human relations and a corresponding relational basis for neurological development, recruiting neuroscience as objective proof of early childhood's influence on adult lives (Rose and Abi-Rached 2013, 196). Specifically, neurological development and later capacity to build interpersonal relationships are highly influenced by the caregiving a child receives during the "critical period" of growth. For foster and adoptive parents struggling to parent their children, the understanding that early childhood relationships with caregivers can impact a child's behavior and development is often an enormous relief. In Japan, in the case of poorly behaved or unmanageable children, these parents are often viewed either as using inappropriate childrearing techniques or as not loving enough to make a child behave. Attachment theory provides an interpretive framework that explains children's behaviors as products of past relationships while simultaneously offering a hopeful path forward through interventions like corrective attachment therapy.

In one of Hennessy's trainings, she asks volunteers to form two circles. Each circle of volunteers bodily represents the neurons within the brains of two babies, Baby A and Baby B. Individual people within each circle stand for neurons responsible for hearing, smell, sight, physical sensation, taste, language, and emotion. Hennessy explains that when neurons stimulate each other, synaptic connections form between them. Hennessy gives each circle a ball of yarn to represent synaptic connections. She reads the stories of Baby A, who is loved and nurtured, and Baby B, who is raised in a child welfare institution and lacks an attachment relationship to caregivers. As Hennessy reads, volunteers unravel and pass the ball of yarn among themselves, performing and embodying synaptic development. "The more synaptic connections there are," Hennessy tells them, "the better the baby will be at processing data, and the more affectionate and smart the baby will be." The purpose of the exercise is to dynamically enact the connections among human relationships, caregiving, brain development, and a child's capacity for love and intelligence.

The wording of this exercise seems to reinforce a deterministic view of sensory input and brain development. At the same time, Hennessy's trainings on attachment disorder portray the complex ways that child development occurs within a densely relational space, in the interstices of crisscrossing social ties. Hennessy would not go so far as to claim that "human beings are essentially reducible to their brains," what Francisco Ortega and Fernando Vidal term "cerebral subjects" (2007, 255). And yet Hennessy's focus on brain development evokes a figure of "neurological humanity" (Rees 2010), one in which the human is defined by the first years of life (the so-called "critical period") (Castañeda 2002). As philosopher of neuroscience Catherine Malabou has argued, "It's not just that the brain has a history . . . but that it *is* a history" (2008, 1).[13]

Baby A, Hennessy tells the group, has nurturing parents and a safe home. Hennessy asks the volunteers embodying Baby A's neurons to enact a script of a day in the baby's life. The person representing the neuron for emotion takes up the ball of red yarn first "because the mother loves the baby." "The baby cries. The mother comes quickly and picks up and hugs the baby, soothing and speaking to the baby. What neurons are stimulated?" Volunteers pass the ball of yarn between emotion, hearing, smell, sight, physical sensation, and language. At the end of Baby A's day, the synaptic connections embodied by the volunteers and their ball of yarn are dense and crisscrossing.

Baby B is not so lucky. Baby B lives in a child welfare institution for infants. "Baby B does not have an attachment relationship with any caregiver," Hennessy says, "and right now the baby is hearing its own crying voice. So let's start the ball of yarn at 'hearing.' Baby B is crying because it is hungry, but no one comes. So we don't need to pass the ball of yarn. Finally, it's time for bottle-feeding. The bottle is propped up against the baby's pillow and the baby sucks at it." Volunteers pass the ball of yarn from hearing to taste and smell. "The baby needs its diaper changed, and it cries, but no one comes." The ball is passed back to hearing. "Finally," Hennessy says, "it's time for diaper changing, and the staff person talks to the baby and smiles at it." Volunteers quickly pass the yarn between emotion, smell, sight, physical sensation, hearing, taste, and language. At the end of Baby B's day, Hennessy shows the audience, Baby B's synaptic connections are much fewer than those of Baby A. In particular, the connections to emotion and language are sparse. "Both babies' basic needs are met, and neither baby is abused or abandoned," Hennessy says. "But I think you all see that an emotional relationship between the baby and its caregiver is imperative for the baby's developing brain."

The training participants learn to understand neural pathways and processes as indices of relationships, instantiated repetitively over time: Baby A's brain is a history of love and care while Baby B's brain is a history of neglect. Parental input literally matters in shaping a child's brain. The participants, unraveling and passing their ball of yarn, construct a "dynamic figuration" (Silverstein 2004, 627) in which they produce a physical diagram in real time that seems to correspond to actual brain structures and reflect histories of care. The culturally and historically specific perspective that children require "input in order to develop fully" (Castañeda 2002, 75) aligns with local logics of parenting in Japan, including the so-called "myth of three years" (*san sai shinwa*), which holds that a child must be cared for full-time by its birth mother, who presumably nurtures the child best, until three years of age. Many participants would find these logics familiar, neuroscience providing an objective basis for commonsense knowledge.

At one of Hennessy's training seminars in Tokyo in December 2009, Hennessy provided a complex view of the ways neglect impacts brain development. This was an embodied brain in a deeply relational space. "Neglect," she told the audience, "is the worst type of abuse because it prevents the brainstem from developing properly." But although attachment disorder may be rooted in the brain, Hennessy represented it as a whole-body problem with physical symptoms. In many cases, Hennessy told the group, attachment disorder might actually be the cause of what is misunderstood as physical or developmental disability.[14] She explained that symptoms of the disorder are rooted in extreme physical and emotional highs and lows: the child's inability to control their own emotions and behavior, inability to calm themselves, not sleeping enough or sleeping too much, not eating enough or eating too much, not defecating enough or defecating too much.

In Hennessy's account, the issue of sign interpretation emerges as a central heuristic, both for caregivers who are self-diagnosing their children as disordered and for children themselves, who must be trained to interpret their own state of being. Attachment disordered children, she said, have trouble evaluating emotions of others based on nonverbal signs and have difficulty with self-expression—the ability to put emotions into words. In the training, Hennessy gave the audience members suggestions for helping their children gain self-awareness and the ability to self-regulate emotions, a process that depended on identifying the differences between what the mind wanted to express and what the body was already expressing. Breathing exercises would, she suggested, help children relax and develop the attention necessary for interpretation: "What is your *body* trying to say [*jibun no karada de nani o iō to shiteiru*]? And how is that different from what your *mind* is saying?" Hennessy asked the audience. Hennessy encouraged caregivers that they could effect a change in their children, first by creating an affective environment that allows the nurturance of security and a sense of safety (*anshinkan o sodateru*), and then by engaging in practical therapeutic techniques.

Hennessy maintained a biomedical and scientific orientation toward the relationship between body and mind, stating in one of her books for Japanese caregivers that the concept of *kokoro*, which can be translated variously as heart, mind, or spirit, is actually the functioning of the brain. Thus, to understand the concept of trauma, or "injuries to the kokoro," one must first look to the brain (Hennessy 2006, 32). This perspective is reinforced in Hennessy's use of brain images in her trainings and publications. But despite these repeated insistences to attend to the brain in a developmental context, Hennessy understands the child—and the brain inside—in a holistic manner, embedded in the environment and in relationships with caregivers. This is clear from the illustrations in her books (2004, 2006), which feature bubbly pink brains inside children moving and actively engaging in the social environment. Further, Hennessy's exercise with yarn to simulate synaptic connections is a visual and visceral iconic enactment not only of brain development but also of the affective field that a well-attached child might be understood to experience. The volunteers in Hennessy's exercise trace out points in a dense social network that envelops the child's mind, body, and embodied brain.

The explanatory model for attachment disorder that Hennessy develops points, in turn, to particular solutions. Hennessy's trainings were suffused with policy recommendations and criticisms of Japan's focus on institutional care in early childhood. She argued that children should be able to remain in state care long after age eighteen, since the brain is not fully developed until a person is in their early twenties; since the first six years of life are the "time for attachment," children should not be moved between institutions during this time; and state policy should encourage a system that allows for long-term attachment relationships, particularly during these critical years. The view of the human central to Hennessy's model of development and attachment points to a particular ethical orientation that should, in turn, shape state care practices (Rees 2010; Goldfarb 2015).

Developmental Logics

Theories about child development and cultural personality informed the explanations people gave me about the prevalence of large-scale group care in Japan. Some said that Japanese people, as such, are intensely group-oriented, and thus an appropriate venue for child socialization is institutional group care.[15] However, those who had spent a lot of time either being raised in such contexts or as staff in large institutions, tended to highlight that, ironically, large-scale institutional care tends to produce people who deal very poorly with interpersonal interaction, specifically difficulty trusting others and maintaining long-term relationships.[16] Others argued that group care, particularly the use of institutions to care for infants, causes attachment disorders and developmental disability.

These discourses emerged, in different ways, one day when I was visiting a small group home in a prefecture northeast of the Tokyo area run by a child welfare worker named Nakai Mitsuo. The group home accommodated six children and three staff members and was located in a quiet residential neighborhood. The home was new, affiliated with a large child welfare institution, and opened as part of an initiative to offer individualized care to a small number of children who were struggling in the large-scale care context. I was visiting with two men: Hanashima Shin'ichi, a man in his fifties who had grown up in a child welfare institution and was now an activist and foster parent, and Hanashima's friend, Ishida Masao, the director of a progressive child welfare institution in the same prefecture. Nakai, Hanashima, and Ishida were part of a network of individuals working to improve the child welfare system in Japan. (I describe Ishida's institution as progressive because, realizing that his institution had many problems, including abusive behavior among children and among staff and children, Ishida had hired a man (in)famous for being a whistle-blower at other institutions to help him in his reform efforts. Hanashima and I visited Ishida's institution the day after visiting with Nakai.)

We had been talking for a couple hours in the group home when the children began returning from school. A little boy poked his head into the dining room where we were sitting. "Reo-kun is a first grader," Nakai told us. "He lived first in a baby home and then in a child welfare institution." Reo glanced shyly at us and then took refuge in another room to start his homework.

"It is so strange [*fushigi*]," Hanashima suddenly exclaimed. "These children aren't institution kids at all [*shisetsu no ko jya nai*]!"

Nakai knew exactly what Hanashima meant, and he laughed. The group home was only five months old, he reminded us. "But a couple months ago, these *were* 'institution kids.' For example, a visitor would arrive, and they would all rush to the door. 'Who is it, who is it? Whose mother are you? Pick me up, pick me up [*dakko, dakko*]!' They don't do that anymore."

"*That's* an 'institution kid'?" I asked.

"You know," Nakai said. "They come flocking over to any new person. It's attachment disorder behavior, no reserve [*enryo*] whatsoever."

Despite its lack of subtlety, Nakai's description reminded me of a visit to a different child welfare institution, where my friends Reina, Sora, Akio, and Kenji had grown up. I was visiting the institution with Reina, accompanied by Yukari, one of Reina's friends who was working at a different institution. We had just arrived and were walking through the playground to the administrative office. A few girls, seven or eight years old, approached us eagerly. One girl promptly took Yukari's hand and continued with us. Yukari laughed, pleased, and addressed the girl by name, asking how she was doing; it turned out that the girl had previously lived at the institution where Yukari worked. Upon Yukari's greeting, the girl, clasping Yukari's hand, glanced upward and squinted confusedly at Yukari's face. "Don't you recognize me?" Yukari asked. "I took care of you before you came here." The girl cocked her head to the side and said, unconcerned, "Nope." She interlaced her fingers with Yukari's as we continued across the gravel field. For this little girl, Yukari was as good as any other stranger: a hand to hold while walking across the playground.

I remembered how upon arriving at the institution where Reina had grown up, we were led by a staff member into the residential section of the building. Within a moment, a space that had seemed sleepily quiet exploded into cacophony. Elbow-height children were everywhere, pulling on my bag, attaching themselves to our legs. One little girl threw herself into my arms, asking, "Who are you, who are you?" as she inspected my earrings. Runny noses, tangled hair and coughs, energy. Arms outstretched. "Pick me up, pick me up [dakko, dakko]!" Each of us had a child on the hip as we navigated this hallway, a staff member chiding the children to be quiet. I felt intense relief to leave the children behind as we climbed the stairs to the second floor. These children—like many of the children at Chestnut House—were indeed what Nakai and Hanashima would call institution kids. I imagined that the atmosphere must have been similar at the institution where Nakai had been working, where children in his group home used to live.

Nakai was proud of the way that the children under his care had become more secure (*anshin*) after transferring to the group home. "They really have changed since coming here. Their sleeping changed! They started sleeping longer, deeper.

And they got *taller.*" One of the elementary school boys grew six centimeters in five months. "Think about it," Nakai said. "At the institution they didn't sleep well, they were anxious [*fuan*], they were lonely [*sabishii*]. Here they eat, they sleep, they aren't anxious, they are secure."

Hanashima nodded. "Growth hormone is activated by sleep," he pointed out. Hanashima himself had grown suddenly—twenty-six centimeters in two years—after leaving the institution where he had lived until age fifteen. He had always been the smallest in his class and was a constant target for physical abuse from the other children. Hanashima's modes of discussing his own experience often verged on the clinical, with references to growth hormone, brain development, attention deficit disorder, memory trouble, and dissociative symptoms, but his explanatory models were also highly experiential. He once explained to me that the reason he had been so small while living in the institution was because he was trying to protect himself. If he was small, maybe no one would notice him.

Harumi, one of the young group home residents, arrived home from school and stood by Nakai's chair for a while, introducing herself after some prompting. After she left the room, Nakai told us that Harumi had been in institutional care her entire life, placed in a baby home immediately after birth and then transferred to the child welfare institution. She was selected to live in the group home because the child welfare institution staff were unable to deal with her. She was constantly crying, she couldn't sleep, she refused to go to school, and she had a host of attachment disorder symptoms (Nakai was not specific about these). Now at the group home, Nakai told us, she developed a close relationship with a particular staff member and had grown "really tall" since moving in. While at the child welfare institution she had been placed in special education, but now she was good at studying, could write kanji, do math. Nakai indicated the vocabulary words and math equations written on pieces of paper taped to the wallpaper. Harumi had just recently called a friend on the phone for the first time.

I highlight these accounts for several reasons. The first is that Nakai's experience with the children in his care, and Hanashima's own personal experience, are not unusual in the context of literature on child welfare and development. There are a plethora of studies exploring the ways that placing children in institutional care, specifically at very young ages, can negatively impact their physical, neurological, and psychosocial development, and related studies highlight the risk of institutionalized children developing attachment disorders (Rutter et al. 1998; Zeanah et al. 2003; Browne et al. 2006; Johnson et al. 2006; Browne 2009).[17] Child welfare reformers in Japan and other places cite these studies to advocate for deinstitutionalization and, most pressingly, for the deinstitutionalization of infants.[18]

One fierce advocate on this front has long been Tsuzaki Tetsuo, the professor who introduced me to Chestnut House. For instance, when he presented as a keynote speaker at a symposium in March 2010 in Tokyo, Tsuzaki forcefully argued that Japan disregards international standards for child rights, including the United Nations' Convention on the Rights of the Child, which Japan ratified in 1994. These standards, he said, are based on research showing that institutional care for infants and young children actually creates disabilities and developmental disorders. "As you know," Tsuzaki told the audience, "in the Convention it is clearly written that 'family-style care must be prioritized,' but the stipulations in the World Report [on Violence Against Children] are even more clear: 'The placement of a child under three years of age in group care is the equivalent of violence perpetrated by the state.'" Japan's practice of placing infants in institutional care—long-term, for child welfare purposes, instead of adoptive or family-based foster care—was "systemic abuse." He indicated the bold red text on his PowerPoint slide. "If an individual perpetrates abuse or neglect, it's a human rights abuse, it's a crime. But if the country perpetrates it, it's welfare work."[19]

These critiques exist alongside recognition that children who have been deinstitutionalized and placed in safe, supportive adoptive homes often exhibit the kinds of "catch-up growth" Nakai and Hanashima described, including physical bodily growth and even an increase in measured IQ. For his own part, as a deeply ethical humanist and good friend to many former state wards, Tsuzaki did not believe that all children raised in institutional care had been irredeemably damaged. He also believed that moving children from institutional care to family-based care, even later in life, could be beneficial. This is a position substantiated by a wide range of studies on the effects of institutionalization on development and the potentially remediating impacts of subsequent family placement (Rutter et al. 1998; Vorria 2006; Nelson et al. 2007; Dobrova-Krol et al. 2008).

For Tsuzaki and other reformers, too few placement options in Japan offer the kinds of support that benefit children. It is difficult to imagine, if one has not spent time in these spaces, what it affectively feels like to work, live, or do research in these child welfare contexts. I offer my own recollections on the contrasts between the quiet space of Nakai's group home and the cacophony of Reina's former residence to offer readers a small glimpse of my own embodied experience in these spaces. I do not propose a simple or unidirectional relationship between forms of care and the developmental outcomes of children. The point is, people who spend time in these spaces tend to develop their own theories that link the affective dimensions of caregiving spaces, the interpersonal relationships these spaces afford, objective measures of bodily development, and subjective measures of embodied experience.

The Space a Parent Should Have Filled

In this final section, I focus not on the ways caregivers or advocates interpret bodily signs but instead on one person's subjective exploration of his own bodily experience of kinship's absence. Hanashima Shin'ichi's account encourages us to consider the diversity of ways that kinship and its absence can be embodied and theorized on the ground, the complexity of which blurs material and immaterial categories of experience. His narrative illuminates how phenomenological theorizations of the body—which highlight the body as both subject and object to itself—can also incorporate scientific knowledge and intersubjective context (Merleau-Ponty 1968; Csordas 1990; Hacking 1996). My analysis is guided by Hanashima's own exegesis of past and present events.

Hanashima had lived his entire infancy and childhood in Japanese child welfare institutions. He had never been raised by his parents, and he had experienced abuse in the institution where he grew up. Although his current life was successful and rich, by most measures—with a stable job, a companionate marriage, one biological child, and one foster child—his experiences in state care continued to indelibly mark his life, and he still sometimes experienced traumatic flashbacks. He worked tirelessly to campaign for the placement of infants in family-based foster and adoptive homes rather than in institutions, and he was deeply involved with an organization whose goal was to eliminate abuse within child welfare institutions.

My conversations with Hanashima quickly moved to intensely personal philosophical questions. He often grappled with the topic of parental figures for children who had not been raised in families, a subject that he found particularly problematic given his own personal history and his reading of literature on attachment and child development. He wondered whether people who grew up without parents possessed some sort of inherent, indwelling (*naizaika*) sense of "parent" that might orient their actions in the world; in one context, he had articulated this as a question of whether one possesses a parent who resides in one's heart or spirit (*kokoro ni omou oya*). While I often discussed cultural dimensions of kinship ideologies in Japan with Hanashima, he was also interested in topics that seemed universal, psychological, and neurological. In what follows, I focus on Hanashima's experiences as he described them to me in many hours of interviews, more recently in 2013 and also from conversations in 2010. He articulated the absence of kinship connections in an exceptionally physical way, making use of his own embodied perceptions as he thought alongside child development and attachment scholars like John Bowlby and Mary Ainsworth.

In response to his own question about an indwelling parent, Hanashima noted, "I personally don't have a parent who resides in my heart." He was curious whether other people who had never experienced parental care did, unlike him, possess an internal parent figure. His voice catching, Hanashima explained, "I've *always*—to put it frankly—it's like I've always had this feeling of a hole open in my chest [*mune ni ana ga aiteiru*]. It's anguishing. Probably, by all rights, there has always been this place left open in my heart for the parent who should have filled that space [*watashi no kokoro no naka ni hairu beki oya*], a parent or someone who would have raised me. But I have lived this entire time without someone filling that space." Hanashima said that he had read accounts of institutional care and foster families from other countries, and he noticed that the expression *a hole in the heart* appeared often. "I've had that feeling my entire life," he told me.[20]

"That sounds like it hurts."

"It does, it hurts so much! There are times when it *physically* hurts," he replied. His statement reminded me of Elaine Scarry's description of other bodies' suffering: "Vaguely alarming yet unreal, laden with consequence yet evaporating before the mind . . . unseeable classes of objects such as subterranean plates, Seyfert galaxies, and the pains occurring in other people's bodies flicker before the mind, then disappear" (1985, 4). The physicality of Hanashima's pain, like its emotionality, remained beyond question and evaluation by external observers.[21]

Hanashima hypothesized that his own Christianity (he was raised in a Catholic institution) might have filled some of the space long left open. His belief that everyone has a space within that should be filled by a parent figure indicates a visceral sense of a universal need to be parented, to be cared for by someone whose existence would dwell within their own throughout their entire life. Notably, Hanashima did not focus on kinship based on blood ties or biological connection, as many of my interlocutors in Japan tended to do, but rather on the persistent role of a caring someone.

Hanashima's own embodied sensibility hews quite closely to attachment theorists, whom he had read, and provides compelling grounds for thinking about the ways that kinship's absences might be materially, psychologically, and neurologically embodied.[22] He referenced Mary Ainsworth's canonical experiments, the Strange Situation Procedure. The Strange Situation experiments were designed to evaluate a child's "attachment type" by examining the child's proximity-seeking behavior to the parent after the parent leaves the child alone or with a stranger and then later returns. Ainsworth's research was based on John Bowlby's (1953) attachment theory, which posited that "attachment behaviors observed in infancy are evidence of the development of an internal working model of social relations" (Gaskins 2013, 33): in other words, key relationships with important caregivers are understood to shape the child's self-image, which will in turn shape the child's expectations for relationships with other people. Bowlby developed the concept of the "secure base," in which (in its ideal-typical form) an infant is able to check in with a parent while exploring new surroundings. If the child has a secure base, so the theory goes, the child will be able to encounter novel situations and also know that their needs will be met. Children without this sense of security, attachment scholars argue, live with the internalized expectation that their needs will only be met sporadically and unpredictably, or that their needs will cause in the parent a sense of alarm or panic, or that their needs will not be met and the child cannot depend on anyone (other than the child's own self) to fulfill basic needs (Bowlby 1982 [1969]; Levy and Orlans 2014). Another important scholar of whom Hanashima is likely aware, but did not mention, is Allan Schore, who posited that a major parental role is to help an infant regulate and organize their affect and emotions.

Hanashima developed his own notion of the parent that inheres in one's heart or spirit by thinking alongside attachment scholars about his own experiences. "If a parent leaves the room, the [securely attached] child will cry, right? When I thought about those [Strange Situation] studies, I thought, 'Ah, what about myself—do I have an internalized parent?'" Hanashima seemed to be wondering whether he himself had a secure base. But it wasn't just himself he was thinking about. He was also considering his foster child, who had been identified as attachment disordered. He explained that his idea of the internalized parent also meant a person's awareness and memory of the parent's way of thinking, the things the parent said, and parental discipline. If the parent has been internalized, Hanashima posited, this internalized parent should exist within a child over a child's whole life. Without an internalized parent to act as the child's moral compass, that child is extremely difficult to discipline. A child with an internalized parent can live and act independently, Hanashima explained, but a child without will be dependent and unable to inhabit social rules and expectations. He argued that he himself had no internalized moral compass—it was simply logic that told him that if he did something bad, he would lose his job. He conceded, however, that his religiosity might play a substitute role. Perhaps God was Hanashima's internalized parent, we speculated.[23]

Motivated by both his own embodied sense of lack and by his reading of child development literature, Hanashima had developed a firm model for child welfare. For him, it boiled down to "not creating people who have no one [*dare mo inai hito o tsukuranai*]." People with no one were most likely to commit crimes, he said, and those people were also the most difficult to socially rehabilitate. His personal goal to place infants and very young children in family-based settings rather than institutions was, then, a wide-reaching goal to place a parent figure inside each child. This parent would live inside the child's heart (*sono kodomo no kokoro ni sumu*). Hanashima pointed out that in his own activities, he never wavers: he insists without exception that babies should be placed in households, not institutions. "It's because for me, inside me—I understand. I understand the cause of my own suffering, the cause of my own difficulty in living [*ikizurasa*]."

Hanashima is one of the most fervent child welfare reform activists I have encountered, and his singularity of focus and conviction impresses even those who disagree with him.[24] Although Hanashima makes use of attachment theory, trauma theory, and neuroscience in his appeals to Japan's Ministry of Health, Labour and Welfare, I find Hanashima's most compelling evidence to rest on his personal, and highly visceral, experiences of lack. In a 2010 interview, Hanashima described his first visit to an institutional baby home in Japan, the cribs like small cages or pens (ori no yō) lined up one after another with solitary babies lying behind tall railings in each one. "When I saw those, it was—agonizing—those babies had been abandoned, thrown away, and I saw that my former self—of course I have no memory of that time, but as one would expect, there were no adults there, just children all lined up alone, and I saw them and it was myself, too, it somehow overlapped, it was agony. I felt I had to somehow help these children, but it was also connected to a need to help my former self."

Despite recurrent flashbacks from which he still suffers, Hanashima has mostly managed to process his experiences of abuse in the institution where he grew up. Those memories, he said, are now "sepia-colored," and while scars remain, they are old. But the one topic that remains an ever-present source of suffering, a topic he speculates he will be forced to deal with his entire life, is the fact that as a child he had always been alone; there was never anyone there for him (dare mo inakatta).

At the same time, it is Hanashima's sense of internal emptiness that provides him energy for his activist work. (Indeed, in a 2019 conversation, Hanashima emphasized that he did not want me to understand his experiences of suffering as a weakness or lasting sorrow. Rather, his stories of suffering are his "fighting story": the source of his strength.) He had always enjoyed physics, and if he had had the financial resources to go to university, that is what he would have studied. He said, "It's like the physics concept of the Dirac sea—the idea of limitless energy that is also a space of nothingness.[25] Within myself, from that place of total nothingness, from that completely empty part, that's where I draw energy to continue my activism." In the process, he said, and despite the long perception of himself acting totally alone, he has also discovered that he is surrounded by people who support him. Hanashima's embodied sensibilities are exquisitely attuned to relationality and particularly to the absence that he experiences as a productive but painful presence.

Kinship relationships can be explored through both embodied presences and absences, which leave material traces. Institutional caregivers at Chestnut House understood children's bodies to reflect social ties, conveying the degree to which children have been left "just as they were when they were born": both caring interventions and neglect inscribe indelible presences through embodied practices and bodily memory.[26] Developmental transformations—the loss of baby teeth as Noriko "grew up" for her caregivers—draw into relief the material, biological, and interpersonal ways that kinship ties might be embodied. Hanashima understood his own condition holistically, making use of international expert knowledge on child development, attachment theory, trauma theory, and neuroscience to give texture to his own culturally and historically specific—and very bodily—experiences.

While kinship ideals in many ways align with David Schneider's old notion of "diffuse, enduring solidarity" (1968) or Marshall Sahlins's more recent articulation of kinship as "mutuality of being" (2011, 2013), otherness and difference, hierarchy, and violence are also very often at the heart of how kinship is known and experienced (Yanagisako and Collier 1987; Stasch 2009; Goldfarb and Schuster 2016; Goldfarb and Bamford, eds., 2024). The lived meanings of kinship, which sometimes hew far from cultural concepts of kinship as mutuality, are sometimes best understood through exploring the absence of meaningful kinship ties and the ways that the experience of neglect shapes future relationships. The cases I have described highlight the often normative and normalizing ways that locally relevant epistemologies, specifically conventional and specialized knowledge about child development, inform how my interlocutors identified and interpreted material signs of caregiving relationships in a context where parental ties were lacking.

I have suggested that cultural anthropologists should pay serious attention to all sorts of embodied processes in order to better understand the interactions among bodies, interpersonal relationships, minds, sociality, culture, neurology, affect, technology, emotion . . . as these shape us as social beings. For instance, research on the field of epigenetics leads one to wonder what it can possibly mean to discuss nature (understood as genetic predispositions) as separate from nurture (understood as the input of cultural surroundings, parenting, food, etc.), when gene expression changes over time and is indeed heritable, based on factors like stress, exercise, drug use, and early life adversity (Niewöhner 2011; Lock 2015; Lock and Palsson 2016).[27] We should attend to both the historical contingency (Muller-Wille and Rheinberger 2012) and the conceptual incoherence of imagining that nature and nurture could be held as discrete objects, where nature is understood as prenatal while nurture takes over as postnatal (Keller 2010, 74; Ingold 1990, 2004). Biology should be understood not as innate physiological characteristics but rather as part of "the entire gamut of ontogenetic or developmental processes by which humans and other animals become skilled in the conduct of particular forms of life" (Ingold 2013, 4). Further, embodiment as a concept should be both historicized and pluralized in an effort to understand the diversities of embodied experiences and the ways these experiences are shaped by politics and culture (Farquhar 2002, 5). This chapter has illustrated ways that cultural anthropologists might welcome material, embodied, and biological processes as interlocutors and work toward theorizing relational embodiments beyond the nature/nurture divide.

In his essay "Belief and the Body" (1990), Pierre Bourdieu writes, "The body believes in what it plays at: it weeps if it mimes grief. It does not represent what it performs, it does not memorize the past, it *enacts* the past, bringing it back to life. What is 'learned by the body' is not something that one has, like knowledge that can be brandished, but something that one is." Readers may be uncomfortable with the ways my interlocutors objectified the bodies and behaviors of the children in their charge, as these processes so often hew toward pathologization and direct us to normative models of caregiving and socialization. I suggest that these accounts also illuminate new ways to understand how embodied life and well-being is inherently political (Farquhar 2002; Farquhar and Lock 2007). Interpretations of the ways that bodies "enact the past," in Bourdieu's terms, direct us toward envisioning other sorts of futures in which the very same linked domains of family, medicine, and the sciences of child development could inform welfare models that support ongoing transformations in the context of relationships. A model in which child welfare and well-being are in less fragile relation. A model of welfare that produces people who have people.

THE END OF THE WORLD

The Catholic child welfare institution where Hanashima Shin'ichi lived until he was fifteen years old was encircled by a tall cement wall. The children's school was on the institution's campus, so they rarely left those confines.

HANASHIMA SHIN'ICHI: There was a sensation that did not dissipate until I was at least twenty years old. It was the sense that beyond one kilometer in all directions in front of me, there was nothing. For so long I had lived within the boundaries of that wall. I had no sense that the world would extend outward beyond that distance. So when I was on the train, once we started moving, I would become incredibly anxious—as though—if we continue to move beyond that point—

KATE GOLDFARB: Ah—you had no idea where you would end up.

HANASHIMA: Right . . . like there was some kind of termination, a precipice. . . . This sensation continued in me for so long. I would become so anxious. I battled these feelings of anxiety within myself anytime I went anywhere. I would stare at a map with all my might and tell myself over and over again, "*See, the world continues up ahead.*"

THE POLITICS OF CHANCE

Tanpopo was a Tokyo-area self-support group created for and by youth who grew up in Japanese child welfare institutions. At the time of my primary fieldwork, the organization was located in a rented apartment near a bustling train station, across from a small shrine; it was one of only a few similar groups in Japan.[1] The apartment featured a cluttered kitchen, where group members cooked family-style meals; stacks of donated foodstuffs and clothing; shelves of books, organization newsletters, and government white papers; a cluster of musical instruments and a dart board; and a dining room table surrounded by chairs. Tanpopo began as a child welfare study group in 2006 and was designated a nonprofit organization in 2008. Staff members were hired to assist its constituency, mostly young people who needed help registering for public assistance, finding work, dealing with mental and physical health concerns, or renting an apartment without a guarantor (a common problem for young people without family members to act in this capacity). The group's stated objectives were to help facilitate stability in four domains: mental health, necessities of daily life, finances, and community. In the afternoons, staff members met individually with young people or with visitors. The evenings were often energetic and noisy, with people making dinner, playing video games, working on job applications at the dining room table, and taking phone calls.

My friend Reina had introduced me to the organization in March of 2010, and with the permission of the director, I began participant-observation field-work at the organization the next month, until I returned to the United States in December 2010. This was a space designed for young alumni of state care but also frequented by researchers, journalists, volunteers, and members of other welfare-related organizations. Belonging felt, to me, to be mediated most by continued commitment to participate in the group's community—to help shop for and cook the evening meal, to fold newsletters, to problem-solve with group members, to sit and chat when nothing in particular was going on, to be there before and after perfunctory visits from local dignitaries who hoped to perform their sensitivity to child welfare issues. At the time of my fieldwork, there were perhaps fifteen careleavers who tended to join evening meals and events, plus the director and a few staff and a few regular volunteers, including researchers like myself. This community was hyper-researched. Any given day, there might be a visiting sociologist or child welfare professor sitting in, or a reporter from the national broadcasting agency filming or taking notes. The people who directly appear in this chapter were the three group members with whom I conducted extensive interviews, a project I approached only once I felt that we knew and trusted one another.

One quiet midafternoon, I was sitting at Tanpopo's dining room table drinking tea with Iida Momoko and Chiba Naoki. Momoko was the director of Tanpopo at the time and was twenty-six years old. Naoki was a thirty-three-year-old man who had recently begun to participate in the group. The three of us sat cradling our teacups in our hands and chatting. Then, as if suddenly remembering something, Momoko stood up and removed a huge piece of paper from a cupboard, opening it on the table in front of us. The paper was a board game that she and some other group members had created. It was a game of chance, in which luck determined a player's success or failure (fig. 11).

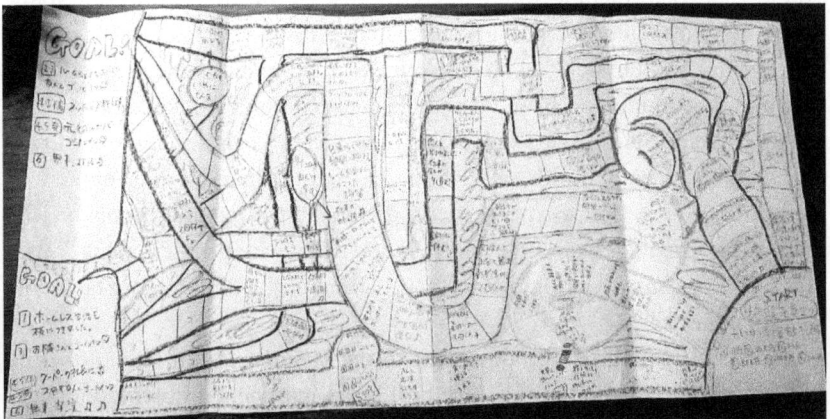

FIGURE 11.   The Tanpopo game. Photograph by author.

Players started with their pieces at the lower right-hand side: "Start: Leaving the Institution." The players rolled dice to determine how much money they had in savings at the time of independence from state care. Those who rolled a one had no money. Rolling a two awarded a player ¥200,000 (around $2,400 as of 2010, the time of research), a three awarded ¥400,000, a four awarded ¥800,000, a five awarded ¥1,000,000, and a six awarded ¥2,000,000. A player's starting monetary status determined which path they followed as they subsequently rolled the dice to determine the number of squares to advance. The green path, on the bottom, was for players who started without savings. "Can't find a job." "Parents take you in and you become a *neet* [a young person living with parents who has no job]." "Experience the homeless life. Get sick. Rest one turn." "Your friend helps you get a part-time job." "You get arrested for eating at a restaurant and not paying. Go back five squares." Players who rolled a two lived with a friend, and their path was marked by the ebb and flow of that relationship: "Talk with a friend about the future. Advance one square." "Your roommate steals all your savings. Rest two turns." Players who began with the most money started off being awarded a scholarship to go to vocational school and lived alone in an apartment. "Get isolated at school. Rest one turn." "Make friends at school." "Can't find a part-time job. Rest one turn." The other tracks were similarly combinations of positive and negative outcomes: "Get fired because of skipping work without calling." "Spend all your savings on an expensive present for your lover. Skip two turns." "Your lover cheats on you. Rest one turn." "Get a venereal disease from your girlfriend. Return to start." "Your neighbor brings you beef and potato stew and you feel loved. Advance two squares." "Appear in a porn film. Receive ¥300,000." "Get food poisoning. Rest one turn." "Start thinking positively and get a haircut. Advance three squares." "You stop caring about anything. Return to start."

No matter what course a player was on, the final outcomes, the "Goals" on the left side of the board, were still determined by a role of the dice. "Get married to your roommate." "Stay working at the supermarket forever." "Become homeless." "Get married to a fabulous person." "Become the head of the supermarket." "Graduate."[2]

I envisioned the Tanpopo members crowding around the paper to draw the game, filling in the blank boxes. In places, the writing unmistakably bore Momoko's hand. I could practically hear her husband, with his irreverent sense of humor, cackling mischievously as he wrote some of the more colorful entries.

Naoki stared at the game board. "It's all chance, isn't it? Do you guys, like, play this and cry, or what?"

Momoko laughed. "No, of course not! It's fun."

For Naoki, the game's dark humor all too accurately depicted events that occurred in the lives of young people leaving state care—events that in many ways depended on chance. Indeed, the Tanpopo game crystalized the ways that Japan's child welfare system as a whole disproportionately depends on chance in shaping positive or negative outcomes for state wards. At the same time, young people in Japan are encouraged to think of themselves as agentive, self-responsible subjects who must take control of their lives.

Conversations and arguments at Tanpopo often highlighted the ways group members perceived chance and agentive action. Later that same day, another group member, thirty-two-year-old Matsumoto Taichi, arrived around five p.m. after he got off work. Matsumoto was always full of dreams and schemes. On this evening, he wanted us to give him feedback on a PowerPoint presentation he was planning to give to a local community leader whom he hoped would support one of his projects. His latest idea was to start a program that would offer Japanese cultural experiences to foreigners visiting Japan but that would also somehow benefit young people from the child welfare system who were under-educated and under-resourced. The optimism underlying Matsumoto's schemes was always matched by equal parts naivety and vagueness, and Momoko was direct with him: How could Matsumoto hope that a local business leader he didn't even know would support a plan only vaguely sketched out, without a successful track record of making these initiatives happen? The last point surely smarted for Matsumoto, who often talked about the importance of actually implementing one's plans. Matsumoto, chastened, replied that since he had never had the opportunity to go to university, he has to borrow other people's strength to actualize his dreams.

Earlier in the evening, when Matsumoto was telling us about his plans, Naoki had suddenly queried, "What was your upbringing like? Normally people who were raised in child welfare institutions aren't as . . ." Not as passionate, full of plans.

"It's because Matsumoto is a hungry spirit [*hangurī seishin*]," Momoko interjected.

The term *hungry spirit* became a catchphrase in conversations with Momoko, Matsumoto, and Naoki. The term implies desperate striving and single-minded ambition toward a goal. All three of them explicitly theorized their own orientations toward agentive action by way of narratives regarding their pasts, specifically the role of contingency and chance in both opportunities and losses. These theorizations provide a way to interrogate the assumptions that underlie the Japanese child welfare system itself and the discursive representations about self-responsibility and agentive action in Japan today.

On the one hand, the fates of children in the system are vulnerable to contingent forces far beyond their control, and they learn from experience that they have little power to change their own situations. On the other hand, these same children are emancipated from the system sometimes as early as fifteen years of age and twenty at the latest, and are suddenly required to make their own decisions and take independent action in order to live. This system of care and emancipation is, I argue, rooted in a deeply non-empiricist view of experience. Despite the fact that most of us depend on our past experiences to guide our expectations for the future, the child welfare system demands that youth leaving care break with a past of dependency and social marginalization in order to care for themselves in society, with minimal or no state assistance. This situation is complicated by the fact that the young people engaging with Tanpopo identify themselves as *tōjisha* (a "person [directly] concerned" with a minority category).[3] The term has historically implied self-advocacy, self-support, self-determination, and empowerment, a subject position that sits uncomfortably with reform-oriented claims that the state has harmed these individuals while they were in care, or that the state should provide more now that youth are "independent" (McLelland 2009, 196; McLelland 2011; Goldfarb 2015).

Experience itself is often privileged within social science analyses and to authorize minority movements, a focus that makes sense within our modernist view of experience as the "foundation of human agency" (Desjarlais 1994, 888). The work of the eighteenth-century empiricist philosopher David Hume, rooted in theorizations of experience, remains salient (Hume 1977). Hume argued that the possibility for human action is based not on rationalization or reason but through our experiences observing consistent effects stemming from consistent causes. According to Hume, we can act in the world because we have made observations about it, and we hazard a guess that these observations will guide us consistently. However, even as our action in the world depends on believing that consistent actions should lead to consistent reactions, we ourselves understand that there is no assurance of this fact beyond our previous experiences. The necessity to rely on empirical examples of past events in conducting action in the present is an expression of faith but also, Hume suggested, the only way we can actually act in the world.

Momoko, Matsumoto, and Naoki inhabited divergent perspectives regarding the empiricist base for action that Hume described, but their situations together illustrate how difficult it is to maintain faith in action without a history of support from others. In line with contemporary neoliberal values as well as common logics of tōjisha empowerment, Momoko embraced a notion of self-responsibility (*jiko sekinin*) through struggling on (*ganbaru*) to overcome past experiences. Yet, in order to embody a self-responsible and striving identity, Momoko was also forced to suppose the past to be only contingently connected to the future. Recognizing past failures, she realized she could move forward only if she assumed the future would not resemble the past. Chance offered the possibility of change and escape from former constraints. Momoko's embrace of contingency's possibilities illuminated the desperation at the heart of a life lived struggling with little assurance beyond her own drive. Her orientation was perhaps a virtue but certainly a necessity, for the state care system guaranteed only contingency—from the quality of residential placements to the degree of material and social support afforded to each state ward—and Momoko's struggles were long based on this shaky ground.

Matsumoto seemed to embrace a similar empowerment model in which he started with a goal and backtracked to identify the necessary requirements for meeting that goal. However, he often explicitly identified support from other people as a condition for any real or hypothetical successes. As Naoki correctly assumed, Matsumoto did consider his own past to be a resource. Both experiences of suffering and positive relationships with others became, in Matsumoto's telling, assets to be leveraged toward an uncertain future. Despite his optimistic self-presentation, Matsumoto's account of important events in his past was threaded through with loss. His successes often hinged on contingent connections and chance meetings, which surely reinforced his perception that accomplishments depended on borrowing other people's strength.

Naoki took an explicitly critical and empiricist stance, arguing that past events of failure and disconnection predicted only more of the same. He articulated a position that self-responsibility is impossible for people who have never received adequate care. He discursively constructed a model of himself in which because of state caregiving failures, his past lived actively in his present, circumscribing and limiting his future possibilities. Naoki's own negative past experiences and personal history of failures made it clear to him that he could not possibly risk action in the world, an orientation that foreshadowed his ultimate ejection from the tōjisha group oriented around self-help.

These three seemingly divergent approaches to life after state care draw attention to twin crises within Japan's child welfare system. The activism and critique underlying Momoko, Matsumoto, and Naoki's orientations to the world highlight a political crisis of a welfare system that does not provide adequate care. Their perspectives also articulate an existential crisis, the ways in which welfare systems are often profoundly unlivable. All three suffered from periods of depression, and I knew that both Momoko and Naoki had attempted suicide.

In theorizing experience, my friends denaturalized the conditions of their own social marginality and simultaneously critiqued the structural constraints that shaped their lives. Their stories—singular accounts that share qualities with those of so many other people from state care in Japan and beyond—illustrate the need for comprehensive social support and the danger of assuming self-responsibility as an antidote to social and economic precarity.

A Tōjisha Group in the Japanese-Style Welfare Society

People who grew up in Japanese child welfare institutions may consider them-selves an "invisible minority," and, over the past two decades, self-support groups like Tanpopo have emerged in many Japanese cities to provide a place where those who grew up in child welfare institutions can gather.[4] These groups are understood as tōjisha communities: groups for people who share a set of com-mon circumstances that mark them as different from the rest of Japanese society.

Experience authorizes membership in tōjisha groups, but the ways each mem-ber takes up the concept of experience entails different personal and political stakes. The children and youth who grow up in child welfare institutions in Japan are disadvantaged in many ways. They are socially marginalized by their lack of kinship affiliations, they are economically and often educationally underprivi-leged, and their pasts are characterized by repeated separation from caregivers. Many have faced abuse and neglect. Young people who grew up as wards of the Japanese state but are made newly independent from state care upon reaching adulthood struggle with social norms that posit self-responsibility (jiko seki-nin) as a requirement for social belonging. Youth leaving state care often overtly grapple with the ways that contemporary values of self-responsibility in Japan are predicated upon densely social networks of care and support as a basis for "independent" action. For youth emancipated from state welfare services, pur-suing goals and working toward a lifestyle independent of state aid may seem impossible. Tanpopo was a site where the political possibilities entailed in join-ing a group marked by one's experiences in state care met with the interpersonal hazards of a history of social exclusion.

Japan's child welfare system is constituted by community organizations, pri-vate volunteers, religious groups, state-run bureaucracies (government-run child guidance centers and a small number of public child welfare institutions), state-certified foster parents, and privately owned social welfare corporations that are funded by a mixture of national and local state resources, and which run their own child welfare institutions (Goodman 2000; Bamba and Haight 2011). Wards of the state would typically interact with many of these service providers. While the Japanese government is attempting to expand its family-based foster care program, the majority of children in Japanese state care are still placed in child welfare institutions and sometimes live in institutional care for many years.[5] Upon emancipation from the system, youth who lack support networks in the form of family or foster parents often find themselves isolated from their peers and face economic, educational, and social disadvantages (Hinata Bokko 2009; Nishida 2011; Children's Views and Voices and Nagase 2015; Nagano 2017; MUFG 2021).

Rather than referring to the welfare state, Japanese politicians developed the term *welfare society* to indicate the ways state welfare in Japan is premised on families, communities, employers, and private and volunteer services bearing the burden of service provision, with the state stepping in only when all other options have faltered (Garon 1997; Takahashi and Hashimoto 1997; Goodman 1998; Kono 2005; Walker and Wong 2005; Hook and Takeda 2007; Goldfarb 2013; Oka 2013). The Japanese-style welfare society is comprised of a heterogeneous mix of public, private, and quasi-private institutions and voluntary services. This contemporary formulation is broadly consistent with historical policy statements about social welfare in Japan, from the restoration of the Meiji emperor in 1868 and the creation of a unified state through the interwar period. For instance, the Japanese government's first national ordinance addressing social welfare, in 1874, focused on the importance of "self-help and family care rather than any state responsibility" (Takahashi 2003, 96), and the 1898 Civil Code "mandated that households had a 'duty of support' [*fuyō no gimu*] toward their needy members" (Garon 2010, 321). In the time of economic growth immediately after World War II, bowing to pressure from the American occupation forces, the Japanese government slowly increased welfare spending.[6] However, as Japan entered an era of persistent low economic growth at the start of the world oil crisis in 1973, Japanese authorities became convinced that "the welfare state had become a disadvantage to the competitiveness of other advanced capitalist countries" (Gould 1993 quoted in Kono 2005, 119–120). At this point, discourses surrounding welfare focused on the excesses of "Western welfare states" that encouraged "dependency" on the government (Goodman 2002). Japanese political discourses favored an expansive welfare state only during the short-lived economic boom of the late 1970s and early 1980s. Upon intimations of recession, Japanese policy officials reversed course, proposing a Japanese-style welfare society that depended on a traditional social safety net: family, community, employers, and voluntary associations.

In Japanese policy discourses, limited welfare provisioning was represented as appropriate for Japanese people as such, who supposedly cared for their own and had tight-knit families, and whose communities were said to nurture those within (Garon 2010). These resources were discursively framed as cultural wealth that obviated the need for extensive state welfare provisioning, the excesses of which, pundits argued, would bring Japan into further decline. Neoliberal policy discourses, specifically surrounding the ideal of self-responsibility (jiko sekinin) and the requirement of the family to care for its members, reinforce an image of a citizenry that cares for itself largely independent of state support.[7] Despite a valorization of independence, neoliberal policies have "pushed individuals to become more reliant on their families," highlighting the contradictory ways that state policy both pathologizes and requires certain forms of dependence (Alexy

2020, 11; Borovoy 2012). This is "an ideology of 'care through abandonment,'" in Jason Danely's words, which creates "both an array of possible dependencies as well as ways to fall through the cracks" (2014, 161).

The dependency of private or voluntary welfare services on state funding, and the state's use of voluntary and nongovernmental organizations, continues today. The public-private funding of these organizations complicates easy comparisons to increasingly privately funded welfare services elsewhere, but Japanese discourses focusing on private sector provisioning, rather than dependence on the state, are consistent with broader neoliberal movements (Greenhouse 2010). I follow other theorists of neoliberalism in East Asia to argue that while neoliberal trends in Japan have their own cultural and historical specificities, contemporary discourses of self-responsibility in Japan closely articulate with a neoliberal ethos in general (Song 2009; Reitan 2012; Allison 2013).[8] As such, although this analysis is in many ways specific to the Japanese case, it speaks broadly to the personal and political stakes of theorizing selves as disembedded from broader networks of support. Representations of self-responsibility elide a person's actual dependencies and interdependencies with other people, family, volunteer organizations, and private and state services.

In this context, what are young people without the support of family to do in cases of need? At a basic level, self-support groups like Tanpopo attempt to fill some of these gaps—if only by providing social support and knowledge regarding the pragmatics of applying for public aid.[9] Tanpopo, as a tōjisha group, was an organization of people understood to be the same as each other by virtue of how they differed from others in society. Momoko and a few like-minded friends had created the group as a setting where youth with similar institutional care backgrounds could gather and support each other. It was to be an *ibasho*: a place to be oneself, to return to in times of need, a space for sociality and commensality, for "collectivized forms of survival and care" (Allison 2013, 128). They embarked upon this project without knowing whether participants would share a sense of identity or be able to learn to trust each other; yet the fact that their backgrounds were so different from normal peers made them similar to each other. These factors exemplify a tension underlying tōjisha communities: while group members can mobilize personally and politically around a common tōjisha subjectivity, this idealized vision tends to erase differences and does little to recognize the ways diverse subject positions emerge from putatively similar experiences (Yoneyama 1995; McLelland 2009).

The chance-driven Tanpopo game threw into relief how a specific orientation to past experience and future possibilities structured participation in the group. The events written into the board game expressed the precarity of the lives of Tanpopo members, which paralleled the capriciousness of the Japanese state in its engagements with state wards. Indeed, many people who spent time in state care described the workings of the welfare state, which stands in loco parentis for the children under its purview, as erratic and arbitrary, echoing Akhil Gupta's analysis of bureaucratic aid that may "repeatedly and systematically produce arbitrary outcomes in its provision of care" (2012, 6). The political project underlying Tanpopo was to increase higher baseline standards across the welfare system, which would decrease the role of chance in determining whether a child had a good or a bad experience in state care.

Good Can Come Out of Misfortune, if One Struggles On: Momoko's Story

Momoko had lived in a group home with her younger brother and sister for seven years before graduating from high school, and before that she had spent time in a large child welfare institution in Osaka, living intermittently with her mother, who had a history of epilepsy. Momoko speculated that her mother had a developmental disability related to frequent seizures. Her mother moved around a lot, sometimes leaving the children with their often-violent father, sometimes taking the children as she ran from him (Kuwajima 2019). The siblings grew up in and out of child welfare institutions. Although Momoko had long been aware of the chasm separating her and her siblings from children who lived with normal parents, this feeling of difference grew more acute when she entered high school.[10] In an interview, she explained how she felt cut off from her classmates by virtue of her family situation. "I had an intense feeling that our household situations were totally different. When I entered high school, it was like—'Ah, everyone is going to go to university supported by their parents, aren't they.' I was furiously working part-time jobs to save money and prepare for independence when I left care. Our baseline circumstances were totally different. The sense that from here on out I would have to live entirely alone, that's not something my classmates would understand." This is why, Momoko said, she initially felt the need to have a place where people with similar backgrounds could gather, a group predicated on that difference from mainstream society.

Momoko emphasized that the conditions of the lives of Tanpopo members would be the same as each other (*jyōken ga issho*), and this equivalence would enable the development of a community that understood each other. Thinking about herself and the other Tanpopo members with respect to her former classmates, Momoko reflected:

> When those baseline conditions are different, it's just . . . difficult. The start line is different. And it *looks* the same, but—it's different from a [visible] disability, for example. This is something you can't see with

your eyes, and it may *look* like the same start line. And everyone else—they're starting *incredibly* ahead, and we—well, even in the beginning, all those things that one gets from a family—we haven't been comforted [*iyasaretenai*], we haven't received sufficient education or rearing, we have economic difficulties, mental health difficulties, we don't have anything to rely on [*yoridokoro mo nai*]. For other people it's common sense [*atari mae*] that one would have a parent, but for us, even if we *have* parents, they're not *normal* [futsū] parents.

The Tanpopo board game reflects this radically different start line: all players begin at the point of graduating from institutional care, a marker of difference from mainstream high school graduates. Their life paths diverge, with distinct benefits and disadvantages, based on a pragmatically crucial factor—the amount of money they have when they leave care, since they have nowhere to turn for help—and the vicissitudes of chance.

The ways Momoko theorized the role of chance clarifies her portrayal of the Tanpopo board game in the face of Naoki's dismayed reaction. Momoko refused the past's power to define the future. In her view, a major intention of the group was to overcome the various past traumas that group members putatively held in common. She had taken as a personal motto a set phrase, *jinkan banji saiō ga uma*, which might be translated as "inscrutable are the ways of heaven," "the future is unpredictable and changeable," or "good can come out of misfortune." For Momoko, this phrase expressed her belief in the ability to improve one's own lot through effort. For her, while the future may not resemble the past, good is possible only through self-discipline, constant striving, and luck.

In a 2010 publication about her experiences (not cited here to protect Momoko's confidentiality), Momoko wrote that from her childhood, she had always been struggling on (ganbaru), and she simply does not know how to live any other way. But at the same time, there was sadness behind her sense of always struggling. Perhaps eventually, Momoko reflected, the day would come when she did not need to struggle. At the same time, she concluded, "If I hadn't struggled to the point I am at now, I wouldn't be here today." Momoko closed her book with a note of advice, saying that although past deprivations may not be one's own fault, there is nothing to do but get over it and move on. The purpose of Tanpopo, she wrote, was to encourage each other in this process, to struggle on together.

In much of Momoko's book, she appears to be speaking directly to other Tanpopo members, using herself as an example of how they, too, might struggle on despite their tribulations. While Momoko's self-representation might seem impossibly disciplined, she also worked politically to represent the needs of former state wards to the Ministry of Health, Labour and Welfare so that others might struggle less. Behind her rosy representation of chance opportunities lay frustration with the systematic creation of arbitrary welfare outcomes. Her focus on constant struggle illuminates how her wager—that the future would not resemble the past—was born of desperation.

Momoko had also experienced existential despair. At the end of her book, she described a period of time after she had started Tanpopo and gotten married, when the pressure she placed on herself seemed unbearable and she attempted suicide. Her husband found her before it was too late. The experience of being saved by him made her reflect on the ways one's ability to exert effort is undergirded by the support of others. Although her book encourages Tanpopo members to struggle on as well, the anguish she describes is likely familiar to her readers, many of whom lack the support that Momoko had in her husband.

In some ways, Momoko seemed the model self-responsible subject, and many of the Tanpopo members saw her as improbably successful and competent (*shikkari*), an impression that she likely hoped to temper through her book. Some people criticized her as being harsh to others in leadership roles, although I saw her as a perfectionist and knew she was even more critical of herself. But these qualities were always tempered by deep empathy and care for others. Despite seeming soft-spoken, her reactions to the stories of group members revealed the fury she felt on behalf of others who had experienced poor treatment in state care. For instance, one day Naoki was telling me about how his father had left Naoki a collection of old coins as his inheritance. One of the institutional staff members told Naoki that he would take care of the collection so it wouldn't get stolen, and he took it. Naoki later heard that this staff member had been showing a coin around, saying that Naoki had given the coins to him. When I asked what happened in the end, Naoki just replied that the staff member had made the coins his own (*jibun no mono*). Momoko, who had been listening from the kitchen, burst out, "*Appalling!* This makes me furious! [*Saiaku! Hara ga tatsu!*]" Her moments of alignment and care suffused interactions with members of Tanpopo, from the birthday cakes she prepared to her gestures to include everyone in conversation and respond to their needs, like covering someone with a blanket as they napped under the low table next to the dining room. At the same time, in response to people's stories (often told humorously) about topics like excessive drinking or job loss, I heard her say more than once, "I often wonder how you all make do, anyway . . . [*Minasan, dō yatte seikatsu dekiru no ka, yoku omou*]."

Within Tanpopo, Momoko was a caring, motherly figure despite her young age. She was friend, counselor, and social worker to the group members, most of whom had complex and layered problems: mental health concerns, social anxiety, difficulty maintaining relationships in personal and work life, health problems and work injuries, conflict with family members, and trouble finding employment. Some group members called her cell phone regularly and depended on her for daily advice. Momoko's own sense of responsibility—extending far beyond the need to care for herself—verged on parental. Her hope to meet long-unmet desires was confronted by seemingly limitless need.

A Hungry Spirit: Matsumoto's Story

"It's the same as with muscle," Matsumoto told me with a chuckle. "If your spirit has been tempered from the time you are small, you are stronger than a normal person." Momoko had once apparently told Matsumoto that his "power" came from having been given the "old-fashioned" rearing of his father, to whom he said he had been close, but who was very strict. His father was of the pre–World War I generation and had himself been strictly raised. Matsumoto supposed that his father's methods of discipline would probably be described now as abuse. "But you know, if you think about it objectively—as a child when you do something bad, and you get locked in a closet as punishment, and you're calling out to have the door opened but no one opens it—it's scary, but you also have time to think about yourself, right?" In Matsumoto's words, I heard echoes of what another friend called his "fighting story," as he admonished me not to feel sorry for him but rather to understand the source of his strength (chap. 4).[11]

Matsumoto's descriptions of his home life expressed empathy for his parents' struggles. The family had lived in a poor community in Gunma prefecture. They received welfare support. His mother suffered from mental health trouble that he understood as rooted in a life of hard work that broke her body and spirit. His father was older and suffered from kidney disease and spent long periods unemployed. Matsumoto was ill when he was young and described himself as a challenging child: his parents were either dealing with his asthma and eczema or his penchant to be a "mood and trouble-maker" (he said this in English). He had a brother two years younger who seemed to play a minor role in the family dynamic and who was stuck at home with their parents even after Matsumoto had been placed for care in a local hospital, from which he commuted to school, as his home was not a healthy environment. He lived at the hospital from fifth grade until the spring of his first year of middle school, when his mother passed away (she was probably in her forties, Matsumoto speculated). Sometime around then, he and his brother were moved to a child welfare institution. His father passed away the following year.

During this time, there was a schoolteacher and a doctor at the hospital who took interest in Matsumoto, and he described these two men as important role models. He was famous in both institutions—surely because of both the intractable difficulties in his home life and his chronic health problems, but also because he had a big personality. He would cause trouble, which demanded the attention of these adults, but also charm them with interesting questions and the direct, humorously innocent way he approached the world. These men were invested in him because he demanded much of them. From them, he said, he received love.

Based on his relationship with these role models, Matsumoto desired to go to university, and he somehow assumed that his parents would be able to assist him in actualizing this goal. Then his parents passed away. "My parents had been unbreakable support pillars for my spirit. When they vanished, everything in front of me went black." At that moment, all he could think was that somehow he would have to keep living. In his characteristic style of reasoning, Matsumoto outlined this thought process: If he had to keep living, then he needed power to live. So, what was that power? For one, it was work: he had to save money. To get a good job, he would have to go to school. (The child welfare institution he was initially placed in was one that almost uniformly did not send children to high school. Matsumoto's resolve to continue his education beyond the compulsory level of middle school was itself significant and required him to change institutions after graduating from middle school.) The people who had been supporting Matsumoto were now gone. To the degree that he had no support, he would have to create his own experiences and find a way to set himself apart from other people. This moment of resolve was, he said, the start of his drive to create and actualize a "vision of an unknowable future" (*shiranai mirai no bijon*). This was the quality Naoki had noticed in Matsumoto, which Momoko had called his "hungry spirit."

While he depended on the support of schoolteachers, Matsumoto knew he could ask nothing of the child welfare institution staff. The institution, for Matsumoto, was "clothing, food, and shelter" (*ishokujū*). The work of staff members, he explained, was to manage the children and keep them out of trouble, not to help them try new things. For instance, Matsumoto said, the children at his institution were prohibited from part-time work. But he knew he needed to save money, so he lied about his whereabouts and took part-time jobs.[12] In contrasting the role of institutional staff with that of parents, Matsumoto said that parents "sow the seeds of their children's talents, but staff members pluck the buds that grow from these seeds." Humans grow by challenging themselves, he continued. But challenge causes trouble, and staff are more concerned with manageable charges.

In accounting for his own past, Matsumoto described goals he defined and worked toward, many of which ended in varieties of failure, but others whose successes were entirely due to his creativity, persistence, and willingness to ask much of other people. For instance, he had been very involved in his high school student government because there were specific things he wanted to change about the school, and he eventually became student body president (a striking achievement for a young person in state care). He was interested in computers and suspected that computer skills would be important in his personal development, but he couldn't afford a keyboard, so he created a keyboard out of paper and taught himself how to type. He leaned on the teachers at his high school for help with university entrance examinations and studied with dedication, but he was not accepted.

Finally, Matsumoto explained in detail how, a few years after graduation from high school, during which time he worked unhappily for his uncle's company in Kyoto and lived in that company's dorm, he dedicated himself to learning programming with the goal of becoming a systems engineer; he still dreamed of saving enough money to attend university. He enrolled in a vocational school and studied programming every spare minute. In the end he failed the exam. He was wandering dispiritedly through the streets of Shin Osaka, in the neighborhood of the company where the exam had taken place, reflecting on his desire to work in information technology. "I suddenly turned back the way I had come and returned to the company, where I located a person in human resources. 'I just took your exam and I didn't pass—but—more than anything, I want to work toward becoming a systems engineer, and with that goal I badly want to learn to be a programmer—and so—please, will you give me a job?' Well, the HR person must have been impressed by my ambition [*netsui*] or something—and hired me. That was my IT debut."

I was moved by Matsumoto's story and told him so. He was so willing to make himself vulnerable to the whim of people he viewed as able to help him, and in moments like these it paid off. As Matsumoto later noted, "It's about transforming a pinch [*pinchi*] to a chance [*chansu*] and turning that chance into one's own development." At another point he noted, "You have to make your own plan, and through the actions you take, you create the future you want [*jibun ga motomeru . . . mirai o tsukuru*]."

Months after our interview, as I was working to develop my own definition of the term *hungry spirit*, I had an interesting online exchange with Matsumoto. When replying to my question of how one might define *hungry spirit*, he wrote that *hungry* meant "to plant" (*ueru*, 植える), and this was connected to continuing to seek the thing that one hoped to actualize. I was confused by his translation and then realized that the Japanese word *ueru* also meant "to be hungry" but was written with different characters (飢える). When I asked Matsumoto to elaborate, he explained that "*ueru* (植える) means to receive seeds. I think it's about inheriting the hopes either of the people living alongside you or of your ancestors. It's about actualizing the dreams that these people couldn't attain themselves."

In many ways, Matsumoto positioned himself as a good neoliberal subject, creating something out of nothing, making plans and taking responsibility to work toward his dreams with single-minded determination. But that was not the entire story. Matsumoto was exquisitely attuned to the importance of relationality in any sort of success. His dream to go to university was due to the presence of his role models, and his achievements that mattered most were due to chance connections and his ability to impose upon and ask for care from another person (a form of dependency, *amaeru*, often celebrated as quintessentially Japanese [Doi 2014]). He even understood the notion of being a hungry spirit as part of a broader set of relationships in which one takes on the dreams of others. Matsumoto's references to talents and hopes as seeds and buds, including his critique that institutional staff pluck these buds rather than cultivating them, articulate with the Japanese term *to raise* (*sodateru*), which can apply to nurturing either a plant or a child. To me, Matsumoto's hunger often felt desperate, seeking, insatiable, and simultaneously impossible to pin down or actualize—less a project or a goal than a diffuse desire for relationality in which he could both care and be cared for (Borneman 1997).

Being a Former Child: Naoki's Story

When Naoki first started visiting Tanpopo, it was with cautious optimism that he might have finally found a community that understood him. After his mother left him and his father, Naoki had lived briefly with his father and then later with an uncle, and finally in two different child welfare institutions before he aged out at eighteen. He had spent the majority of his childhood at a large public institution in rural northern Japan, in which the staff members were nonspecialized government workers.[13]

Naoki had a keen sense of not having been protected and cared for in a way that would enable him to live as a successful member of society. Naoki's first major complaint about his institution was that the staff did nothing to intervene in the endemic violence among the children, and thus the children knew they had no one to protect them.[14] Naoki's second major complaint was that the residents had been prohibited from working part-time jobs, which would have allowed them to save money for their exit from state care and given them experience acting independently. Without savings, young careleavers often have no option but to work at a factory with employee dorms or to depend on a friend, lover, or relative for housing support.[15] Because life in child welfare institutions is generally highly structured, young people raised in these environments often have little opportunity to develop the ability to make their own decisions. These were points Naoki returned to again and again in his discussions with me and with others.

Although Tanpopo's premise was that the members would see themselves as similar to each other, Naoki claimed that inter-child violence and the prohibition on part-time work differentiated his experiences from those of other Tanpopo members, whom he viewed as more successful than himself. (Others in the group found his perspective intensely frustrating, as many group members, including Matsumoto, had had similar experiences in state care.) He indexed these forms of perceived difference with coined terms: he took two conventional words and added the prefix *moto* (元), which means both "former" and "foundation" or "origin."[16] Naoki began calling himself a *moto tōjisha* to distinguish himself as a more legitimate or original tōjisha, thereby undermining the possibility for a cohesive group identity and problematizing what he perceived as homogenizing tendencies within the tōjisha category. Further, because he understood his inability to act as an adult—specifically, his inability to search for and obtain a job—in contrast to other Tanpopo members, he characterized himself as different in this way, too, by using the term *moto kodomo*, or "former child." A moto kodomo was, Naoki explained, a person whose age was that of an adult but whose inner self (kokoro) is that of a child. For a moto kodomo, having been a child remained a central quality of nonchild (but not yet adult) life.

In an interview, he explained that while children are malleable (*sunao*), adults who have had their own histories of failure now fear making attempts to improve their lot. "Right now there are increasing numbers of systems of care for children. But what about former children [moto kodomo]? Children who weren't raised properly. Now, those former children, now they are adults, aren't they?" Although the child welfare system has improved dramatically in recent years, he correctly pointed out that there are no comprehensive social services for people who grew up in the system and have become, as the years passed, adults. The only true resolution, Naoki argued, is to provide programs to compel adults to recover from past deprivations and traumas (*kyōsei saseru*). While Naoki did not suggest the types of services he felt should be provided, his desire to be forced to change illustrates his difficulty imagining independent action.[17]

By focusing on the importance of part-time work, Naoki argued that an inability to participate in the labor market while he was growing up prevented him from becoming a self-governing individual who effectively engaged in capitalist regimes of accumulation. If state welfare programs barred youth from the very establishments that would later determine their success or failure, while simultaneously placing them in situations where they were unable to learn independence, how (he asked) could the state—indeed, society in general—expect these people to work?[18] The same went for taxes. "I don't want to pay taxes," Naoki said. "That money goes to pay for the things that messed me up to begin with [*ore o okashikushita*]. I'm not grateful." Naoki's arguments underscored what he saw as the essential contradiction of a wealthy capitalist society with insufficient welfare programs: no one should be surprised, he argued, that Japan's child welfare system produces people who require welfare to live. (These points were echoed, unbeknownst to Naoki, by participants of many of the child welfare related symposia I attended). Naoki's arguments explicitly contrasted with Momoko's self-position as a responsible contributor through her activities in Tanpopo; as a liaison with the Ministry of Health, Labour and Welfare; and through her past work experiences, and Matsumoto's pragmatic orientation to the importance of work as a way to improve one's lot in life.[19]

The hungry spirits of Momoko and Matsumoto verged on the incomprehensible for Naoki. To have a hungry spirit implies desperate striving, with a thin line between success and total failure. In order to have a hungry spirit in the first place, he argued, one must have someone or something to depend on (*tayori ni naru mono*). For most people this would be a parent, but it could also be knowing that one has a place to live for sure; homelessness was a constant specter to Naoki. In order to strive and take risks, Naoki argued, one needs something to provide a sense of security (*anshinkan*), a place to return in case of failure.

Action, in Naoki's mind, was linked directly to the degree of support one could claim from others. In contrast to Matsumoto, who also knew this poignantly but focused on cultivating these relationships on his own, Naoki articulated this point as a critique of a society that celebrated self-responsibility without providing the social support for action. The way Naoki represented himself to me and to Tanpopo members was deeply shaped by a sense of being terribly alone and of having been alone. He cited the institutional staff's failure to protect the children from inter-child violence as an example of the instability of his own basis for action. However, he said he understood that if the staff had intervened, their workload would have increased. The staff's self-responsibility benefited them but harmed the children in their care. "Someone tells me, 'self-responsibility' [jiko sekinin]—that's just unreasonable [*mucha*]," Naoki said, his voice catching. "In a normal household, the parent takes some kind of responsibility. But institutional staff . . . Whatever happens to that child, it has nothing to do with them, does it [*kankei nai jyanai*]? If things go badly, well, that's just unlucky, isn't it? Unhappy, isn't it?" Naoki thus argued that the self behind self-responsibility is constituted first and foremost by others—specifically caregivers—taking responsibility for a child. Unluckiness and unhappiness appear entangled in logics of disengagement, in which a staff member's detachment from a child's fate means that the child has nowhere to turn in case of failure. According to Naoki, the child learns that the only safety is in not acting at all.

For Naoki, the concept of former child (moto kodomo) embodied his argument that it is unreasonable to assume that an individual with an impoverished background can act proactively without support. In an email, I pressed Naoki to specify his use of the term. He explained, "There are people who say, 'Support [*shien*] for children is important!' But these are the same people who say to adults who weren't raised well and currently want support, 'You're an adult, so do your best by yourself [*jibun de ganbare*].' I think, 'Okay, if that's the case, even if you leave a kid alone and neglected [*hotte oite*], that kid will one day reach adulthood.' So when you say 'do your best by yourself,' that means it's unnecessary to provide support? This is utterly mistaken. . . . I use the term *moto kodomo* to explain, 'The person who is currently struggling was originally a child. Can you really say that support isn't necessary?'" Naoki's invocation of the past-in-present through the term *former child* pinpointed what he saw as the hypocrisy of well-meaning arguments for increased care for children without a concomitant push to care for people who grew up as wards of the state. The biological process of growth and development occurs whether or not a person is given care. One day a neglected child will have become an adult, but this does not mean that this adult does not require assistance.

Naoki considered himself a moto kodomo, in contrast to the many adults participating in Tanpopo who had somehow emerged from circumstances similar—but crucially different, he was quick to argue—from his own. Around six months from his original contact with Tanpopo, Naoki had become completely alienated from the group. Constant discussion of his own troubled past provoked another member to tell him that he was not welcome back until he, Naoki, found a job. Naoki retreated to the solitude of his apartment and became, as he had been for a period in the past, a *hikikomori*, a shut-in, meeting no one and communicating through email via cell phone with only a few.[20] Naoki's previous framing of himself as a moto tōjisha proved an accurate premonition when he became a former member of the group.

Naoki, with an empiricist's attention to his own past experiences of failed action and failed relationships, refused to continue to hazard action. Although he took the risk of engagement in Tanpopo, acknowledging that the past is not always a sure rule for the future, the results of that experiment illustrated to Naoki that his habits of engagement in the world were too durable. As he had predicted, failure was certain. During a period of intense depression after his expulsion from Tanpopo, Naoki sent me occasional lengthy cell phone text messages and finally explained that he had attempted to commit suicide. According to Naoki, his inability to complete that task as well confirmed his understanding of himself as someone who—even at the moment of deepest personal anguish—was still unable to act.[21]

On my second visit to Tanpopo, as I was just getting to know Momoko and Matsumoto (Naoki had not yet started attending the group), Momoko suggested that the group members come up with a way to write my name in Chinese characters (kanji) to document my presence in the guest book. Each Chinese character has multiple possible pronunciations, and when naming a child, parents generally choose characters with propitious meanings whose combination could be pronounced as a legible Japanese name. Matsumoto carefully wrote down everyone's contributions for me on the back of a Tanpopo flier. Some of the names could have actually been Japanese names pronounced "Kate" (*keito*), like 京都 (generally read "Kyoto," as in the Japanese city, but the first character can also be read "*kei*"). Others were fabulously ridiculous—to my amusement, one group member came up with 毛胃止 ("hair," "stomach," "stop")—like a cat hairball! Momoko's choice was typically classy: 恵富 ("blessed" and "fortune"), an auspicious baptism that may have equally expressed her hopes for me as my past and present privilege. Matsumoto's was 恵糸 ("blessed" and "thread"). While a typical Japanese name would not generally use 糸 as one of its characters, Matsumoto explained that this character indicates "a multitude of connections (en) and chances." 糸 is part of the character for *en* (縁), which implies chance connections, fate, and relationships to people and places (chap. 1). Both Momoko and Matsumoto gifted me names rooted to their sense of possibility and hope: Momoko blessed me with fortune, intimately connected to wealth but also to chance, and Matsumoto gave me en, the fated threads that brought me to Tanpopo but that also represented the wealth of human connections that do in fact enable my personal and professional lives.

In the context of the child welfare system, where the only guarantee is contingency and the relationships granted by the system are generally not ones that can substantively support former state wards, my friends at Tanpopo engaged these politics of chance in different ways. Each articulated critiques of the system that highlight how their struggles are indeed products of the politics of care in Japan. Their accounts also highlight the difficulty of making do and the difficulty of surviving, much less flourishing, in this context.

While Naoki understood the past as a rule for the future, Momoko hoped that the future and past are only contingently related. For Naoki, the sense that failure would necessarily occur meant that there was no reason to act, and conversely, action should be taken only when success was certain. Success was never certain for him, and thus for him action was impossible. For Momoko, on the other hand, action was possible and indeed necessary precisely because past experiences do not inevitably determine future outcomes, and thus contingency and chance offered possibility. Matsumoto, an optimist in the face of Naoki's pessimism, understood his own basis for action to be the relationships that supported him in the past and offered him models for the future. He did indeed "borrow the strength" of others to work toward his goals in a way that both made explicit the necessity of relationships as a foundation for stability, and that highlighted the fragility of self-making projects in the face of constant precarity.

Despite what seems to be a self-defeating orientation to life, the social isolation resulting from Naoki's exit from Tanpopo should be "understood as the product of specific *structures and processes of disconnection*" (Ferguson 2009, 316, italics in original). Naoki's inability to act directs us to attend to his lack of social ties that would constitute security. Further, his isolation should be understood similarly as the result of social forces that in many ways overdetermined the outcome of his engagement with Tanpopo but that also knit together the disconnections Naoki experienced in institutional care with his later disconnection from broader society. Indeed, while I continue to be in contact with Momoko and Matsumoto, Naoki stopped replying to my emails during his period of desperate isolation, and then his email address stopped receiving messages. Momoko asks me every time I see her if I have heard from Naoki. I never have.

The above accounts demand a critical examination of the broader pragmatic and affective stakes of discourses of self-responsibility in a contemporary Japan in which welfare regimes provide insufficient support and services are often terminated at the moments people need them most. Nongovernmental projects like Tanpopo fit tidily within the context of the so-called Japanese welfare society, which posits that family and community structures should provide for the needs of the people, with the state stepping in only where these nongovernmental forms of support have failed. Momoko's perspective on life—that one makes one's own future through effort—is pragmatic in the context of Japan's welfare structure, where terms like *self-responsibility* are mobilized to describe what might be understood as both a virtue and a necessity.

At the start of this chapter, I briefly discussed the empiricist philosopher David Hume and his thinking on experience. Hume proposed that people use their past experiences as a guide to understand how particular actions typically lead to certain effects, and it is the accumulation of experience and then habit that allows us to negotiate and take action in the world. However, even the best empiricists cannot know for sure whether consistent actions will lead to consistent effects. We merely act with the trust that this is so. For in fact we can't avoid trusting. If we didn't risk this trust, we would not be able to act at all (Hume 1977; Rutherford 2009).

The Japanese child welfare system, as part of a broader welfare state underpinned by ideologies of self-responsibility, requires a perverse orientation toward experience as a guide for action. Despite their differences, for both Momoko and Naoki, trusting that the future would resemble the past precluded them from taking initiative. Matsumoto's celebration of chance connections as a resource for the future appears simultaneously naïve and pragmatic. The Japanese child welfare system, in its current incarnation, systematically creates structures of experience in which radical contingency offers the most dependable opportunity for action. This is a situation that most people, empiricists that we are, would find untenable, and requires real effort and indeed suffering to transcend.

Interlude

MATSUMOTO'S FAMILY DIAGRAMS

Matsumoto Taichi used a specific documentation technique when he was taking notes or thinking things out: mind mapping. At the start of our interview, when I asked him to visually document his family, he produced two parallel images: a diagram that looked like a fairly normative genealogy (fig. 12), with circles above the

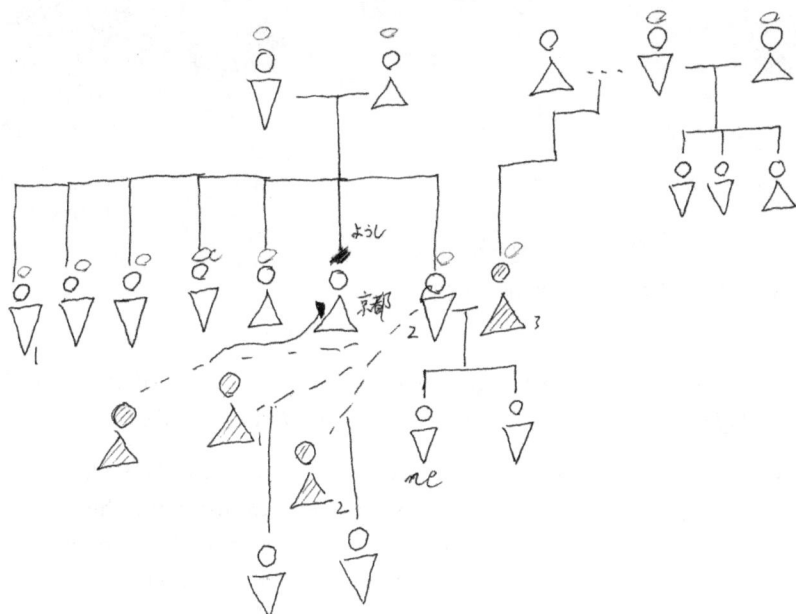

FIGURE 12. Matsumoto's family diagram.

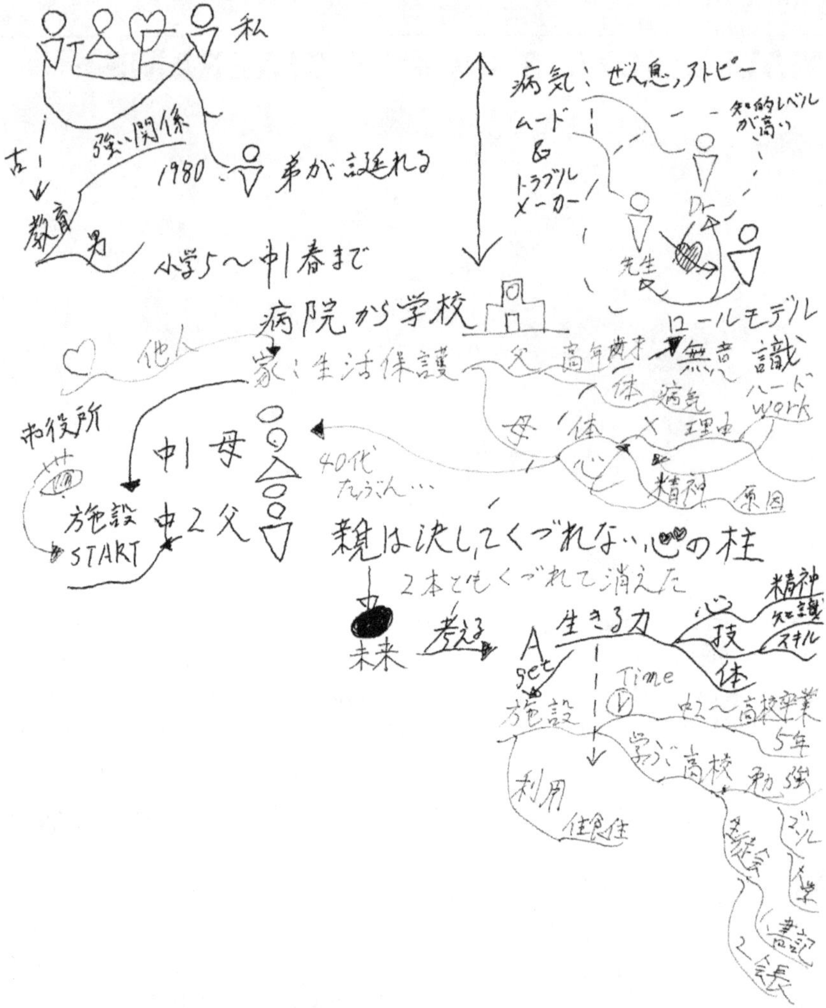

FIGURE 13. Matsumoto's mind map.

heads of people who were no longer living, and an image (fig. 13) that tracked the content of our interview and the progression of time through his life.

- Matsumoto (私) documents his birth with a heart to signify not love between his parents but rather the connection (en) that linked him to them. A curved line connects him to his father to mark their strong bond.
- A vertical arrow tracks the status of Matsumoto's childhood ailments (asthma and eczema) and his relationships with key role models, a teacher and a doctor.

- He had lived in the hospital and commuted from there to school, and writes, "public assistance" to indicate his family's welfare benefits. Wavy lines extending to the right point to the causes of his parents' ill health.
- An eye indicates the evaluative gaze of city hall: the welfare officers who decided he and his brother should be placed in a child welfare institution.
- Matsumoto's parents' deaths are indicated by the figures with angel halos. "Parents are unbreakable support pillars for [my] spirit," he wrote, inserting small hearts into the character for "spirit" or "heart" (*kokoro*).
- Their deaths prompted the emergence of his hungry spirit as he strategized how to acquire the power to live (*ikiru chikara*).

KNOWLEDGE AND NARRATION

The colored pencil box bore a white paper label, the kind used to mark children's belongings in elementary school. Written over smudged characters was the name Fujisaki Nozomi. The name that had previously been erased was Ōta Nozomi. Nozomi had had other names in the past: Ebara Nozomi, and before that, Mori Nozomi, which was the name on her birth certificate. Ōta, Ebara, and Mori were all names of strangers. At the time of writing, this young woman goes by Ōta Nozomi, the legal name on her family registry.

When I met her in 2009, Nozomi was in her early twenties and lived at home with her parents, Fujisaki Hiroko and Eiji (see interlude, "Genealogical Returns").[1] Hiroko and Eiji were technically Nozomi's foster parents, who had taken care of her on weekends since she was three and then raised her as a daughter since she was six. She referred to them as Mom (*okāsan*) and Dad (*otōsan*). Nozomi had no memory of her biological mother, and she had lived in a baby home and then a child welfare institution before being placed with the Fujisaki family. Between moving in with them at age six and entering college, Nozomi had gone by their last name, even though it was not her legal name. Ōta was the family name of the biological mother Nozomi had never met and the name Nozomi had to use for official documents and processes like school registration.

The colored pencil box with its smeared, overwritten label; a family registry and a birth certificate documenting different names; university transcripts and child welfare case files. For Nozomi, these material instantiations of a core aspect of her identity—her name—reflected both an odd mutability and a strangely underdetermined quality because their referents were unclear. What did the fact of these name changes point to, whose names were they, and what sort of context did these create for Nozomi's own identity? Although she had memories from her early life in the institutions, there were many things she could not recall and many things she could not forget because she had never known them.

Research on early childhood memory—particularly childhood experiences before age four, a period Freud described as characterized by "infantile amnesia"— highlights how children create a sense of autobiographical memory through iterative discussion with parents and other family members, who "scaffold" the child's understanding of event and time (Edwards and Middleton 1988; Nelson and Fivush 2000; Rose 2012). Cognitive psychologists and others studying memory show that individual memory does not live within the mind of an individual; human memory "incorporates external resources" like places and material objects as a sort of archive that indexes certain events and emotions (Harris et al. 2008; Sutton 2008; Barnier 2010; Sutton et al. 2010). Physical spaces, photographs, documents like birth certificates, even technologies such as smartphones, like the people around us, are sources of information, confirmation, and contestation when it comes to remembering personal pasts (Barnier 2010; Brown and Reavey 2014).[2] In this sense, individual memory bears many similarities to collective memory in that both are collaboratively created, depend on differential power structures that enable certain sorts of memorialization practices over others, and rely on material and discursive artifacts and practices to be taken as legitimate indices of the past (Halbwachs 1992; French 2012). Scholars of narrative and memory explore the processes by which children learn to maintain a sense of themselves over time, but this research almost universally assumes ideal-typical family relationships, dense social ties, and the maintenance of personal documents like photograph albums as this scaffold (Cook-Cottone and Beck 2007).

What happens to people's understanding of their own past and their current selves when these multifarious scaffolds are absent or inconsistent and when either basic facts about the past are unavailable or the context for them is unclear? Cases in which these resources are absent, unavailable, or underdetermined invite us to consider the stakes of certain types of knowledge for identity, selfhood, and experience. Stories from those who were raised in the Japanese child welfare system, like child welfare systems elsewhere, force us to question common assumptions about the ways we make memory, the preconditions for memory, and the status of memory in constituting a sense of self. In this chapter, I bring together two very different types of accounts from people who grew up in the Japanese child welfare system—that of Ōta Nozomi, and a man I call Edward—with discussion of a child welfare practice that is intended to ameliorate these gaps and fissures of self-knowledge. This child welfare initiative,

Life Story Work, highlights how documentation practices impact experiences of temporality and personal identity.

In a cultural context that privileges knowledge about biological relationships, a lack of such knowledge is rendered pathological.[3] We should consider how empirical knowledge of biological family is only one way of knowing truth about personal pasts, but it is the way that is most often held up as valuable, indeed as a right, in the child welfare context. Within this cultural framework, the absence of such knowledge is often experienced as deep existential lack. Yet cultural discourses surrounding identity must not necessarily center knowledge of genetic relatedness, or roots, as the most valuable form of ontological truth. This particular configuration linking certain sorts of knowledge practices with certain understandings of identity are, like all cultural practices, contingent. This chapter centers the very real experiences that link epistemological projects of knowledge gathering and creation to certain kinds of ontologies, ways of being, and selves.

What's in a Name

Pierre Bourdieu's essay "The Biographical Illusion" focuses on the proper name as a tool that maintains the artifice of unitary personhood, an anchor for the ever-moving target that is a person's evolving sense of self over time.[4] The name is one technique we use, he argues, to naturalize the idea that people have individual life histories that an anthropologist or sociologist could collect. Bourdieu writes, "The proper name is the visible affirmation of the identity of its bearer across time and social space, the basis of the unity of one's successive manifestations, and of the socially accepted possibilities of integrating these manifestations in official records, curriculum vitae, *cursus honorum*, police record, obituary, or biography, which constitute life as a finite sum through the verdict given in a temporary or final reckoning. . . . [It is] indifferent to circumstances and to individual accidents, amidst shifting biological and social realities" (2000, 300). If the proper name is *support* and maybe even *substance* of social identity, "indifferent to circumstances," as Bourdieu proposes, Ōta Nozomi's ever-changing social designation should give us pause.

I had known Nozomi well for five years before I interviewed her. Her family was one that I became closest to during my initial fieldwork, from 2009 to 2010, and I often spent the night at their house, sometimes sharing a room with Nozomi. That comfortable intimacy made it difficult for me to propose an interview. I hesitated to put myself in a position to know things about Nozomi that her parents continually wondered, concerns they had confided during my interviews with them. I had tentatively suggested an interview with her before leaving Japan in 2010, but she gently demurred. During a visit in 2014, however, she said she thought she could do it. Things had changed. Most significantly, she had found out that her biological mother had died (without Nozomi having ever met her), and she had for the first time been in contact with her biological mother's kin. Unlike her two siblings growing up (both also foster children of Fujisaki Hiroko and Eiji, none of them genetic siblings), Nozomi had been the one child who had not known anything about her family of origin. In contrast to her brother's caseworker, who made regular appointments to talk to him, Nozomi's caseworker was rarely in touch. The fact that Nozomi had no known kin was one reason Hiroko and Eiji had eventually asked whether she would like to be adopted, but she said no.

In the following discussion of our interview, I focus on two points: Nozomi's understanding of her family name and the reasons why she had declined to be adopted by the Fujisaki family. Her account sheds light on the ways a lack of knowledge about the past, specifically biological kin, can indelibly shape the present and future in a context like Japan where genetic roots are perceived as the ultimate form of truth about self.

Nozomi had started going by Hiroko and Eiji's family name after joining their household, and I brought this up early in our conversation.

"You started going by Fujisaki, right?"

"Yeah," Nozomi replied. "But at the institution, my name kept changing anyhow."

"Really?"

"Uh hmm, like when my mom . . ." Nozomi trailed off. "First it was Mori Nozomi. Then Ebara Nozomi in preschool. Then Ōta Nozomi when I started elementary school. When I went to the Fujisakis, I became Fujisaki Nozomi. So you know, I didn't feel any sense of discomfort [iwakan] [when I started using the Fujisaki name]."

"So this was marriage, divorce, remarriage . . .?"

"I have no idea, but I guess I was like, 'Huh, it changed again.' It changed all the time. All the things I owned, I had to have my name written over and over again." Given that all personal items are labeled in a child welfare institution, this relabeling must have been a significant project.

"Hmm, I wonder why."

Nozomi replied briskly in a stage whisper, as though to indicate that there was no use speculating: "Dunno [wakannai]. But if I wanted to ask at the child guidance center, I suppose I could."

"If you wanted to . . .?"

"But I'm scared and I can't ask [demo kowakute kikenai] . . .?"

Nozomi had the feeling that only bad memories had been documented. Repeated name changes pointed to stigmatized practices of divorce, at the very least (Alexy 2020, 120).

Later, I asked her if she had ever wanted to meet her biological mother. "No way," Nozomi replied. "Not once. And my name kept changing, too."

"Divorce, remarriage, divorce, remarriage . . ."

"Probably. But I don't know."

I suggested that even though she had never met her biological mother, as an unmarried person she would still be entered into the Ōta family registry. I wondered out loud who Ōta was. Nozomi explained that it was her biological mother's unmarried name, which is also the name on her biological grandmother's and mother's graves. This was even though the family name on Nozomi's birth certificate was Mori. "It's like, huh, you can *do* that kind of thing?" she said, referencing her biological mother's peripatetic movement between family registries with Nozomi dragged along in the wake.

Despite Nozomi's repeated insistence that she had no sense of discomfort (iwakan) about the repeated name changes, she turned to this fact to explain why she had had no interest in meeting her biological mother, someone who would apparently do what Nozomi perceived as a somewhat shady practice of documenting her daughter differently in different moments of bureaucratic reckoning. Material objects like items Nozomi owned, as well as an entire span of official documents, bore traces that made clear how little Nozomi could count on even this most basic element of identity to be either support or substance of her social personhood (Bourdieu 2000, 300). These name changes, these facts about her past, were underdetermined indications of something she didn't even care to speculate about. It was too uncomfortable to imagine asking for information about this history because one never knew what sort of unsavory past events these names might index.

Later in our conversation, Nozomi told me something I had already heard from her parents: that they had asked if she would like to be adopted, but she had declined. "It's not like I was waiting for my biological mother to come and get me. But you know, you meet, you resolve your feelings. . . . Anyhow, I'm not going to be adopted. 'Ōta' is fine. Plus, I might get married sooner or later, so what's the point?" Nozomi was also waiting to hear back from her biological mother's older sister, whom she had met once and who had promised to set up a meeting with her mother's younger sister. These were important, as yet undetermined events on Nozomi's horizon. Regarding a potential adoption, Nozomi said, "I haven't processed my own feelings yet. I need to meet my aunt's younger sister—my mother's younger sister. And I need to ask them things, and maybe at that point I will want to be adopted, or maybe not, I don't know. But it's like, once I *know* the

Ōta family, then I can move on? Somehow to throw them away without knowing anything about them, it's like a waste, it's sad or something. My mother went
out of her way to choose the name Ōta. . . . Precisely because my mom is dead it
feels important to figure this out for myself before moving on to the next thing."

I asked what an adoption might mean to Nozomi. "It's something that *I* would
get to decide, and I want to decide carefully," she replied. "When my name kept
changing, that was something that my parent just decided, and basically I didn't
care, you know, but this is something I can decide for myself." She knew adoption
would make Hiroko and Eiji happy and would probably even make herself happy.
But this opportunity to make the decision or not seemed worth lingering on.

Nozomi turned to one point that she had long wondered about. For three
years, between ages three and six, she had lived during the week at a child welfare
institution and went to the Fujisaki household only on weekends, a type of foster relationship designated as *three-day fostering* in Japan. This arrangement was
because her biological mother would not consent for her to be fostered long-term
or adopted. The child guidance center must have finally received consent because
in the fall of her sixth year, Nozomi was transferred from the institution to the
Fujisaki household full-time. Nozomi never knew why her biological mother had
opposed family-based foster placement.

"That's what I would like to know," Nozomi told me. "It's not like I wanted her
to come and get me, I just would like to ask what sort of feeling or expectation
she had"—some kind of hope, perhaps, that prevented her from wanting Nozomi
to be put in full-time family-based care.

In fact, there was also the matter of Nozomi's given name, which meant "hope."
What did it mean that her biological mother had chosen a name loaded with such
positive and future-oriented affect?[5]

It would have been emotionally difficult to meet her mother, should she ever
have had the opportunity, if she had been adopted into another family registry.
Laughing, Nozomi said, "It's like, I'm not your daughter, but I'm your daughter,
actually I guess I'm not your daughter."

Suddenly, Nozomi suggested that maybe her mother had been waiting to meet
the right partner, after which she could take care of Nozomi again. "It's something
I just thought of, not something I've been thinking all this time," she asserted, to
forestall any assumptions I might make. "But I don't have a clue [*wakaranai*]. I
don't know [*shiranai*]." She said this crisply. Closing this part of our conversation,
she repeated, "Well, whatever. I have no idea anyhow [*wakannai shi*]."

The limits of Nozomi's knowledge, the tension between her desire to speculate and her frustration with the impossibility of confirming these speculations,
were poignantly evident. Insisting that it was fruitless to wonder, she wondered
nonetheless. Consistently powerless as a child to choose her own family affilia-

tion, she maintained that she hadn't cared about her family name changing until now, when she could make the decision herself. She knew it might be a happy thing—both for her parents and for her—to become part of the Fujisaki family. But until she knew more about the Ōta family, she could not imagine giving up that affiliation and moving on.

Life Story Work in (Japanese) Practice

Parts of my memory are just missing. I must somehow gather information about the time before I was old enough to remember anything, to make connections between the time I was born and my present self (Yamamoto et al. 2015, 3).

It is with this quotation that Hirata Shūzō, one of the editors of the first detailed manual on conducting Life Story Work in Japanese (published in 2015), begins the book's preface. For Hirata, a researcher focusing on Life Story Work (LSW), these words exemplified the necessity of a child welfare mechanism to ensure that children were able to connect the dots between periods of time in their lives. Being unable to do so, in his observation, was the root of much of the anxiety and loneliness suffered by young people raised in the child welfare system—people who did not have family members to collectively document their childhood, who did not own photographs or drawings that documented periods of their life. For these people—like Ōta Nozomi—periods of time in their lives were simply missing.

The central element of LSW is the collection of specific pieces of information about a child's life, which would be entered into a book (the Life Story Book) for the child to keep. Child welfare workers describe LSW as an important aspect of subjectivity, a claim based on the assumption that people have trouble remembering who they are and where they came from if they have no one with whom to remember. Documented memory takes ontological and epistemological priority when a person has no long-term caregivers to help remember, and keep remembering, together and over time.

In 2024, over 2,300 Japanese infants and toddlers were cared for in baby homes (institutions for children up to age two), many of whom would be transferred to institutions for older children, as was the case with Nozomi. Approximately one-third of children living in family-based foster care and one-quarter of children living in institutional care had become wards of the state before the age of three years old (Yamamoto et al. 2015, 11–12; MHLW 2022, 257). Consider that young children are initially separated from biological parents and family members, then potentially placed in multiple institutional and/or family-based foster care settings; approximately 70 percent of children in family-based foster care and 20 percent of children in institutional care placements have no contact with biological family members (Yamamoto et al. 2015, 12; Kodomo kateichō 2024, 44). Consider, too, that institutional caregivers have a high level of turnover, such that a staff member who has worked at an institution for over three years is often referred to as a "veteran" (Goodman 2000). Even the majority of case-workers rotate every few years, as government employees are usually required to change practice fields and locations multiple times during their tenure. Japanese social welfare caseworkers tend to have massive caseloads, and many of them do not make regular contact with children. While files are kept for children at the child guidance center overseeing their case, children may not know that they can request information regarding their families or the reasons they were put into care, or they may be afraid to ask, for fear of what they might find out. Nozomi's situation, then, was not unusual. The result is that children often do not have any single caregiver or caseworker who has known them for an extended period, particularly during their first few years, and many grow up without knowing basic information about their family's situation or their early lives. This might be experienced as an acute gap in a person's story of self.[6]

Life Story Work was introduced to Japan in the early 2000s by a group of social workers and researchers, inspired by its use in England. Beginning in the 1950s in Europe and the United States, social workers had begun creating Life Books for children who were placed in foster and adoptive care that documented basic information about their family histories. In the 1970s, this practice shifted to include a focus on ameliorating children's confusion regarding their out-of-home placements and was understood as a tool to help children develop narratives of their upbringing. Efforts to document basic facts about children's lives were rein-forced by new child welfare laws in England in 2002, which stated an objective to guarantee the provision of information to children about their backgrounds. Contemporary social work practice that engages these ideas is now generally referred to as Life Story Work or sometimes Memory Work, the material out-come of which would be a Life Story Book containing information, pictures, and drawings, ideally collaboratively created by a child and their caregiver(s). Some LSW, explicitly conducted for therapeutic purposes, is referred to as Life Story Therapy.

Although elements of LSW are required of social workers in England, and it is also commonly practiced in Australia, practitioners in other parts of the world implement it ad hoc, and social workers writing on the topic perceive it as an undertheorized and somewhat ill-defined social work tool. At base, LSW depends on an understanding of recordkeeping and documentation and making basic information easily accessible to children. In England, this is in the context of a system that does comprehensively maintain case files: English social welfare practice requires case files for children in the child welfare system to be maintained for one hundred years. In Japan, however, case files may be destroyed as early as five years after a child leaves care. This orientation toward child welfare recordkeeping is one of the factors that inspired the initial movement to institute LSW in Japan. However, LSW proponents feel there is a long way to go. A 2013 national survey of child welfare institutions and child guidance center caseworkers found that over 41 percent of institutions and over 61 percent of child guidance centers had never once implemented LSW, which the survey defined as "a trusted adult helping a child understand past events, topics related to their family, and to process emotions related to their upbringing" (Yamamoto et al. 2015, 14). In the Japanese government's 2021 careleaver survey, multiple individuals noted in the free entry section that they wanted this support (MUFG 2021, for example 75).

In the Japanese Life Story Work manual, Hirata Shūzō and Narahara Shinya outline five major characteristics of children in Japanese state care that motivate the use of LSW. The first and most basic characteristic, they argue, is that children in state care almost always have voids in the stories of their lives that they desperately want to fill. (From my own observations, this might be because staff members or even caseworkers don't know about children's backgrounds and thus don't speak to the children about them, or because staff members or caseworkers do know, but they are unsure how to tell the children difficult information about their pasts. In some cases the children's own parents have specified that they don't want the children told certain things.) The second characteristic of children in Japanese child welfare that Hirata and Narahara outline is that many children's life stories are characterized by confusion and fantasy—their own interpretations that they have created to make sense of knowledge voids. Hirata and Narahara write that children often think that they were bad or unlovable, and that is why they were removed from their families; they spin unrealistic fantasies regarding their parents; they believe that their foster parents are their birth parents. These fantasies are sometimes protective mechanisms, but other times they are harmful.[7] Third, children in the state care system have a tendency toward negative self-narratives and outlooks, a tendency that begins with the negative event of removal from their family and is reinforced by social stigma, a cycle that furthers the tendency for low self-esteem. Fourth, many of these children have life stories that are fragmented by trauma, a situation that makes it difficult for them to construct a coherent sense of themselves and their own history. Finally, Hirata and Narahara cite research on parent-child reminiscing and the ways that it reinforces a child's sense of shared history and teaches children to articulate their own memories as part of a life story; they point to the lack of such parental figures for most children in state care. They argue that for children removed from

families early in life, all children will have to deal with the first and fifth characteristic: gaps in their life narratives and difficulty filling these gaps because they
lack stable caregivers (Yamamoto et al. 2015, 131–132).

Publications on LSW guide caregivers on the three main steps of conducting
this work, which are designed to ameliorate the problems Hirata and Narahara
describe. First, caregivers are instructed to collect as much information about the
child's history as possible. The Japanese manual outlines the types of information
that should be gathered: biological parents' names, birthdates, and occupations;
the conditions of the child's birth, including any illnesses; places the family lived
and descriptions of the neighborhoods; and family medical history. Other things
to collect are documented accounts from the parents; a genogram or family tree;
photographs; and stories about the child from the parents or former caregivers
(Yamamoto et al. 2015, 37). Notably, one item mentioned multiple times in the
LSW manual is information on the origin of a child's name, a topic elementary
school aged children in Japan are often told to research for class assignments
(36). After gathering information, the caregiver is instructed to help the child
understand what has been discovered, with the objective that the child will be
able to reframe their own vague stories of the past and identify ways that negative
self-perceptions or patterns formed early in life tend to direct them in nonopti-
mal ways (Rose 2012, 30).[8] Finally, the caregiver is instructed to help the child
document these details of the past in a physical book, including photographs and
drawings created by the child, which can be kept between state care placements
and which the child can reference in the future.[9]

Given the sensitivity of this process, literature on LSW notes that there is the
potential for a child to be retraumatized. While many children in state care have
had pasts that are somehow traumatic, LSW proponents argue that the informa-
tion-gathering process helps children work through these experiences. Saimura
Mari (her real name), a social worker, professor, and researcher who contributed
to the 2015 Japanese LSW manual and has been heavily involved in advocating
children's right to know their past, emphasized to me in an interview that if you
do not know, recognize, and accept your past, that past will come "chasing after
you." For her, the potential benefits of the work outweigh the risks; LSW is not
intended to be therapy but is rather a social work tool to protect a child's best
interests, which she believes is the provision of information that is not otherwise
guaranteed by Japanese law (see also Yamamoto et al. 2015, 35, 56). The Japanese
LSW manual highlights concerns caregivers might have, specifically regarding
retraumatization or children acting out after learning disturbing information
about their past. But in Japan, there is often a dearth of professional training for
caregivers, short staffing in institutions, inaccessibility of overworked caseworkers, and shortages of mental health care for children in the child welfare system.

Thus, at the present time, there is little a practitioner can do to ameliorate these very real concerns. They must simply trust the conviction that children should be provided information and the possibility to process emotions regarding their past.

Tokunaga Shōko (her real name) worked for ten years as a residential staff member at two different institutions for preteen boys with extreme behavioral problems. She has written extensively on Life Story Work, and she is one of the editors of and contributors to the Japanese LSW manual. Shōko notes that there is simply not enough capacity to practice LSW in Japanese child welfare institutions in the ways that it is practiced in England and Australia (Tokunaga 2011). Rather than the richly detailed protocol common in England, Shōko and her collaborators on the LSW manual suggest two potential models: LSW conducted as part of daily life within institutional, foster, and adoptive care settings, and LSW conducted with a trained therapist in therapeutic sessions. The former model is the sort that she herself practiced as a residential institutional caregiver.

"You have to catch the sign," Shōko told me. When children seem to want to know something about their past, a caregiver should follow up and answer the child's questions as fully as possible, which might require a phone call to the child guidance center or a visit with the child to the child's former institution.[10] If a child was acting out, Shōko tried to help the child make connections between their current (often exaggerated) response to a stressor and a past moment of having experienced something that could explain their current behavior. For instance, perhaps the child vividly remembered being told that they were bad and worthless, a framework that shaped the child's self-perception and actions. Her goal was to help a child understand why they were responding in a certain way, in order to be able to change their self-perception and reactions to be more appropriate or constructive. Shōko's professional focus on clinical approaches to delinquency led her to understand that children may be both victims and perpetrators: in order to escape the negative cycle, they must realize the connections between having experienced maltreatment and their own behavior. She framed this process as the explicitly temporal project of "keeping the past in the past" (*kako wa kako no mono*) (Tokunaga 2011, 52). Thus the type of LSW that Shōko advocated can be understood as a kind of everyday therapy—not psychotherapy and not narrative therapy but a collaborative sharing of information and building of understanding between child and caregiver in the context of daily life.

The Self Posited by Life Story Work

Life Story Work is not often considered alongside narrative theory or even narrative therapy. While narrative therapy is understood as focused on a patient's inner world, LSW does something rather different: it is oriented around collecting social facts (*shakaiteki genjitsu*). Although in the LSW manual Hirata and Narahara propose that LSW should be understood as a specific type of narrative therapy for children in state care, I suggest that the contrast between the two modalities provides insight about the normative assumptions generally made regarding personal history and selfhood.

Anthropologists and philosophers have generally approached narrative as an "activity [that] provides tellers with an opportunity to impose order on otherwise disconnected events, and to create continuity between past, present, and imagined worlds" (Ochs and Capps 1996, 19). Elinor Ochs and Lisa Capps note the importance of the temporal dimension of narrativization, where coherency and chronological sequence become important; for example, post-traumatic stress disorder is often understood as a problem of narrativizing and incorporation into "one's life story" (30).

Like theories of narrative in general, narrative therapy is oriented toward a person's inner state as a meaning-making project, often with the goal of putting singular events into life context. As the Narrative Therapy Centre of Toronto website puts it, "Narrative therapy is a collaborative and non-pathologizing approach to counselling and community work which centres people as the *experts of their own lives*" (italics added).[11] From a medical anthropological perspective, the concept of illness narratives connects to this orientation toward storytelling and narrativization as a therapeutic process of meaning making. As Arthur Kleinman writes,

> Patients order their experience of illness—what it means to them and to significant others—as personal narratives. The illness narrative is a story the patient tells, and significant others retell, to give coherence to the distinctive events and long-term course of suffering. The plot lines, core metaphors, and rhetorical devices that structure the illness narrative are drawn from cultural and personal models for arranging experiences in meaningful ways and for effectively communicating those meanings. Over the long course of chronic disorder, these model texts shape and even create experience. The personal narrative does not merely reflect illness experience, but rather it contributes to the experience of symptoms and suffering (1989, 49).

Cheryl Mattingly's (1991, 1994, 1998) studies of "narrative emplotment" among physical therapists elaborate the ways therapists and patients collaboratively build narratives that trace a trajectory for the patient, helping patients to understand often traumatic interruptions in the context of their lives, such as injury or illness, and to see themselves on a healing path. These narratives shape, rather than mirror, the patient's experience and help patients see life interruptions as part of a larger process rather than, as one of Kleinman's interlocutors put it, "one damned thing after another" (Kleinman 1989, 124).

These brief examples highlight several important common orientations to narrative therapy in Western contexts: narratives are created collaboratively; there is a powerful feedback loop between narration and experience, such that both inform and shape each other; and narrative is seen as a central way that people understand themselves and particular events in a broader life context. Theorists of narrative do not believe these are unmediated representations of some real self. The fact that narratives emerge through hard interpersonal labor and within certain cultural logics of intelligibility are the reasons, after all, that Pierre Bourdieu (2000) called the "life history" a "biographical illusion." As Ochs and Capps succinctly write, "Lives are the pasts we tell ourselves" (1996, 21).

If a basic assumption in narrative theory is that people use narrative to create stories out of distinctive events, the basic assumption in LSW is that the child does not even have knowledge of such events. In fact, one might argue—in contrast to the description of narrative therapy above—that these children are not experts in their own lives at all. Life Story Work, particularly the more limited, pragmatic form proposed for Japanese institutional care, is intended to outline life facts, the bare bones of the context for identity that narrative therapy takes for granted. We might understand this tension using a framework offered by cognitive psychology. Narrative makes use of autobiographical memory, defined as "declarative, explicit memory for specific points in the past, recalled from the unique perspective of the self in relation to others" (Nelson and Fivush 2004, 488; Bietti et al. 2014). Life Story Work, however, engages in the collection of semantic knowledge about specific facts: where one was born, what one's father's name was. Semantic knowledge is understood explicitly as the context for declarative or autobiographical memory. According to researchers who support the theory of memory creation as collaborative, a second important context for autobiographical memory is a person's family (or others with long-term relationships to the child), who contribute to a child's own narrativization of the past and take part in "socially distributed remembering" (Hirst et al. 1997; Pasupathi 2001; Fivush 2008; Sutton et al. 2010). Even children who were too young to remember an event might incorporate that event into their own story of self; in conversation about it with intimate others, they may learn "about remembering without actually having to remember" (Edwards and Middleton 1988, 22). Objects, like photographs and official documents, are part of this past interpersonal context (Reavey and Brown 2009; Barnier 2010; Sutton et al. 2010). Life Story Work, thus, addresses a situation in which children have neither semantic context for their own sense of self nor the social and material context understood so widely to be necessary in the creation of autobiographical memory.

Complicating this interpretation further, the life facts documented in a Life Story Book are expressions of situated and contingent knowledge (Haraway 1988). Richard Rose, a social work scholar and child trauma specialist and author of key texts that the Japanese LSW manual is based on, highlights the contingency of perceived personal history. Documented facts might vary dramatically depending on who wrote a case file or who helped a child assemble their Life Story Book. Rose writes, "What do we know about ourselves that is fact? We may say that we know when we were born. How? Well, we have a birth certificate with a date on it. We may say we know who our father is. How? 'Well, I was told he is,' 'He looks like me,' and 'He is in all my photographs when I was little.' Birth certificates are only as reliable as the person who completes the paperwork; I have known plenty of occasions when the birth record has proved to be inaccurate, both in name and date" (2012, 120). And yet despite explicit awareness that these facts may not actually be unmitigated expressions of truth, Rose emphasizes throughout that "we are a collection of stories, they are what defines us" (148). Rose's de-emphasis on veracity stems from his own experience as a social worker attempting to document truths that turned out to be all too specific to his own positionality. He also writes with frustration of children whose beliefs are not recognized as truth by their caregivers (119).[12] Rose thus highlights the interplay between facts and the stories we tell about ourselves, which define us. These facts, true or false, are the context for the more elaborate narratives that people create—the connections "*between the time I was born and my present self*," in the quotation above. Of course the fluidity of fact is not a condition unique to children in state care. However, one might argue that without an interpersonally rich context to deliberate and discuss these facts, the stark documentation in a Life Story Book takes on oversized epistemological weight.

This view of veracity as being situational and constructed is very much in line with constructivist theories of memory, many rooted in the scholarship of Frederick Bartlett, who wrote in the early and middle twentieth century. Although Bartlett became widely relevant only in the 1970s and '80s, his work is now requisite citation for memory scholars. In her history of theories of memory, Alison Winter traces two main views: understandings of memory as literal repetitions of past events, which still persists in some camps, and the view that memory is constructed based on current sensibilities about the self, in which gaps are filled in imaginatively according to a holistic sense of one's past experiences and habitual reactions to them, which Bartlett calls "schema" or "schemata" (Bartlett 1932; Winter 2012).[13] Bartlett's theory "brings remembering into line with imagining" (Bartlett 1932, 214) such that recollection and perception are deeply intertwined mental processes (Winter 2012, 199).

Bartlett would be unsurprised to know that one of the main challenges faced by caregivers in the Japanese child welfare system is that in the absence of facts regarding their families and (inter)personal histories, children tend to imagine content to fill the gaps in their knowledge. In an interview, Tokunaga Shōko, the careworker and LSW scholar mentioned above, described LSW as helping a child "give up the fantasy" of an imagined past. She explained with a chuckle, "In English they say, 'My mom is in prison, not a princess.' If you believe that your mother is a princess, but she doesn't come to see you for three years—then you are waiting for her to come pick you up to the castle, to be raised as a princess. Tomorrow, maybe, or maybe in twenty years. You wait, because you don't know. But Life Story Work helps the child gain realistic ideas about family."[14] Shōko went on to describe her own research on LSW. Her interviewees noted that "giving up fantasies was important for them to engage with new people, attach with new people—because otherwise they keep looking to their past. . . . So yeah, I think giving up—"

Then Shōko interrupted herself. She had looked up the meaning of the Chinese character used in the Japanese verb "to give up" (*akirameru*) and discovered that the verb root means "to make clear" (*akiraka ni suru*). "Can you believe that?" Shōko exclaimed. "It's exactly what I mean [about LSW]."

For Shōko, this discovery solidified her understanding that "unless something is clear, you can't give it up." The ways that constructivists understand memory to work, in which people fill in knowledge gaps with their own interpretations or fantasies, reinforce the power of this "making clear to give up" process and illuminate some of the stakes of the gaps in knowledge that characterize the lives of children in state care.

With the concept of making clear to give up, we return full circle to Nozomi's account. Without clarity surrounding her biological family, she was unwilling to give up the potential of a connection, to move on in a direction that she knew was likely to bring her happiness. This, then, brought her suffering that must be understood in the specific social context of Japan, in which knowledge of biogenetic roots is held as a baseline for self-knowledge and understanding. This lack of knowledge then becomes aberrant, a problem to be addressed through social work or psychological interventions.

Uncanny Mnemonics

This chapter has highlighted the difficulty of autobiographical knowledge and narrative construction in the context of missing information or when documented information (like repeatedly changing last names) bears ambiguous, possibly incorrect, and potentially disturbing meaning. I close with a final example of the difficulties of knowing in a situation where it is unclear whether one can trust one's own memories or deduce the meaning of the material and embodied traces of past events.

On my left leg, there are six straight burn marks.[15]

When I bend my knee, these marks connect and become three. Like marks made from being touched with burning hot metal chopsticks, these three burn lines have always caused me concern.

Thus begins section 10—labeled "Mother"—of "Edward's Memory Diary," an account posted on a website that he created for alumni of Japanese child welfare institutions like himself.[16] Edward is the Christian name of the Japanese man whose story the diary documents. I will refer to him as Edward throughout, although I know him in person by his Japanese birth name.[17]

In elementary school, I was nicknamed "mysterious burn guy." They really named me well.

Why those burns were there, I didn't know.

At the child welfare institution, even when I asked the staff members, they said, "I don't know." One time when I was visiting with family, I tried asking my uncle. "There's no reason Uncle would know a thing like that!" he said in an angry voice, and the topic ended there.

Even now that I'm an adult, I still don't know the cause.

For Edward, the uncanny traces of long-ago burns point to some old act of violence, perpetrated by someone not consciously remembered but once presumably known by Edward and perhaps others. His scars materialize both social relationships and their absence.

Studies of somatization, and particularly bodily expressions of traumatic memory, focus on the body proper as keeper, protector, and involuntary hoarder of past experience, in which specific events are understood as catalysts for later symptoms. For instance, in Bessel van der Kolk's canonical article in psychiatry, "The Body Keeps the Score" (1994) (and later book of the same title), van der Kolk describes the physiobiology that makes the body an important site of attention for clinical psychiatrists. Van der Kolk and others have suggested the necessity of developing diagnostic criteria for developmental trauma that occurs over a sustained period of time, and particularly in childhood, in contrast to post-traumatic stress disorder (PTSD), which implies a single traumatic episode. Developmental trauma resembles Allan Young's theorizing of PTSD as a "disease of time": its "distinctive pathology is that it permits the past (memory) to relive itself in the present, in the form of intrusive images and thoughts and in the patient's compulsion to replay old events" (Young 1995, 7).

This complex of symptoms is understood to result from what Young denotes the "temporal-causal relation" between a past etiological event and present symptoms. These symptoms themselves, in the case of flashbacks, may be the experience of the past in the present. Flashbacks, then, enfold time upon itself, layering cause and symptom. As Allison Crawford points out, however, only some connections between bodily experience and a past moment of trauma might be clearly indexically related: for instance, the recollection of the smell of smoke in the case that the trauma was a fire. Other times, symptoms "bear no clear relationship to the event." Either way, symptoms "can make people feel haunted by something out of their control or comprehension" (Crawford 2010, 707).[18] Therapeutic interventions often involve counseling that assists sufferers in processing traumatic events so that they can be consciously recalled but no longer intrude upon daily life. But what happens when a trauma cannot be named, labeled, recognized, and ascribed meaning? What happens when the absence of social ties becomes an embodied source of suffering?

Edward's mysterious scars were traces of a past event that could not be recalled and refer to a now unknown past relationship. Edward brings up the topic of his scars at the beginning of the section where he introduces his mother, whose existence he learned of when he was in first grade. In his online diary, Edward writes (as quoted above), *Even now that I'm an adult, I still don't know the cause.*

He continues: *One time, my friends and I were comparing the things we were afraid of. "Ghosts." "Teacher." "Dogs." Suddenly I chimed in with complete confidence. "The most scary thing is not knowing what you yourself are doing."*

He follows this statement with a description of how one day he was taken from his child welfare institution to meet his mother for the first time. She lived in a hospital with chains and bars securing the doors. When he entered her room, she approached to hug him but he stood there stiffly. *For some reason, I was scared of my mother.* The structure of his documentary practice—the section heading "Mother," the introduction of his mysterious scars, his discussion of his fear of insanity, and the description of his own embodied fear when meeting his mother—intimates a causal connection between his unknowable scars and the woman attempting to hug him, enacting a suspicion he is reticent to elaborate, that cannot be confirmed or denied by anyone he knows. It is a dual knowing and not-knowing, a "truth, in its delayed appearance and its belated address, [that] cannot be linked only to what is *known*, but also to what remains *unknown* in our very actions and our language" (Caruth 1996, 4, italics added). Even as Edward's suspicions and what he does know give structure to his narrative of his scars, their cause is ultimately unknowable. His scars embody the silences and gaps in knowledge in his own history.

Like a Life Story Book of his own richly narrativized (and sole-authored) creation, Edward's online memory diary proceeds chronologically, except in one important aspect. Edward's fifteenth section, titled "SA," chronicles two years of sexual abuse from the head priest affiliated with Edward's Catholic child welfare institution. He closes this section with this statement: *But the strange thing was, I completely forgot all of this. Until 23 years later, when my own child was born.* True to linear narrative conventions, Edward chronologically incorporates his retrospective memories of abuse within the account of his time at the child welfare institution. Then, mirroring the detemporalized nature of his actual memory, the following section—entitled "Flashback"—transports readers to Edward's midlife.

After aging out of the child welfare institution, Edward had gotten married and had a son. Every night, he bathed the boy. One evening, as Edward and his one-year-old son were playfully flinging bubbles at each other, his wife called into the room, saying that she had taken the boy for a checkup and the public health nurse had told her to make sure the boy's genitals were thoroughly washed.

I reached out my hand to wash my son's penis.

And right before my eyes, scenes from 23 years before suddenly expanded in front of me. The priest's body, my own emotions at the time, holding that *in my hand, it was all brought back.*

I cried out.

In a single moment, I remembered it all. The things at the time that I hadn't had the knowledge to understand, now I clearly understood, I knew what had happened to me.

I suddenly began to weep.

That I had had such a past . . . !

. . . It seemed incredible that I had forgotten a thing like that.

Edward's days became suffused with the reexperience of scenes from that past. His fevered library research gave him the label of sexual abuse for what had happened to him. At the same time, he writes, after that day in the bathtub, *It was as though I had been split in half. I still felt intense love for my child, and at the same time, I was consumed by jealousy for him, for I had never been loved in the way that I loved him.*

Edward felt that he was going insane.

And yet Edward's sensation of being split in half, loving his son and jealous of his son for his own love, was also mediated by intensely embodied sensations of oneness with his son. When he held his son close, their heartbeats would synchronize. When his son tripped on the playground and scraped his knee, Edward himself felt intense pain in his own knee. If Edward's body had heretofore "kept the score" of old traumas, his body was also the medium through which he experienced the social relationship that (literally) mattered most.

The doubleness that haunted Edward's relationship with his son—where his son was self but also other, where Edward simultaneously loved his son and was jealous of his son for being loved—mirrors the doubleness of Edward's sense of time. It took Edward years to learn to ride the waves of flashbacks that still occasionally came. Reading scientific and popular literature on trauma helped him process his own memories without the help of counseling or medication. Edward's son is now a young man, and Edward is active in advocating for child welfare institutions without violence. However, these engagements continue to bring him face to face with this double self of the past-present. Spending time with other people who were raised in child welfare institutions can prompt sudden flashbacks. Merely hearing about what he calls "good institutions"—child welfare institutions supposedly without violence—or seeing a child who appears happily situated in a foster or adoptive home can engulf him in anger and sorrow. If these children are happy, why aren't *all* children happy? If these children are cared for, why wasn't *he* cared for? Personal loss and jealousy press hard against Edward's own role as the advocate and father he never had.

Edward used a bodily metaphor to explain how a lack of caregiver has shaped his sense of time. "If you have a long history with someone," Edward told me, "that history leads you to think that in the future there will be some continuity." This is the case whether or not these are relationships of kindness or abuse. But for children cared for by institutional staff who come and go, there are few continuous, durable interpersonal relationships. Not knowing whether a person will be there in the future—tomorrow, or next year—means that a child lacks, Edward told me, a sense of their *own* future.

While Edward engages with psychoanalysis and theories of trauma to give a name to his flashbacks and pursues writing projects that narrativize and represent his past and present, his story also illustrates nonsemiotic and nonrepresentational ways of being in the world. Flashbacks may be references to a past event, but they are themselves not precisely representations—they are lived repetitions, events in and of themselves (Caruth 1996, 115). In these relivings, one can be both subject and object to oneself, what Maurice Merleau-Ponty has called "intertwining" (1968). In the words of William Mazzarella, Edward's is an "affective body" that "preserves the traces of past actions and encounters and brings them into the present as potentials" (2010, 292). A psychoanalytic perspective might assign stable-seeming meanings to Edward's experiences of sexual abuse and its aftermath, meanings that seem to be expressed and reified in Edward's writing project. However, the impossibility of assigning stable meanings to his scars and the open-ended and emergent bodily connections he felt with his son illustrate the multiple registers through which bodily experience articulates with intimate relationships.

Edward's narrations of embodied self are characterized by the temporalities of traumatic memory and the gaps and absences of his "being-in-the-world" (Csordas 1994), where embodied memories fold back on themselves, recursively bringing childhood pasts to bear in the present. His engagement with the materiality of his body contrasts with the project of Life Story Work, which encourages children in state care, moving between transitory caregivers, to document their pasts in Life Story Books, in a linearly normative and normalizing structure. Childhood pasts and adult presences are materialized in bodies and paper trails, in bureaucratic detritus like Nozomi's state documentation in the family registry of a stranger. While the Life Story Book project relies on linear recollections of a child's experiences to document who that child is for later reflection, Edward's story highlights the affective excesses of nonlinear and nonrepresentational embodiment, where both the presence and the absence of durable interpersonal ties live and are relived in the body. Neither Edward nor Nozomi are able to give up attachments to these opaquely known pasts because they lack the information that would make their pasts clear.

At Chestnut House, some children entered the institution with the most minimal of possessions. It is a lonely image, a child entering a new home with all their belongings bundled into one plastic sack. The accounts in this chapter explore the personal and interpersonal stakes of lacking information about one's past as well as the ways that objects that index the past—documents, belongings, bodies—may not do so transparently. This chapter has explored how memory is created and experienced through dispersed engagements with objects, bodies, and other people, a perspective that exemplifies the ways that social connection and disconnection are materially experienced, evidenced, and instantiated.

Despite its focus on documenting the past, the Life Story Book's utility is explicitly future-oriented, toward the maturing self that wants to remember the past in order to know who that self is. The project is oriented around a concept of the self as experiencing and remembering, rooted in empirical and temporalized events, that prioritizes a particular sort of knowing and, in turn, pathologizes a lack of this knowledge. The "self" evident in Life Story Work contrasts with other views of the self, particularly in Western contexts, as "a fiction constructed on personal memories" (Young 1997, 253; Bourdieu 2000; Desjarlais 1994). This contrast reminds us how contingent certain formulations of selfhood are, as they link particular ways of knowing with particular modes of being. The accounts in this chapter press back on assumptions of a self that exists in some stable form through the scaffolding of event knowledge.

When a child's caseworkers or caregivers gather information about a child's past, these are often not forms of knowledge that a child acquires from experience. This is, of course, the point. Life Story Work is intended to allow a child to incorporate into a narrative of self the information contained in the Life Story Book, both in the absence of personal, direct experience and in the absence of a consistent caregiver who can remember in dialogue with the child. Yet, if "we are our stories" (Rose 2012), the need for Life Story Work highlights the contingency of the basis for selfhood that many of us take for granted, a sort of selfhood normalized by Life Story Work.

Asymmetrical distributions of care are evidenced in narratives and in bodies. Life Story Work in child welfare prioritizes representational documentation in the absence of long-term caregivers. This project, compensation for presumed practices of dialogic memory making in normal families, reinscribes this normal family as a reality elsewhere, an ideal distant from the lives of the children using these books. While I am critical of the ways family is often unreflexively valorized within both Japanese and international child welfare, accounts like Nozomi's and Edward's highlight the intensely visceral longing many of my interlocutors felt for a family where they felt they fully belonged, a family that was safe, caring, and lasted over time.

In their article "Vital Memories," Steven Brown and Paula Reavey write, "If memory is considered as a distributed system . . . which encompasses both other people . . . and material artefacts (i.e. diaries, photographs), then accessibility becomes a collective project. This is especially the case where we have responsibilities for the memories of others" (2014, 332). Institutions play a role too, as they "recruit or take hold of individual and collective modes of remembering" (Brown and Reavey, 2014, 334).

What does it mean to have responsibility for the memories of others? I close by suggesting that we consider the individualized and psychologized perspectives of memory presented in this chapter as also part of a collective, communal memory system (Halbwachs 1992). How might we better take collective responsibility as part of a distributed relational system? This is a form of social obligation and good social care, with profound existential and ethical stakes.

Conclusion

Children in child welfare institutions still experience discrimination. I guess for people who themselves don't live in institutions, it's hard to understand institutionalized children. But I hope more people come to understand that children in institutions are simply children without parents by their side. I hope that [one day] they won't be assumed to be pitiable, that they are evaluated on equal terms. I pray that children in child welfare institutions will be able to live the same way as other children in the community and can come to be glad to have been born.

—Governmental careleaver survey, free entry: "What do you hope to communicate to the country and to the government?" (MUFG 2021, 112)

Child Welfare in the Worst of Times

Despite their diversity in form, child welfare systems across the world are too often poor at cultivating social networks for people who need them most. Japan's child welfare system, like many others, does not facilitate children developing and maintaining long-term relationships with caring others. This core problem—the rootlessness that many of my interlocutors identified—is encapsulated by a social media post by one of my research contacts who grew up in Japanese institutional care. In spare prose, he lamented how he never knows who to list as an emergency contact or a guarantor on job applications and apartment contracts. He was someone who emerged from the child welfare system with no one to count on.

Vastly different child welfare systems are too likely to produce common poor outcomes.[1] For instance, people who have experienced state care are disproportionately more likely to have lower educational attainment, poorer health, poorer employment opportunities, more involvement in criminal justice systems, mental health problems, homelessness, involvement in gangs and sex work, and suicidal tendencies (McCall and Groark 2015; Gypen et al. 2017; Nagano 2017; Nemtzov 2019; International Care Leavers Convention 2020). In Japan, family-based foster care is often celebratorily framed as a better alternative to dominant placements in institutional care. More data are needed to compare outcomes for youth from institutional versus family-based foster care in Japan, but my own ethnographic research foregrounds the finding that young people in state care benefit from long-term relationships with caregivers, which are often difficult to cultivate in an institution. Yet the North American system, in many ways opposite of Japan's, dependent on family-based foster care, small group homes, and adoption, produces substantially similar failures in social care.

The COVID-19 pandemic highlighted the vulnerabilities of the world's most underserved people. Current and former wards of the state—any state—are undeniably described by that category. Child welfare advocacy organizations conducted their own research during the pandemic, attempting to grasp its impact on their constituents. In what follows, I briefly discuss survey data collected by the International Foster Care Alliance (IFCA) Japan team, which is comprised of youth from care and professional team members including academics, and data collected by FosterClub, an Oregon-based advocacy and research organization for young people in and from foster care.[2] Commonalities of experience are loss of employment, food and housing insecurity, enormous burdens on mental and physical health, and difficulty obtaining governmental support.

The Japanese IFCA survey, which opened in late May 2020 and closed in mid-June 2020, collected responses from 425 former state wards from across the country (reporting from 39 out of 47 total prefectures) with an average age of 23. The survey results paint a picture of youth from care living in deeply insecure circumstances that preceded and were exacerbated by the pandemic. Even before the pandemic, only 25 percent had full-time jobs; over 50 percent had been working part-time or contract jobs, and about 12 percent were unemployed. After the start of COVID-19, 35 percent reported having unstable income, 29 percent reported significant reduction in income, and 5 percent were laid off. One in five respondents reported that they currently had no money. About 20 percent of respondents were facing food insecurity, with 4 percent reporting that they had no food at all. Twenty-two percent were concerned they would lose their housing. The qualitative responses expressed profound anxiety, depression, and isolation; difficulty in accessing medical and social services; and a lack of social support. Many of these young people had no one to turn to for help. The Japanese government, whose rhetoric and practice during the pandemic doubled down on familial responsibility for social welfare, distributed COVID-19 cash benefits to households rather than individuals. Former state wards tend to have strained or absent relationships with their families of origin, and many did not receive governmental support during the pandemic (IFCA Project C 2020).

Despite systemic differences from the Japanese child welfare system, American and Japanese data highlight the same fault lines and vulnerabilities. FosterClub's survey, conducted in early May 2020, captured results from 613 respondents from 44 states, between the ages of 18 and 24, who had spent an average of 7 years in care. Thirty-six percent of respondents had been laid off since the start of COVID-19. Almost 1 in 5 respondents reported they had entirely run out of food; more than half reported food insecurity and concern that they did not have enough to eat. Twenty-three percent of respondents were concerned about their housing stability, an insecurity exacerbated by university dorms forcing students to leave. Around 18 percent were insecure in their ability to obtain medical care because they lacked health insurance, were having trouble obtaining care, were going without needed medication, or did not have an internet connection for telehealth appointments. Approximately 20 percent of respondents reported being entirely alone. Half who applied for unemployment benefits did not receive them, and over half reported that they did not receive a governmental stimulus check (FosterClub 2020).

The Japanese IFCA team ended their report with concrete policy recommendations, which are also relevant to the North American context. The two most central were: Governmental support should be focused on meeting the needs of individuals in diverse circumstances rather than assuming affiliation with a supportive family. Second, the child welfare system must do better at helping young people cultivate lasting connections to supportive adults, and not just adults who are already their caregivers. IFCA emphasized the necessity of better supporting and following young people after they leave care and the importance of mental health care. Their final recommendation was to promote authentic engagement from state wards to shape welfare policy.

The normative claim underpinning this ethnography is the argument articulated by my friend Hanashima Shin'ichi: Welfare systems should not produce people who have no one. This claim points to a positive corollary that welfare systems should cultivate well-being through a focus on belonging. One of my central arguments is that Japanese people often understand well-being as relational. So why aren't there more relationship-focused interventions in Japanese child welfare and social policy? It is crucial to attend to the cultural specificities and discourses of self in any context, which implicitly shape social policy and practice (Burgess 2010). In Japan, people find it difficult to conceptualize an individual as having multiple family affiliations. Yet cultivating ties to a caregiver does not necessarily mean foreclosing relationships with other kin. How might children and parents be better supported in preserving their relationships with each other, and how might a parent's ability to care for their children be holistically bolstered? Qualitative research such as this ethnographic study could be more systematically implemented to seek contextually specific answers to these questions.[3] Children and young people need social supports in place before they age out of the welfare system. If relational possibilities are maintained in engagements with the child welfare system, children and young people would be able to choose for themselves what belonging means to them and what relationships they want to preserve.

COVID-19 laid bare social fault lines across the world. Even in the best of times, alumni of state welfare systems are profoundly invisible. The worst of times invite us to think creatively—in ways we have thus far failed to do—about how societies might better support relationships and a social safety net for people who need them most.

Insights for Japanese Studies and Anthropology

Social invisibility, for any group, is not natural or inevitable. In Japan, a country that collects exhaustive data on many aspects of life, perhaps the invisibility of children in the child welfare system is intentional.[4] Families that seem non-normal in their particular cultural context often provoke anxiety, as they push back against dominant forms of power and privilege. Consider, for instance, the ways that anti-miscegenation laws in the United States used marriage and family-building as a racist technology of control, or how same-sex marriage legislation prompts claims from American conservatives that heterosexual marriage will be destroyed. Kinship practices that go against the grain of normative and normalizing cultural practices threaten hegemonic power.

The Meiji Restoration of 1868 marked far-reaching political, economic, and social changes in Japan, including new regulation of family practices. The contemporary family registration system was instated, documenting every person as part of an extended family line (ie) in accordance with samurai customs. Further, "the Emperor was designated by the government as the pinnacle of the formal family system, thus making obedience to the government a moral issue" (Miyaji and Lock 1994, 99). As Jennifer Robertson has written, "The concept of a family-state (*kazoku kokka*) system was invented by late nineteenth-Century idealogues to create a familiar and modern community—the nation—where one had not existed before. Some ideologies stretched out the family metaphor and likened nationality to membership in an exceptional 'bloodline' (*ketto*)" (2002, 192; Gluck 1985). The post–World War II American occupiers viewed Japanese kinship practices as problematically linked to the Imperial family and to war-making imperatives. In the postwar occupation Japanese Constitution, the ie system was abolished, and individuals were required to create their own new family registries upon marriage, highlighting American values of liberal individualism. Despite these top-down legal interventions into family structure, Japanese family practices are still often seen to point both to Japanese identity and to the coherence of the Japanese nation.

For instance, nihonjinron discourses on Japanese identity, which John Lie defines as theories of national culture that point to "essential elements about Japanese people in contradistinction to others" (2001, 52), depict Japanese people, definitionally, as prioritizing blood relationships in families. Culturalist notions that blood ties define family in Japan portray adoptive, foster, and chosen families as exceptions to a rule. These perspectives deny internal diversity and the fact that culture itself changes over time. I have approached the concept of Japaneseness from the sides and margins in order to explore how nihonjinron discourses are constituted as central to the definition of Japanese people as such but also speak so poorly to many people's experiences in the world.[5] There is no unchanging Japanese self that is somehow linked to a specific, narrow view of kinship norms, and while some people personally hold beliefs that uphold these perspectives, many do not. Yet people inhabiting nonnormative family forms experience stigma and discrimination at the worst, and at best, their families are not easily recognizable by others.[6]

Declining birthrates and divorce are often mobilized in popular discourse as evidence of the disintegration of the Japanese family and a threat to the Japanese nation. Pronatalist policies are portrayed as a backstop against the existential peril of extinction; it is common to see media graphics representing an ever-dwindling young population supporting the crushing weight of Japan's elderly. The realization that Japan was dealing with a less-than-replacement birthrate—the so-called "1.57 shock" in 1990—prompted new policies under the rubric of alleviating an impending population crisis (Roberts 2002; White 2002). Divorce is often represented as the result of transformed gender norms that connect women's desire to work to this demographic transition, pointing to anxieties about social dissolution (Alexy 2020). Educational subsidies, the creation of new day care services and community parenting centers, partial subsidization of infertility treatments, and subsidies for each child born have become central to governmental public policy. However, liberalizing immigration laws to alleviate work shortages and increase the number of children born in Japan has not been embraced as a solution to the problem. Although the government is invested in increasing the Japanese population, the ideal supported by contemporary policies is that of a married Japanese couple bearing their own biological children. Other reproductive practices are represented as problematic for national identity. For instance, in a well-known 2007 court case, a Japanese couple used their own gametes and hired an American surrogate, who gave birth to twins in the United States. The Japanese Supreme Court held that the surrogate was the legal mother of the twins, who were denied Japanese citizenship.[7] This case illustrates one way that reproductive practices have the capacity to disrupt conventional notions of citizenship and kinship.

When I began this research, I saw nonnormative kinship practices as profoundly troubling this kind of national-cultural rhetoric of identity in Japan, which seemed to explain why these practices were so culturally policed and legally suppressed. However, this interpretation risks further reifying Japanese identity and culture, as if there is no room for difference and diversity. Here in this conclusion, I would suggest something different: Practices such as adoption, fostering, and institutional care in Japan offer productive friction for oversimplified notions of Japaneseness, highlighting the contingency of the ideological constructs of family and household, denaturalizing them and suggesting a way to broaden categories of relatedness.

Kinship technologies are tools of recognition but also tools of inclusion. By attending to semiotic techniques for understanding relatedness, we see the tensions that arise when certain sorts of relationships are not initially recognized as a type of family—but we also learn the inherent flexibility of the category itself. In other words, although we might recognize a family based on previous types of other families we have seen in the past, new categories can be created that allow new moments of recognition. Discourse offers ways to reframe kinship, to popularize and pluralize new understandings of family, and to disseminate these perspectives; portrayals of adoption, family-based fostering, and institutional care are increasingly popular in Japanese fictional and nonfictional media. Legal mechanisms are also kinship technologies, through which emerge new ways to recognize and reconfigure relationships. Legislation was passed in 2020 to specify that married recipients of donated gametes would be considered the legal parents, rather than the donor.[8] Same-sex marriage is not legal in Japan at the time of writing, although a spring 2021 ruling determined that the ban on same-sex marriage is unconstitutional.[9] Dual custody, which would split custody rights between two parties and allow a child a legally legible affiliation to two families, was made possible in a May 2024 Civil Code revision.[10] This transformation could profoundly shift the domains I have traced in this ethnography, in which individuals are understood as able to have only one formal family affiliation. These diverse elements of kinship technologies—which also include engagements with physical things (land, houses, Buddhist altars, records, and personal belongings)—are an important aspect of the way people know themselves to be connected to one another. Despite rhetoric about the inviolability of blood ties, kinship relationships are profoundly contingent. Most centrally, this ethnography has shown the ways that kinship is a matter of practice and of doing.

Embodied selves grow relationally, such that kinship should also be understood as an important aspect of bodily life, with biological entailments: bodies are situated within relational environments. Ethnographic research illuminates the lived meanings of the ways people understand their own and others' embodied experiences. This ethnography has tracked both externally "objective" transformations in bodies and selves that can be observed by others and correlated with changing relational contexts, as well as subjectively experienced embodied life that is given meaning by past and present narrative practices and engagement with popular and scientific discourse. I have intentionally left the borders of these categories underdetermined in an effort to shake up the oversimplified ways many of us think about biology and the body. Changes in body size, the loss of baby teeth, left-handedness, a person's habitual way of using chopsticks, perceiving brain structure to mirror relational contexts, experiencing oneself as a former child, the feeling of having a hole in one's heart—these are embodied experiences that cast into relief the historical and cultural specificity of bodily life, the excitable interconnectedness of biology and social existence, and the dynamic articulations between forms of knowledge (of self, of child development science) and the ways these shape lived experience. Further, despite both scientific and lay discourses about human fates governed by genetic and environmental inputs during specific periods of development, my ethnographic data highlight relational environments as transformative throughout life, disrupting deterministic models of development. This book has thus illustrated multifarious ways that overly delimited understandings of nature and nurture, biology and culture, constrain our understanding of human experience, and urges readers to reconceptualize what it means to live embedded in relational environments.

My interlocutors often used two words to describe their goals for children in the child welfare system: *anzen* and *anshin*. These terms, "safe" and "secure," share the character for "ease." On the one hand, being safe and secure seems like a rather minimal goal and could be interpreted as pointing to a sort of bare provision of clothing, food, and housing (*ishokujū*). But taking these terms' most expansive meaning, they direct us to the definition of well-being that has informed my analysis. Ease in life is cultivated holistically, through a sense of wellness in one's emotional, physical, and social dimensions of experience. Echoing international child welfare norms, Japanese child welfare discourse has recently taken up the concept of permanency as a goal for state wards. Although often written in katakana as *pamenenshī*, one Japanese translation of this term is poignant—*eizokuteki shinrai kankei*, a persistent or lasting relationship of trust—and points to the stability and ease of a relationship in which one can believe. Feeling safe and secure in the world means feeling rooted, tethered, knowing that there are people out there for whom your existence matters. Safety and security emerge through positive, supportive relationships. Theorizing welfare and well-being as a consequence of relationships, I have shown, offers a powerful window into socioemotional and bodily life in a context where relationships themselves are too often attenuated and fragile.

Both kinship technologies and embodied experience offer new angles for retheorizing normativity. Families have been understood as normalizing institutions par excellence, in Japan and elsewhere—a domain for state intervention through practices like family registration, medical recordkeeping, and the pathologization and medicalization of intimate practices and childrearing labor, even as ideals of privacy and inviolability hold sway. Families are also a space for socializing children into normalizing discourses and practices (Foucault 1978; Donzelot 1979; Garon 1997; Rose 1999, Frühstück 2003). This ethnography has shown how, at the level of experience, the normal often appears to exist in the negative as something that does not provoke surprise or stigma but also, for many people, as something always over there, not quite here. Normalcy is often an object of desire and aspiration. Processes of *mimetic approximation* apply poignantly to the institutional spaces I have analyzed here but also to the ways people express desire to inhabit unmarked worlds and unmarked subjectivities. Kinship technologies—the process of making recognizable new dimensions of relational life—offer one avenue for expanding the domains that are experienced and evaluated as recognizable family, for queering normative categories, and for welcoming new ways of being and belonging.

Notes

INTRODUCTION

This Introduction draws on material previously published in Goldfarb 2018.

1. In 2021, the dominant reported reasons for children's placement in alternative care were maltreatment (from one quarter to one half of children in various child welfare placements), neglect, and parental mental health troubles (Kodomo kateichō 2024, 33). Poverty is a common denominator for many of these children's families of origin, as well as lower parental educational attainment (Goodman 2000, 55–56). Divorce is one major cause of poverty in Japan, particularly for single mothers, because dual custody has not been possible; custodial mothers are often reluctant to demand child support (Alexy 2020, 152).

2. *-kun* (conventionally gendered male) and *-chan* (conventionally gendered female) are honorific suffixes used for other people's children, just as *-san* is a typical suffix used to refer to a colleague or friend.

3. I am indebted to my friend and research interlocutor whom I call Hanashima Shin'ichi for this core insight.

4. Nihonjinron, literally "discourses on Japaneseness," are stereotypes characterizing Japanese national character or psychology as distinct from other peoples and imply internal ethnic and class homogeneity. These discourses often focus on perduring cultural characteristics and traditions that link Japanese history, cultural institutions, and even geography with the nation's modernity (Lie 2001, 151; Befu 2001). Nihonjinron is produced by both Japanese and non-Japanese people and is famously contradictory: Ruth Benedict, the American anthropologist, wrote in *Chrysanthemum and the Sword* that the Japanese are "both aggressive and unaggressive, both militaristic and aesthetic, both insolent and polite, rigid and adaptable, submissive and resentful of being pushed around, loyal and treacherous, brave and timid, conservative and hospitable to new ways" (1946, 2). Claims that "Japanese people are hyper-relational" and also that "Japan is a society without social connections" are present-day examples of the coexistence of these contradictory generalizations. Rather than focusing on whether nihonjinron discourses are empirically true, I attend to their social and policy effects (Burgess 2010).

5. Many of these actors can be understood as "street-level bureaucrats" (Lipsky 2010).

6. Most Japanese statistics designate children as under age fifteen. "Japan's Proportion of Children to Adults Lowest in the World," May 18, 2022, https://www.nippon.com/en/japan-data/h01320.

7. In Japanese: child welfare institutions (*jidō yōgo shisetsu*), baby homes (*nyūjiin*), family-based foster care (*sato oya*), family homes (*famirī hōmu*), children's psychotherapeutic facilities (*jidō shinri chiryō shisetsu*), youth correctional facilities (a possible direct translation is "child self-reliance support facilities," *jidō jiritsu shien shisetsu*), institutions to support independent living (*jiritsu shien hōmu*), and institutions for single mothers and children (*boshi seikatsu shien shisetsu*).

8. In his 2024 PhD dissertation, Christopher Chapman argues that the Japanese child welfare system should be seen as a "disaggregated system," "a piecemeal conglomerate of competing perspectives and intentions. These dissonances speak to broader trends and lived tensions in the professionalization of casework, valorization of the nuclear family ideal, and local reconfiguring of care knowledge" (2).

9. The Japanese government's own reports highlight the divergences in family placement rates among England, Germany, France, Italy, the United States, Canada (British Columbia), Australia, Hong Kong, South Korea, and Japan, with Japan ranked substantially lowest (Kodomo kateichō 2024, 64).

10. In this framework, social care is actually abuse (Goldfarb 2015, 274). Critics include the Tokyo office of Human Rights Watch and Japanese activists, some of whom are alumni of state care; others are academics, child welfare workers, lawyers, adoption providers, and foster parents.

11. In this ethnography, I specify *family-based foster care* to refer to a child welfare placement in a family, in contrast to group homes or small-scale institutional care.

12. With the revision of the special adoption law in Japan, as of April 2020, children as old as fifteen could be adopted under a system that completely cut ties with their biological family. In the past, this type of adoption was generally open only to children under age six. There have been 500 to 600 special adoptions per year for the last couple decades; in 2022, special adoption numbers were reported at 580 (Kodomo kateichō 2024, 87), still falling short of the government's benchmark for 1,000 per year by 2024 (MHLW 2019b).

13. I arrive at the 19 percent figure by summing the total number of children in family-based foster care (6,080) and family homes (1,718), divided by the total number of children in state care (42,000) (Kodomo kateichō 2024, 5), thus distinguishing between placements in families and placements in small-scale institutions.

14. In 2012, a law was passed allowing for temporary removal of parental rights by family court decision. Before this legal change, every year there were only a handful of family court decisions that forcefully removed parental rights. From 2012 to 2019, there were an average of twenty-seven cases annually where parental rights were terminated by family court decision and an average of sixty-two annually where parental rights were temporarily suspended (Supreme Court General Secretariat Family Affairs Bureau 2020, 3).

15. Because dual custody has not previously been allowed, children of divorced parents have maintained a legal tie to only one parent, in many cases losing touch with the noncustodial parent: the "clean break" standard for divorce (Alexy 2020, 127). The 2024 civil code revision allowing dual custody is likely to change these norms. See also Krogness 2008; Chapman and Krogness 2014; White 2018.

16. From all sides, children in Japanese institutions are engaging with parents, caseworkers, and caregivers as adults who are temporarily invested in their well-being. The child welfare treatise *Children Who Wait* (Rowe and Lambert 1973) describes how children in state care exist in an unending state of anticipation, waiting for decisive action from adults that never materializes. In Japan, children may be understood as waiting for engagement from parents they might not even know. Institutional staff view their own engagements with children as temporary. A staff member (not at Chestnut House) specified, "We are not *raising* these children. We are temporarily entrusted with their care [*azukatteimasu*]." Caseworkers also have short-term relationships with children, as the majority of child welfare officers in Japan are government workers who are transferred to different divisions every three to five years.

17. For English coverage, see "Care Leavers in Japan Struggle to Make Living, Pursue Higher Education: Survey," Mainichi Shimbun, May 1. 2021, https://mainichi .jp/english/articles/20210501/p2a/00m/0na/019000c; "Life after Foster Care No Bed of Roses for Many," Asahi Shimbun, May 1, 2021, http://www.asahi.com/ajw/articles /14341374.

18. About 2 percent of the MUFG sample graduated from university, which popular press coverage compared to a national average of almost 30 percent (MUFG 2021, 36; Asahi Shimbun 2021). However, the survey assessed only people who had left care

between 2015 and 2020 (not a lot of time to graduate from university!). The Japanese government reports the four-year university entrance rate for young people from child welfare institutions only (not family-based foster care or other placements) at 22.6 percent, but does not report graduation rates (Kodomo kateichō 2024, 139).

19. See ann-elise lewallen's *The Fabric of Indigeneity* (2016, chap. 3) for a discussion of blood ties within Ainu communities. Ainu people traditionally reckoned kinship relationships through material objects like textiles. As part of Japan's colonization of Hokkaido, quasi-scientific notions of blood lines and blood quantum have become increasingly dominant ways of documenting kinship for Ainu people.

20. In this context, Nobe Yōko describes special adoption as a systematic way to prioritize love from biologically unrelated caregivers, rather than prioritizing biologically related caregivers who do not love a child (2018, 313).

21. Allison Alexy notes that while most Japanese people perceive divorce as a "uniquely modern problem signaling the erosion of traditional family norms," divorce has historically been common in Japan, peaking in 1883, when it was relatively usual for people to test matches with trial marriages (2020, 17).

22. For international comparisons of compensated and uncompensated labor differentiated by gender, see the Japanese Gender Equity Bureau Cabinet Office's whitepaper: https://www.gender.go.jp/about_danjo/whitepaper/r02/zentai/html/column/clm_01.html.

23. I thank Hilary Holbrow for her articulation of this question.

24. Gender identity and child welfare is another topic about which limited research exists. In 2016, the nonprofit organization Rainbow Foster Care assessed awareness of and responses to gender minority children in Japanese child welfare institutions; see their homepage for research reports: https://rainbowfostercare.jimdofree.com.

25. This discursive practice can be considered "ontological choreography," in Charis Thompson's (2005) turn of phrase, expressing how people reproduce old understandings of relatedness despite their use of new reproductive technologies.

26. This project brings together "an anthropology of the body and an anthropology of discourses and practices" (Farquhar 2002, 5). I explore the multiple and divergent ways bodies may signify, depending on the characteristics that are taken as signs, and the possibilities of bodily experience as diverse as these signification processes (Kuriyama 2002). People actively attribute meaning to particular bodily phenomena, a process open to historical shifts, local interpretive differences, and culturally specific politics of representation and recognition (Keane 1997; Kroskrity 2000).

27. For a take on aspirations to "nobodyness," see Nozawa 2012; see Oliphant 2021 on the "privilege of being banal."

28. Over the long course of this project, I obtained research ethics board approval from the University of Chicago, Harvard University, McMaster University, and the University of Colorado Boulder; provided written consent forms for everyone I interviewed; and audio recorded oral consent. I have substantial training in Japanese and conducted my own interviews without translation. Unless otherwise noted, all translations from the Japanese in this book are my own.

29. Race was not always invisible within the Japanese child welfare system. In the immediate aftermath of World War II, mixed-race orphans were publicly represented as a social crisis, specifically children identified as half Black. Kristin Roebuck highlights how, while one in ten children of Western fathers and Japanese mothers were indeed state wards, representing these children as kinless was a racial nationalist tactic to show mixed-raced (and particularly Black) people as unassimilable in Japan, justifying segregation and overseas adoption. Roebuck dubs these groups "orphans by design" (2016, 193). Japan's history of inviting Brazilians of Japanese ancestry to work in Japan and then incentivizing them to return to Brazil, is another example of the ways blood ties do not

necessarily point to national and cultural membership. See Tsuda 2022 for a discussion of "co-ethnic racism" directed at return migrants from Brazil. By contrast, in contemporary discourses on Japanese child welfare, race and ethnicity disappear from official statistics. Michael Rivera King discusses a unique 2011 survey conducted by the National Association of Child Guidance Centers, according to which 1.5 percent of children in Japanese state care were not Japanese nationals, and an additional 0.4 percent were not registered in the family registration system; 1.6 percent had a non-Japanese father, and 4 percent had a non-Japanese mother (2021, 37). Buraku people, or *burakumin*, are not an ethnic minority, but buraku populations are similarly not marked in child welfare statistics. Buraku people are "a group identified by an occupational, a spatial, or a genealogical relationship to historically stigmatized labor such as meat and leather production." The category is "contagious" because people can become identified as burakumin by virtue of work or residence or by marrying into a family historically identified as burakumin (Hankins 2014, 2–3).

30. While some foster parent friends have fostered non–ethnically Japanese children, and one family described ongoing support of an ethnically Korean mother and her children, race and ethnicity were mainly highlighted when people described their desire to remain unmarked as adoptive or foster parents: non-Asian children would be legible to onlookers as out of the ordinary.

31. Many of the children were not immunized at Chestnut House because medical procedures required permission from holders of parental rights. In only a few cases, the institutional director held sole parental rights and could unilaterally make medical decisions for the children.

32. Foster parents can register under four different categories: regular foster parents (*yōiku sato oya*), foster parents for children with special needs (*senmon sato oya*), foster parents with intention to adopt (*yōshiengumi sato oya*), or kinship caregivers (*shinzoku sato oya*). Many register under multiple categories to increase their chances of placement. As reported in 2024, a regular foster parent would receive 90,000 yen for each child plus living expenses of 53,710 yen for older children and 62,020 yen for younger children (all per month), in addition to school and medical expenses (Kodomo kateichō 2024, 14). Foster parent families have slightly higher than average incomes, and about 40 percent of foster parents both work (MHLW 2019a, 146). Japanese foster parents are disproportionately Christian (Goodman 2000, 16–17) or members of the Japanese new religion Tenrikyō (Omori 2016).

33. The pseudonym Tanpopo, which means "dandelion," was chosen by the director of the organization.

1. KINSHIP TECHNOLOGIES

This chapter draws on material previously published in Goldfarb 2016a.

1. This is his real name; all quotations are from a public presentation.

2. Quotes in this section are my translations of audio-recorded conference proceedings.

3. These are "pragmatic semiotics" (Silverstein 1993; Stasch 2009), self-reflexive regimes for interpreting signs in the world that people actively use in daily life.

4. Nobe Yōko (2018) denaturalizes the phrase "for the sake of the child," asking who benefits from contemporary Japanese rhetoric about blood ties. In a context where adoption is increasingly common and people often use the phrase *transcending blood ties* to describe the creation of adoptive and foster families, Nobe asks why and with what stakes there is simultaneous rhetoric linking a child's identity to knowledge of biogenetic origins.

5. In the North American context, ascriptions of "nefarious motives for fostering" focus centrally on "fostering as a commercial endeavor" (Wozniak 2002, 203). Wozniak writes that for social workers, "economic need often implied a lack of parental/affective

motivation" (2002, 206), and social workers tended to measure a foster parent's "potential for success" by "their distance from economic necessity" (2002, 207). This ideological framework undergirds low monetary compensation for foster caregivers, whose motivation can be understood as "pure" only if financial compensation is a "token" (Wozniak 2002, 214; Zelizer 1985).

6. This is also the case for adult adoption. In son-in-law adoption (*mukoyōshi*), families without sons might adopt the husband of a daughter, which requires the man to enter the family registry of his spouse and take her name. This process has a reputation for being pitiful even though men who are adopted into their wives' families are generally not candidates as heirs in their families of origin (Paulson 2010). The adoption of adults may also connote efforts to circumvent legal norms. Elderly people might conduct adoptions to decrease the overall amount of inheritance tax applied to an estate (inheritance tax decreases the more inheritors there are) or adopt with the promise of exchanging inheritance for elder care. Extramarital lovers can be adopted, which means that the portion of inheritance designated for a legally married spouse and children would decrease. One member of a same-sex couple can also adopt the other in order to produce legally binding ties (Bryant 1990).

7. Scholars have also cited this saying as a way to explain unease surrounding the quality and origin of donated gametes for use in infertility treatment (Lock 1998, 225).

8. This desire is mirrored in Karl Jacob Krogness's (2011) findings that Japanese people idealize "normal" family registries (*koseki*) that will not reveal irregularities like divorce or adoption.

9. These foster parents were not part of my intimate network of research contact friends, and I never met these women's families.

10. These accounts echo Danielle Wozniak's descriptions of American foster parents feeling that they were "violating a cultural norm of motherhood and family" by taking in racially different or numerous same-age children, and receiving money for this care work (2002, 86). Many of Wozniak's interlocutors found it easier to "pass" by not identifying themselves as foster parents or to preserve ambiguity about the relationship, "maintaining the possibility or illusion of familial relations (such as a stepparent relationship, adoption, or extended family relation)" (2002, 87).

11. Goffman quotes the narrative of a "criminal" who surprised someone with his highbrow reading selections: "'Fancy that!' they say. 'In some ways you're just like a human being!'" Goffman provides the further example of a blind person whose facility managing day-to-day affairs provokes shock: "His most ordinary deeds . . . are no longer ordinary. He becomes an unusual person. If he performs them with finesse and assurance they excite the same kind of wonderment inspired by a magician who pulls rabbits out of hats" (1963, 15).

12. Many people understand the term *kokuchi* (confession) to carry negative connotations. More neutral is *teringu* (based on the English word *telling*).

13. To a certain extent, one of my interlocutors told me, debates surrounding the confession of adoption in Japan are irrelevant: "No matter what, if you look carefully at the family registry, you will be able to find out." The family registry contains different proof than the household registry: the former lists all unmarried children who share the family name, and *special adoption* is marked with reference to the constitutional bill that ratified the process in 1987 (adoption became possible in 1988) (Hayes and Habu 2006; Krogness 2008).

14. Many people working in adoption in Japan argue that children have the right to know their own background, a right violated by adoptive parents who do not tell the truth of a child's past (Rakugi 2006). Notably, Hamabata and Abe were two of the adoptive parents I interviewed earliest in my fieldwork, while I was very much an anonymous

foreign researcher. Later in my research, I attempted to follow up with both of them for further interviews, but both gently demurred. By this point I was ensconced in this community of foster parents and saw both women regularly at trainings and other events, and I suspect that my familiarity with this community by then dissuaded them from further participation in my research. (Neither asked me not to use their interviews.)

15. In the case at hand, in which nonbiological kinship is articulated in material terms, there are many levels at which these kinship technologies reinforce an impression of "familyness." In Peircean semiotic terms, the relationship between parent and child comes to be iconic, a (literal) matter of resemblance; but this similarity is also indexical, a result of causal interactions between parents and children over time, like the caregiving relationships that Yamanta tells us make parents and children come to look alike. Further, this relationship might be ultimately understood as symbolic, subject to the arbitrariness of social conventions in selecting the qualities relevant to calculating similarity itself and entailing future unexpected effects.

16. Studies of transnational and transracial adoption are useful to consider in the context of Japanese adoption and fostering. When ethnicities of adoptive parent and child are different, this difference must be incorporated into a coherent model of family (Howell 2006; Dorow 2006; Yngvesson 2010; Kim 2010; Deguchi 2013). For Howell, "kinning" describes the process by which a "previously unconnected person is brought into a significant and permanent relationship with a group of people that is expressed in a kin idiom" (2006, 63). Howell suggests that a key process occurs to "kin" a child in the case of international adoption: a "fundamental change" is understood to occur *inside* the child as they are kinned while the child's outward appearance remains the same as before, different from that of the adoptive parents (2006, 69). The child becomes internally, substantially one of the family while visually marked as "other."

17. The sense of compulsion motivating adoptive parent-child bonds is one also highlighted in non-Japanese narratives of adoption. Barbara Yngvesson's discussion of international adoption in Sweden, bracketed by her own experience as an adopter in the United States, is peppered with references to compelling, nonlogical forces.

18. This analysis is based on a publication by a Wa no Kai member (Rakugi 2006); it is thus a snapshot of this organization's practices in the early 2000s.

19. Wa no Kai was unusual among Japanese adoption organizations, which historically have not emphasized values of semiopen or open adoption.

20. This framing of the obligatory, nonchosen nature of ties of "nature" or "substance," in contrast to "voluntary" ties of law, is central to David Schneider's (1968) argument in *American Kinship*.

21. *Kizuna's* meaning is generally taken as a beneficial connection, but the word also means "fetters," "bonds," or "shackles."

22. This contest is part of a larger phenomenon, the annual listing of trendy words that are commodified as "language superstars that highlight cultural moments of mass interest" (Miller 2017, 48).

23. This disaster also provoked intense debates about how much the people of Tōhoku should be compensated for losses of property, livelihood, and life from both the Tokyo Electric Power Company (TEPCO), whose nuclear power plant was damaged in the tsunami and continues to present overwhelming concerns regarding environmental and health impacts of radiation, and the national government. Discourses regarding the resilience and connectedness of the Tōhoku people seem to excuse both TEPCO and the government from responding to the area's need for support.

24. *Japan Today*. 2012. "'Kizuna' Takes Many Forms in Post-disaster Japan, Including Marriage and Infidelity," January 17, 2012. http://www.japantoday.com/category/kuchikomi /view/kizuna-takes-many-forms-in-post-disaster-japan-including-marriage-and-infidelity.

25. Terebi Iwate. 2011. "'Shinsai koji' ni shien no wa" ["The Supportive Circle for Disaster Orphans"]. News Plus. April 27, 2011.

26. NNN News. 2010. "Ai no sato oya kosodate" ["Childrearing by Loving Foster Parents"]. March 9, 2010.

27. My interlocutors described regression as "akachan gaeri," returning to babyhood.

28. If kinship technologies assist people in learning to see some types of relationships as family, there are other ways that people "learn not to see as real or legitimate families that do not meet the heteronormative patriarchal structure, and they learn not to acknowledge as family members kin not recognized by law" (Patton-Imani 2020, 16).

2. APPROXIMATING A HOUSEHOLD

This chapter draws on material previously published in Goldfarb 2017.

1. While Kitahara specifically mentioned sexual assault, in Japan the term *child abuse* does not readily connote sexual abuse, which is still not commonly discussed. See Goodman 2000, chapter 6 for discussion of well-known abuse cases within Japanese child welfare institutions and Onchōen 2001 for an in-depth study of systemic child-child and staff-child abuse in the Onchōen child welfare institution of Chiba, Japan. The 2005 Minimum Standards for Child Welfare Facilities formally prohibited abuse of children by staff members in child welfare institutions and required the provision of a method to address children's complaints. The 2008 Child Welfare Law included, for the first time, abuse within institutions under the category of child abuse (Goldfarb 2013, 152).

2. Chapter 5 focuses on Tanpopo and the stories of Naoki and Matsumoto.

3. Family-run institutions in particular are likely to have long-tenured staff, so this depiction is not universal. Child welfare institution staff have difficult jobs. Kameda et al highlight the mental health burden on staff members caring for children with histories of trauma, disrupted attachment, and difficulty building interpersonal relationships (2014, 149). Both staff members and resident children often grapple with unresolved grief and loss, pointing to the need for better mental health care support for caregivers and children in state care (Ide 2022).

4. The term *household-like* was initially used to describe family-based foster care and in some cases adoption—contexts that one might reasonably describe as an actual household. The term then began to be used in reference to family homes, a system begun in 2009, where foster parents and support staff care for up to six children. But then the term began to be employed in reference to small-scale child welfare institutions that boasted household-like environments, like Chestnut House (MHLW 2011). Along these lines, SOS Children's Village locations in Japan are described as foster care, while in almost every other country they are considered institutional care (Michael Rivera King, personal communication, March 28, 2021). In this way, the term *kateiteki* came to refer to any small-scale care, whether an institution or an actual family, presenting inflated statistics for "foster parent etc." placements (Kodomo kateichō 2024, 62). Notably, the same categorization issue is present in the United States and Canada. A study discussing the extent of institutionalized children under age seventeen worldwide notes that "data for North America is difficult to identify as they refer to all children in public care as 'fostered,' rather than restricting this term for children placed into professional surrogate families" (Browne 2009, 5).

The Japanese government's most recent report on the state of child welfare breaks down these categories more minutely into a spectrum (Kodomo kateichō 2024, 3). The report distinguishes between "institutions," unqualified by a descriptive heading; "favorable household-like environments" (ryōkō na kateiteki kankyō) of "small-scale institutions," which include community-based group homes or small-scale group care within a larger institution, of groups of between 4 and 6 children; "child-rearing environments the same as a household" (*katei to dōyō no yōiku kankyō*), under which are listed adoption, family homes, and family-based foster care; and finally, on the right-hand side, "household" (*katei*) described as "upbringing by actual parents (*jitsu oya*)." This is the second state-of-the-field report by the new Japanese Children and Families Agency, created in April 2023, which unfortunately doubles down on "household" defined normatively by biological kin relations.

5. For an alternative use of the concept of mimesis in a Japanese context, see Levi McLaughlin's theorization of the Japanese religion Soka Gakkai as a "mimetic nation," as it "makes itself intelligible and attractive by emulating the institutions, activities, and ideologies perpetuated by nation-state enterprises" (2019, 19).

6. If relationships between staff and children persisted over time, it was despite—not because of—the institutional form.

7. Kitahara's description evokes early twentieth-century notions of the household (katei) that emerged in Meiji-era reform movements to democratize and rationalize a properly modern family, specifically through dining practices (Sand 2003). Jordan Sand argues that dining tables helped constitute a modern Japanese "family circle" as a bounded group. While past use of individual dining trays with the family arrayed before the patriarch "manifested a strict hierarchy of authority," Sand writes, "it was an open structure, since the ring could be expanded to accommodate any number of participants. A common table, on the other hand, created a focus of limited size for a closed and intimate family circle, delineating inside from out at the same time that it implied greater equality within. Peripheral household members, particularly servants, were placed on the outside" (35).

8. The process of increasing small-scale care has been slow. As of 2022, only 17.5 percent of institutions had 30 or fewer children; 60.6 percent housed over 41 children; and there were 5 institutions that housed between 121 and 150 children (Kodomo kateichō 2024, 46).

9. Within Japanese child welfare institutions, children above elementary school are often divided according to gender and further divided in one of two ways: either horizontally (*yokowari*) according to age cohort or vertically (*tatewari*) so that children of many different ages share the same space. Horizontally divided groupings have the disadvantage of separating siblings who are in different age cohorts, and younger children do not benefit from stimulation by older children. However, this organization avoids a problem endemic in vertically divided groups, which is that age-based hierarchies among children in institutions are often abusive and coercive.

10. Temporary care (*ichiji hogo*) facilities in child guidance centers house children of all ages in a relatively small space. Because of staffing shortage and safety concerns, the children are not able to attend school during the period they are in temporary care—and some children are in temporary care for over a year.

11. Youth correctional facilities were formerly called *kyōgoin* (juvenile reformatory) and currently are euphemistically called *jidō jiritsu shien shisetsu* (institution to support independence).

12. This was not a Goffmanian vision of a "total institution" cut off from the community (Goffman 1961). See Rasell 2020 for a similar discussion about child welfare institutions in Hungary.

13. Ninety percent of child welfare institutions in Japan are privately run and managed by social welfare corporations that receive government funding (a set amount per child, which differs depending on the child's age [*itaku hi*]) to pay for upkeep and staff salaries.

14. The concepts of *inside* and *outside* (*uchi* and *soto*) are firmly ensconced within discourses of Japaneseness (nihonjinron) that posit specific qualities as central to Japanese character and psychology (Borovoy 2012). Household structure and beliefs about dirt and

cleanliness (Ohnuki-Tierney 1984), language use demarking inside and outside (Makino 2003), and differentiations of behavior as that appropriate for inside or outside, front or back (Lebra 1976), are examples cited by scholars to illustrate the cultural centrality of these concepts in Japan.

15. To comply with labor laws, the staff were considered off duty while the children were at school or sleeping, but in reality they might end up caring for a sick child, doing administrative work, attending trainings, and meeting with the children's social workers in their off-duty time.

16. By the summer of 2012, only one residential staff member of the originally hired staff remained as a caregiver at Chestnut House (two staff members had moved to administrative roles).

17. The institution's houses were connected duplexes, and part-time workers would alternate where they prepared the food. This meant that every other night, the food was delivered fully prepared.

18. This perspective aligns ideologically with gendered expectations regarding food preparation and care in Japan (Allison 1991).

19. Attention to professional boundaries seemed particularly acute to me in my ongoing interactions with current and former Chestnut House employees as they related to children who were still at the institution (structural insiders for current staff but outsiders for former staff) and children who had left because they aged out of the system or had changed placements (structural outsiders to both current and former staff). Tetsu remained in regular contact with current staff, and he was fully up to date on the status of the children. I heard years later from another staff member that he did visit the institution once, but he was treated as a *kyakusan* (an outsider or a visitor) by the then-director. His pragmatic self-representation in our interview was, I think, a product of that moment in his life, as he grappled with both his own sorrow at leaving the children and the pleasures of new parenthood, and an expression of the professionalism he embodied as a seasoned care worker.

20. Young people who do not continue to high school must leave the child welfare system after the conclusion of compulsory schooling (middle school) at age fifteen. In general, youth age out of the system after completing high school at age eighteen, but care can be extended in certain circumstances, sometimes when a young person proceeds on to university or when they require extra care (for instance, in the case of a disability) (Kodomo kateichō 2024, 177).

INTERLUDE: GENEALOGICAL RETURNS

1. This is not a story Nozomi ever told me herself. Nozomi's own accounts appear in chap. 6.

2. Nozomi's insecurity in her foster family reflects a structurally overdetermined sensibility. In response to a question from foster care researcher Danielle Wozniak in the American context, about whether a young woman in foster care ever felt a sense of belonging while in care, Wozniak's interlocutor responded, "You would have to be crazy to let yourself feel like you could belong when you are only a foster girl" (Wozniak 2002, 223).

3. NORMAL ASPIRATIONS

This chapter draws on material previously published in Goldfarb 2018.

1. Merry White notes that in North America, people say "starting a family" to mean having children, whereas in Japan, children continue a family (2002, 99).

2. The Japanese imperial family is often depicted in popular media with genealogical diagrams, which is one reason people are familiar with this graphic form.

3. Unmarried adults may also create their own individual family registries to legally separate from the registries of their parents, a bureaucratic representation of the liberal individual par excellence! (See White 2018.)

4. It is possible that the family began as a *bunke*, a tertiary branch of the main family line, started by a son who was not the honke successor.

5. See Nakane 1967 for discussion of household property, inheritance, and sibling relationships.

6. A social welfare scholar and government official once commented to me that people who have worked in childcare or as teachers are often the most promising foster parents because they understand that "a stranger's child can be cute." Tetsu's easy recognition of the lovability of strangers' children was a quality not to be taken for granted.

7. These Japanese government statistics are available at https://www.e-stat.go.jp/dbview?sid=0003411618. The rates for the United States and United Kingdom are cited in Hertog 2009.

8. For discussion of the difficulty of maintaining sibling relationships in state care, see Rasell 2020, chapter 4.

9. Sora's story has many commonalities with the accounts of other interlocutors who had grown up in institutions. Two less common characteristics are Sora's (like Reina's) high level of education (King 2012; Nagano 2017) and the length of out-of-home placement: the national average is about four and a half years, but Sora was in care for twelve years. Reina spent her entire life before graduating high school, excluding some summers, in institutional care.

10. Similarly, in her research on male irregular workers, Emma E. Cook argues that while precarious employment conditions seem to offer a chance to destabilize normative gendered expectations for employment, "many couples appear to be unable to take these conditions as an opportunity to create alternatives." Instead, they "continue to hold onto normative ideas while negotiating the complexities of intimate relationships in a precarious landscape" (2019, 144). In a similar vein, Michelle H. S. Ho highlights how female-to-male crossdressing interlocutors reject LGBT identity politics and instead "value the 'normal'" (2020, 105). Social precarity may offer conditions that demand retheorizing normativity in Japan (Ho 2020, 115).

4. MATERIALIZING RELATIONSHIPS

This chapter draws on material previously published in Goldfarb 2015 and Goldfarb 2019.

1. This woman's perspective is substantiated by scientific studies on child development in the context of institutionalization (Rutter et al. 1998; Vorria et al. 2006).

2. Handedness has been explored by anthropologists as epitomizing symbolic classification practices and normative social views (Needham 1960; Hertz 1973 [1909]).

3. I share commitments of "bioethnography" to "conduct analyses that suspend in advance prevalent domaining practices that designate some phenomena (like blood-lead levels) as biological/natural, and others (like family meals using lead-glazed ceramics) as social/cultural" (Roberts and Sanz 2017, 750).

4. For example, the notion that parent and child bodies come to "share the same flesh" (Weismantel 1995, 695) or "their blood becomes progressively more similar" (Carsten 1994, 40). See also Counts and Counts 1983, Carsten 2004, Howell 2006, Leinaweaver 2008, Bamford 2009, Stasch 2009, Goldfarb 2016a.

5. Progressive projects to celebrate culture over nature as the basis for human worth reproduce a gendered and unequal narrative about humanity (Ortner 1972).

6. Masa and Rie had atypical careers as foster parents because they were relatively young, had no children of their own, and were willing to take older children. Because few

foster parents are willing to take children older than middle school, foster parents like these were valued resources for child welfare placement officers.

7. Brad Weiss's study of "plastic teeth" (1996, chap. 6) offers an alternative perspective about the importance of teeth as a medium of social engagement.

8. Of "local biologies," Lock writes, "This concept does not refer to the idea that the categories of the biological sciences are historically and culturally constructed (although this is indeed the case) nor to measurable biological difference across human populations. Rather, *local biologies* refers to the way in which the embodied experience of physical sensations, including those of well-being, health, illness, and so on, is in part informed by the material body, itself contingent on evolutionary, environmental, and individual variables. Embodiment is also constituted by the way in which self and others represent the body, drawing on local categories of knowledge and experience. . . . The material and the social are *both* contingent—both local" (2001, 483–484).

9. I note that "dialectic" and "interactions" imply the separability of biological and cultural processes, while I argue in favor of the concept of "intra-action": the ways biological and cultural dimensions manifest precisely through their mutual entanglement (Barad 2007). For a counter description from Lock herself, see Niewöhner and Lock 2018, 691.

10. This blurriness is itself evinced in culturally specific ways. For example, eugenic scientists in Japan during the interwar era focused on socialization and habits of women of reproductive age—which were understood to be hereditary—rather than sterilization (Robertson 2002).

11. Tim Ingold would argue that these bodily effects are explicitly biological: "those specific ways of acting, perceiving and knowing that we have been accustomed to call cultural are enfolded, in the course of ontogenetic development, into the constitution of the human organism, then they are equally facts of biology" (2004, 215).

12. Attachment theory has only recently obtained prominence as a psychological tool and explanatory model in Japan, in large part due to Hennessy Sumiko's efforts. However, it has a long-contested place in Western culture, within human development focused social sciences, and in psychological anthropology. Naomi Quinn and Jeannette Mageo's edited volume *Attachment Reconsidered: Cultural Perspectives on a Western Theory* (2013) provides a smart and incisive analysis of attachment theory, which has been criticized for assuming a fixed number of normative, optimal attachment types regardless of culture, and for conducting evaluations in clinical environments out of context from a child's normal social sphere. Studies of attachment patterns in Japan specifically have labeled Japanese children as "insecure-ambivalent," and critiques (focusing, among other things, on the fact that it is odd to imagine an entire population as insecurely attached) might lead one to believe that attachment theory is not relevant in Japan (Quinn and Mageo 2013, 14–16). However, knowledge of attachment theory has been revolutionary for many of my interlocutors. The many trainings on attachment that I have observed in Japan or that target a Japanese audience do not focus on these critiqued narrow concepts of culturally specific attachment types but rather encourage a holistic understanding of interpersonal neurobiology.

13. Perhaps these neuroscientific explanations are a mismatch in Japan: Margaret Lock argues that in Japan, "for many people 'person' does not reside in the brain, nor is it exclusively associated with the mind." In fact, "there is no 'center' that takes priority over everything else" (2002, 228). Unsurprisingly, people who were themselves raised in baby homes or conditions of neglect often have trouble embracing the view of the brain and person as determined by early childhood experiences.

14. See Sugiyama 2007 for discussion of the connection between child abuse and symptoms of developmental disability.

15. This culturalist explanation neglected the historical conditions for the emergence and maintenance of large-scale child welfare institutions, which were built to house war orphans after World War II and then continued to be managed as family-run businesses (Goodman 2000).

16. These findings are echoed in studies of Israeli *kibbutz* (Spiro 1972).

17. Studies of epigenetic changes resulting from adverse childhood experiences in institutions have also prompted policy change (Lock and Palsson 2016, 106).

18. I have written on the unintended effects of these discourses, specifically the ways they tend to pathologize people raised in institutional contexts (Goldfarb 2015, 2019).

19. Browne et al. (2006, 486) note that among WHO European countries with available data, France and Spain, along with Russia, Romania, and Ukraine, have the highest numbers of children under three years of age in institutional care; Belgium has one of the highest percentages of institutionalized young children out of the total child population. Japan is thus not exceptional in its child welfare practices.

20. I don't know if Hanashima picked up this phrasing for the first time after seeing it written in overseas contexts or if it was a phrase that had come to him independently. Regardless, it powerfully resonated with him.

21. Hanashima's words reinforce Margaret Lock's argument that "subjective accounts about embodiment involving past and present events must be taken into account to effectively situate biological difference historically, ecologically, and politically in specific times and places. Only then can the extent of the changes in mind and body resulting from violence, poverty, discrimination, and racism be fully appreciated" (2018, 466).

22. These conceptual alliances may be illustrations of the "looping effect" in practice—the ways scientific knowledge is taken up, influences people's perceptions of themselves, and in turn impacts the evolution of scientific concepts (Hacking 1996). In these ways, scientific and embodied self-knowledge are coproduced (Jasinoff 2004).

23. While Hanashima was raised Catholic and speaks openly about his own religiosity, he has never intimated that his child welfare activism is rooted in Christian orientations toward welfare. In fact, while he might understand Catholicism to have helped fill the hole a parent should have filled for him personally, it is clear that to him, religion is but a pale substitute for the parent he should have had.

24. The history of attachment theory has been inflected with activism, and Hanashima's work is part of this lineage. John Bowlby authored his initial study on attachment for the World Bank in 1953, and attachment theory since then has been "infused with Bowlby's ideological fervor for more humane child care. . . . In its assertion that humans could develop only in the context of a tender, sensitive one-to-one bond, attachment theory militated against the dehumanizing tendencies of institutional care in industrial society. . . . In the wake of Bowlby's writings, as a result, attachment theory became a blend of academic school and political movement" (Quinn and Mageo 2013, 26).

25. Wikipedia describes the Dirac sea as "a theoretical model of the vacuum as an infinite sea of particles with negative energy." An online blog in Japanese (http://oshiete .goo.ne.jp/qa/621393.html) points out that while a vacuum is conventionally understood as entirely empty, the Dirac sea model argues instead that a vacuum contains positive and negative energy in equal measure and only appears to contain nothingness.

26. The notion that the absence of relationships is itself an embodied presence is reflected in D. W. Winnicott's description of "the fruits of privation," the results for an infant when the "holding environment" is not "good enough." In her analysis, Maggie Nelson emphasizes how Winnicott sees these results—which Winnicott describes as "going to pieces; falling for ever; dying and dying and dying; losing all vestige of hope of the renewal of contacts"—"not as lacks or voids, but as substantives" (Nelson 2015, 33).

27. Epigenetics "is a process in which the body, understood as coalesced inseparably with environmental forces (macro and micro) from the moment of conception on throughout life, is ceaselessly modulated" through mechanisms that control gene expression (in part through DNA methylation) but "do not involve DNA modifications" (Lock 2015, 151). Lock (2018) emphasizes that scientific research in epigenetics tends to "miniaturize" the environment that is seen to impact gene expression, which makes these impacts easier to measure. Qualitative ethnographic research produces a much broader view of the environment and all its entailments.

5. THE POLITICS OF CHANCE

This chapter draws on material previously published in Goldfarb 2016b.

1. Children's Views and Voices (CVV) is the oldest self-support organization for careleavers in Japan, founded in Osaka in 2001. In 2010, Tanpopo and CVV were two of five such groups in Japan; by 2015, there were eleven groups.

2. Thanks to Fujikawa Fumiko for assistance with these translations.

3. The term *tōjisha* was "originally a legal term referring to the 'parties concerned' in litigation; it is now widely used among minority and civil-rights groups to insist on their right to self-representation and self-determination" (McLelland 2011, 146). The characters mean *this* (当), *matter* or *circumstance* (事), and *person* (者).

4. Only around 0.3 percent of the child population in Japan is in state care. The small population contributes to their invisibility; greater social awareness may lessen stigma and discrimination (Nishida et al. 2011; Children's Views and Voices and Nagase 2015).

5. Although the average length of time in care is around 4.5 years, this statistic does not take into account multiple placements. A 2012 survey of 949 careleavers undertaken by a Tokyo-based tōjisha support group found that 20 percent of respondents had been in care between five and ten years, 19 percent had been in care between ten and fifteen years, and seventeen percent had been in care for over fifteen years. In line with national statistics at the time, around 10 percent of respondents had been in family-based foster care, and the remaining 90 percent had spent time in institutional care facilities (Futaba Flat Home 2012, 5, 7).

6. Legal debates surrounding Article 25 of Japan's constitution, which sets forth citizens' rights to "social welfare and security," resulted in a Supreme Court finding that "strengthened substantially the discourse on the duty of all citizens to provide for their own (or their family's) 'wholesome and cultured living,' weakening the idea of a right to social security for all" and further reinforcing "the idea that the citizen had the right and obligation to work" (Hook and Takeda 2007, 100–101).

7. The term *jiko sekinin* emerged as a catchphrase in 2004 when three Japanese citizens were taken hostage in Iraq; the Koizumi administration called their Iraq trip irresponsible and the ransom demands a burden on Japan, and the hostages were criticized and discredited by claims of their supposed lack of self-responsibility. Miriam Silverberg (2007) notes that "the term had been adopted as one of accusation by those in power eager to abnegate responsibility" and connects discourses surrounding jiko sekinin to militarism and public debates surrounding war responsibility.

8. Hook and Takeda note that the economic crisis of the 1990s and early 2000s led to classic neoliberal reforms, such as the reorganization of the pension system, and discourses surrounding self-responsibility were part of a larger policymaking project to "reshape the relationship between the Japanese state and the citizen." They argue that "this combined to lead to governmental and popular promotion of a self-sufficient life, that is, a life in which each 'productive self' shoulders the responsibility to deal with his or her own economic and social risks without depending on state provisions" (2007, 110, 109).

9. Careleavers ranked their greatest difficulties upon independence from state care as the lack of an apartment guarantor, deep loneliness upon suddenly solitary living, having no one to talk to or from whom to obtain advice, problems with family relationships and difficulty maintaining work and personal relationships, and having nowhere to depend on in case of illness (Futaba Flat Home 2012, 16; Children's Views and Voices and Nagase 2015; MUFG 2021).

10. Hyperawareness of one's difference from normal peers is a common problem for young people in the state welfare system. Children's Views and Voices (CVV), the Osaka tōjisha group, notes that tacit understandings about normal families contribute to tōjisha's sense of social exclusion and their invisibility within others' commonsense frameworks (2015, 15).

11. In their research with youth leaving American foster care, Samuels and Pryce (2008) call this rhetoric "what doesn't kill you makes you stronger."

12. Young people responding to a careleaver survey listed part-time work as their top need in preparing for independence from state care (second and third were the necessity for relevant work credentials and the need for an apartment guarantor) (Futaba Flat Home 2012, 12).

13. Most child welfare institutions in Japan are privately managed with public funds and hire their own staff members. Public institutions are staffed mainly by Japanese civil servants who change positions every few years, from water sanitation to child welfare to transportation, etc. There are very few fully public institutions in Japan, but those that exist have a reputation for being extremely large with limited resources and untrained staff.

14. Naoki's experiences regarding violence within the institution are not uncommon (Japan Federation of Bar Associations 2009; Tsuzaki 2009; Onchōen Children's Support Group 2011; Goldfarb 2013). Bamba and Haight (2011) describe institutional caregivers' desire to *mimamoru*, to watch and protect from afar without direct intervention, also common in the education of young children in Japan. However, inter-child violence in child welfare institutions can reach extremes that seem to demand intervention, even as employees are hampered by insufficient staffing, training, and support. For a personal account, see *"Edwādo no omoide nikki,"* available at http://yogo-shisetsu.info /ganbare/nikki/no001.html.

15. This common solution means that housing depends on a person's ability to continue working; injury or conflicts at work can easily result in homelessness. For detailed analysis, see chapter 3 of Children's Views and Voices and Nagase (2015).

16. *Moto* can be used to indicate an ex-wife, for example, or a former prime minister, in situations where a past state still inflects current meaning and identity.

17. In later conversations with Naoki by email, Naoki made clear that mental health services—particularly counseling and trauma therapy, rather than the ubiquitous dependence on psychopharmaceuticals—was what he most desired. For someone without national health insurance or stable employment, costly private counseling was far out of Naoki's reach. For more on mental health care in Japan, see Kitanaka 2012.

18. Child welfare scholars comment on the irony that young people in state care, who need more support than the general population, are forced to be independent at a younger age than youth who can depend on family (Goodman 2000; Hinata Bokko 2009; Nishida et al. 2011; King 2012). See also a Tokyo survey of former state wards, Tokyo Metropolitan Government 2011, and MUFG 2021. For an American example, see Smith 2011.

19. Naoki did not cite national discourses surrounding irregularly employed young people (*freeters*). However, the way he tethered work practices to alignment with state priorities echoes public discourses regarding the crisis of irregular workers in Japan, whose

labor practices undermine "the norm of a productive self" and who are targeted as objects for "a new set of disciplinary regulations" (Hook and Takeda 2007, 119, 122; for gendered dimensions, see Cook 2016).

20. In contrast to research on hikikomori focusing on familial care as a key aspect of life as a shut-in (Borovoy 2008; Horiguchi 2011), Naoki's case—as a solitary shut-in with no one to care for him—highlights a less explored aspect of social isolation in Japan.

21. This email communication took place after I had returned to the United States. Naoki's willingness to confide in me was in part, I believe, because of my physical and social distance. I introduced Naoki to a therapist who agreed to correspond with him at no charge, but Naoki did not pursue this connection. I have written briefly about Naoki's situation in a review of Anne Allison's text, *Precarious Japan* (Goldfarb 2014).

6. KNOWLEDGE AND NARRATION

1. It is typical in Japan for young adults in school to live with family to save money.

2. This is one reason that Alzheimer's patients often show decreased functioning after being moved from familiar surroundings to unfamiliar care facilities: the physical space that had operated as an implicit memory aid was now lost to them (Barnier 2010). Reavey and Brown (2007) examine the ways that physical spaces, such as a bedroom featuring a door that could be locked, are key mnemonic features in sexual abuse survivors' narratives.

3. I thank Donna Goldstein for offering me this language and, with Junko Kitanaka and Amy Borovoy, for pressing me to consider the normative underpinnings of these sorts of knowledge practices.

4. Elinor Ochs and Lisa Capps point out that the use of "personal names and pronouns imply a unified self," a culturally specific view of personhood. This perspective contrasts "the view that the self comprises multiple, partial selves in flux," which anthropologists have identified as belonging to "small-scale, non-European societies" but have equally embraced more recently "in the postmodern Western world" (1996, 29); and in the context of therapy, for instance, Schwartz 2001.

5. This name is a pseudonym chosen by "Nozomi" and retains the tenor of her actual given name.

6. In some institutions, directors and caregivers have long tenures, and young people who have aged out may be able to return and find people who knew them as babies.

7. One reason children may be afraid to ask for background information is that they may fear that they themselves caused the fragmentation of their family. The fact that their background has not been discussed with them indicates to many children that this past is unspeakably bad. Children may also implicitly know that their foster parents are not their biological parents, but they feel what social workers call a *loyalty conflict* between biological and social parents and hesitate to ask for information.

8. LSW can be considered a process of reeducation: "In helping a child understand the reality of his [sic] life to date, one must find and dispute the irrational, negative beliefs the child holds about himself and his parents in order to allow him to see himself, his life, and the future in a more positive and realistic way" (Aust 1981, 558).

9. Blank Life Story Books are also sold for children to fill in. One version has been translated into Japanese, a project led by Saimura Mari (Saimura 2009).

10. Although this is a point Shōko makes repeatedly to institutional caregivers in trainings, at Chestnut House, staff expressed significant concern that information about a child's past was too difficult for the child to handle, or that the child's parent would be angry that certain information was conveyed. In my fieldwork, I heard many accounts of children's offhand comments—the signs Shōko wanted caregivers to catch—but

institutional staff often simply did not know what to say in response, and thus said nothing. Even engaged and well-meaning staff had difficulty implementing the most basic tenets of LSW.

11. https://narrativetherapycentre.com/about/.

12. See Baynes 2008 on the power of caseworkers to document truths in case files, and Ochs and Capps 1996 on narrative asymmetry.

13. Bartlett's claim that "remembering appears to be far more decisively an affair of construction than one of mere reproduction" (1932, 205), taken seriously by scholars focusing on the social dimensions of collective memory and collaborative remembering, sits uncomfortably with a continued focus on veracity in legal claims like those regarding sexual abuse, a tension made explicit during the "memory wars" of the 1980s (Reavey and Brown 2007; Winters 2012).

14. This interview was conducted in both English and Japanese (Tokunaga Shōko conducts research in England). This quotation was spoken in English.

15. All italicized quotations are my translations from the written Japanese.

16. "*Edwādo no omoide nikki*" (Edward's journal of reminiscences), available at *Ganbare! Yōgo shisetsu shusshinsha*, http://yogo-shisetsu.info/ganbare/nikki/no001.html.

17. At the time of writing, Edward has publicly come out about his experiences, but during my fieldwork his children were unaware of some elements of his past. This chapter uses the name he chose for his online writing.

18. Cathy Caruth offers a Freudian perspective that I find compelling: traumatic repetitions are explicitly connected to the inability to have known them in the moment, but are experienced post facto as "the very incomprehensibility of one's own survival." Repetitions are "the very attempt to *claim one's own survival*" (1996, 64, italics in original).

CONCLUSION

1. It is difficult, however, to empirically define and assess what a "good outcome" is in child welfare placements (Dickens et al. 2019).

2. The FosterClub findings align with extensive coverage by *The Imprint: Youth and Family News* on the impacts of the COVID-19 pandemic on children in the American child welfare system.

3. Foster care researcher, former social worker, and anthropologist Danielle Wozniak writes, "Most research relevant to the crisis in the [US] foster care system has decontextualized systemic problems and has disembodied the subjects of investigation. That is to say, most research has examined specific problems within the system without examining the ideologies and assumptions upon which policies and practices are based, and has excluded consideration of the historical, cultural, and political contexts through which problems are created and identified" (2002, 212).

4. The work of the International Foster Care Alliance (IFCA) is particularly noteworthy in the context of this systematic invisibility.

5. As a refutation to universalizing nihonjinron rhetoric about Japanese people, I am inspired by Naoki Sakai's exploration of the concept of "Japan" (in scare quotes) in a manner that produces, in the words of Meaghan Morris, a "'nonaggregate' Japan . . . by reading from the oppressed or unlivable edges of national space" (1997, xx).

6. Chris Burgess (2010) points out that even if nihonjinron discourses are not reflections of reality, they still impact public policy and have real social effects.

7. "Top Court: No Registry for Pair Born to Surrogate," *Japan Times Online*, March 24, 2007, https://www.japantimes.co.jp/news/2007/03/24/national/top-court-no-registry-for-pair-born-to-surrogate.

8. "Japan Gives Legal Recognition to Parents Using Donated Eggs, Sperm," *Kyodo News*, December 4, 2020, https://english.kyodonews.net/news/2020/12/c99a1016f5ea-japan-gives-legal-recognition-to-parents-using-donated-eggs-sperm.html.

9. "In Landmark Ruling, Court Says Japan's Ban on Same-Sex Marriage Is Unconstitutional," NPR, March 17, 2021, https://www.npr.org/2021/03/17/978148301/in-landmark-ruling-court-says-japans-ban-on-same-sex-marriage-is-unconstitutiona.

10. "Japan's Diet Passes Bill to Allow Joint Custody after Divorce." *Kyodo News,* May 17, 2024, https://english.kyodonews.net/news/2024/05/9d339f1f3d5c-japans-diet-passes-bill-to-allow-joint-custody-after-divorce.html.

Works Cited

Alexy, Allison. 2020. *Intimate Disconnections: Divorce and the Romance of Independence in Contemporary Japan.* Chicago: University of Chicago Press.

Allison, Anne. 1991. "Japanese Mothers and *Obentōs*: The Lunch-Box as Ideological State Apparatus." *Anthropological Quarterly* 64 (4): 195–208.

Allison, Anne. 2013. *Precarious Japan.* Durham, NC: Duke University Press.

Ambrose, Drew. 2014. "Japan's Throwaway Children." *Aljazeera*, October 3, 2014. http://www.aljazeera.com/programmes/101east/2014/09/japan-throwaway-children-20149299271732632.html.

Aoki, Kikuyo. 2012. "*Seikatsu rinshō ni okeru kankeisei enjo e no shinri rinshōteki sekkin*" ("A Psychoclinical Approach to Relational Assistance in Clinical Life"). In *Shakaiteki yōgo ni okeru seikatsu rinshō to shinri rinshō (Clinical Life and Clinical Psychology in Social Care)*, edited by Takashi Masuzawa and Kikuyo Aoki, 70–82. Tokyo: Fukumura shuppan.

Aust, Patricia H. 1981. "Using the Life Story Book in Treatment of Children in Placement." *Child Welfare* 60 (8): 535–560.

Bachnik, Jane M. 1983. "Recruitment Strategies for Household Succession: Rethinking Japanese Household Organization." *Man* 18 (1): 160–182.

Bakhtin, M. M. 1981. *The Dialogic Imagination: Four Essays.* Austin: University of Texas Press.

Bamba, Sachiko, and Wendy. L. Haight. 2011. *Child Welfare and Development: A Japanese Case Study.* Cambridge, UK: Cambridge University Press.

Bamford, Sandra. 2009. "'Family Trees' among the Kamea of Papua New Guinea: A Non-Genealogical Approach to Imagining Relatedness." In *Kinship and Beyond: The Genealogical Model Reconsidered*, edited by Sandra Bamford and James Leach, 159–174. New York: Berghahn.

Barad, Karen. 2007. *Meeting the Universe Halfway: Quantum Physics and the Entanglement of Matter and Meaning.* Durham, NC: Duke University Press.

Barad, Karen. 2010. "Quantum Entanglements and Hauntological Relations of Inheritance: Dis/continuities, Spacetime Enfoldings, and Justice-to-Come." *Derrida Today* 3 (2): 240–268.

Barnier, Amanda J. 2010. "Memories, Memory Studies and My iPhone." *Memory Studies* 3 (4): 293–297.

Bartlett, Frederic C. 1932. *Remembering: An Experimental and Social Study.* Cambridge, UK: Cambridge University Press.

Baynes, Polly. 2008. "Untold Stories: A Discussion of Life Story Work." *Adoption & Fostering* 32 (2): 43–49.

Befu, Harumi. 2001. *Hegemony of Homogeneity: An Anthropological Analysis of Nihonjinron.* Melbourne, Australia: Trans Pacific.

Benedict, Ruth. 1946. *The Chrysanthemum and the Sword.* Boston: Houghton Mifflin Co.

Benjamin, Walter. 1968. "The Work of Art in the Age of Mechanical Reproduction." In *Illuminations: Essays and Reflections*, 217–251. New York: Schocken.

Berlant, Lauren. 2011. *Cruel Optimism.* Durham, NC: Duke University Press.

Bietti, Lucas M., Charles B. Stone, and William Hirst. 2014. "Contextualizing Human Memory." *Memory Studies* 7 (3): 267–271.

Borneman, John. 1997. "Caring and Being Cared For: Displacing Marriage, Kinship, Gender and Sexuality." *International Social Science* 49 (154): 573–584.

Borovoy, Amy. 2008. "Japan's Hidden Youths: Mainstreaming the Emotionally Distressed in Japan." *Culture, Medicine and Psychiatry* 32: 552–576.

Borovoy, Amy. 2012. "Doi Takeo and the Rehabilitation of Particularism in Postwar Japan." *Journal of Japanese Studies* 38 (2): 263–295.

Bourdieu, Pierre. 1977. *Outline of a Theory of Practice*. Cambridge, UK: Cambridge University Press.

Bourdieu, Pierre. 1990. *The Logic of Practice*. Stanford, CA: Stanford University Press.

Bourdieu, Pierre. 2000. "The Biographical Illusion." In *Identity: A Reader*, edited by Paul du Gay, Jessica Evans, and Peter Redman, 297–303. London: Sage.

Bowlby, John. 1951. *Maternal Care and Mental Health*. Geneva, Switzerland: World Health Organization.

Bowlby, John. 1982 [1969]. *Attachment and Loss: Volume I*. New York: Basic.

Briggs, Charles L. 1986. *Learning How to Ask: A Sociolinguist Appraisal of the Role of the Interview in Social Science Research*. Cambridge, UK: Cambridge University Press.

Browne, Kevin. 2009. *The Risk of Harm to Young Children in Institutional Care*. London: Save the Children.

Browne, Kevin, Catherine Hamilton-Giachritsis, Rebecca Johnson, and Mikael Ostergren. 2006. "Overuse of Institutional Care for Children in Europe." *British Medical Journal* 332: 485–487.

Brown, Steven D., and Paula Reavey. 2014. "Vital Memories: Movements in and between Affect, Ethics and Self." *Memory Studies* 7 (3): 328–338.

Bryant, Taimie L. 1990. "Sons and Lovers: Adoption in Japan." *American Journal of Comparative Law* 38 (2): 299–336.

Burgess, Chris. 2010. "The 'Illusion' of Homogenous Japan and National Character: Discourse as a Tool to Transcend the 'Myth' vs. 'Reality' Binary." *Asia-Pacific Journal* 9 (1): 10. https://apjjf.org/-Chris-Burgess/3310/article.html.

Cannell, Fenella. 2013. "The Re-enchantment of Kinship." In *Vital Relations: Modernity and the Persistent Life of Kinship*, edited by Susan McKinnon and Fenella Cannell, 217–240. Santa Fe, NM: School for Advanced Research Press.

Carsten, Janet. 2004. *After Kinship*. Cambridge, UK: Cambridge University Press.

Caruth, Cathy. 2010. *Unclaimed Experience: Trauma, Narrative and History*. Baltimore, MD: Johns Hopkins University Press.

Castañeda, Claudia. 2002. *Figurations: Child, Bodies, Worlds*. Durham, NC: Duke University Press.

Chapman, Christopher. 2024. "Dissonances in Care: Childhood, Well-Being, and the Politics of Welfare in Japan." PhD diss., University of Oxford.

Chapman, David, and Karl Jakob Krogness, eds. 2014. *Japan's Household Registration System and Citizenship: Koseki, Identification and Documentation*. London: Routledge.

Children's Views and Voices and Masako Nagase. 2015. *Shakaiteki yōgo no tōjisha shien gaido bukku (A Guidebook for the Support of Child Welfare Tōjisha)*. Osaka, Japan: Children's Views and Voices.

Collier, Jane, Michelle Z. Rosaldo, and Sylvia Yanagisako. 1997 [1982]. "Is There a Family? New Anthropological Views." In *The Gender and Sexuality Reader*, edited by Roger Lancaster and Micaela di Leonardo, 71–81. New York: Routledge.

Cook, Emma E. 2016. *Reconstructing Adult Masculinities: Part-Time Work in Contemporary Japan*. Oxford, UK: Routledge.

Cook, Emma E. 2019. "Power, Intimacy, and Irregular Employment in Japan." In *Intimate Japan: Ethnographies of Closeness and Conflict*, edited by Allison Alexy and Emma E. Cook, 129–147. Honolulu: University of Hawai'i Press.

Cook-Cottone, Catherine, and Meredith Beck. 2007. "A Model for Life-Story Work: Facilitating the Construction of Personal Narrative for Foster Children." *Child and Adolescent Mental Health* 12 (4): 193–195.

Counts, Dorothy Ayers, and David Counts. 1983. "Father's Water Equals Mother's Milk: The Conception of Parentage in Kaliai, West New Britain." *Mankind* 14 (1): 46–56.

Crapanzano, Vincent. 2003. "Reflections on Hope as a Category of Social and Psychological Analysis." *Cultural Anthropology* 18 (1): 3–32.

Crawford, Allison. 2010. "'If the Body Keeps the Score': Mapping the Dissociated Body in Trauma Narrative, Intervention, and Theory." *University of Toronto Quarterly* 79 (2): 702–719.

Csordas, Thomas J. 1990. "Embodiment as a Paradigm for Anthropology." *Ethos* 18 (1): 5–47.

Csordas, Thomas J. 1994. *Embodiment and Experience: The Existential Ground of Culture and Self*. Cambridge, UK: Cambridge University Press.

Dale, Peter. 1986. *The Myth of Japanese Uniqueness*. New York: St. Martin's.

D'Andrea, Wendy, Julian Ford, Bradley Stolbach, Joseph Spinazzola, and Bessel A. van der Kolk. 2012. "Understanding Interpersonal Trauma in Children: Why We Need a Developmentally Appropriate Trauma Diagnosis." *American Journal of Orthopsychiatry* 82 (2): 187–200.

Danely, Jason. 2014. *Aging and Loss: Mourning and Maturity in Contemporary Japan*. New Brunswick, NJ: Rutgers University Press.

Deguchi, Akira. 2005. "Double or Extra? The Identity of Transnational Adoptees in Sweden." *Culture Unbound* 5: 425–450.

Desjarlais, Robert. 1994. "Struggling Along: The Possibilities for Experience among the Homeless Mentally Ill." *American Anthropologist* 96 (4): 886–901.

Dickens, Jonathan, Judith Masson, Ludivine Garside, Julie Young, and Kay Bader. 2019. "Courts, Care Proceedings and Outcomes Uncertainty: The Challenges of Achieving and Assessing 'Good Outcomes' for Children after Child Protection Proceedings." *Child & Family Social Work* 24 (4): 574–581.

Diprose, Rosalyn. 2002. *Corporeal Generosity: On Giving with Nietzsche, Merleau-Ponty, and Levinas*. Albany: State University of New York Press.

Dobrova-Krol, Natasha. A., Marinus H. van Ijzendoorn, Marian J. Bakermans-Kranenburg, Chantal Cyr, and Femmie Juffer. 2008. "Physical Growth Delays and Stress Dysregulation in Stunted and Non-stunted Ukrainian Institution-Reared Children." *Infant Behavior & Development* 31: 539–553.

Doi, Takeo. 2014. *The Anatomy of Dependence*. New York: Kodansha International.

Donzelot, Jacques. 1979. *The Policing of Families*. New York: Pantheon.

Dorow, Sara K. 2006. *Transnational Adoption: A Cultural Economy of Race, Gender, and Kinship*. New York: New York University Press.

Dower, John W. 1999. *Embracing Defeat: Japan in the Wake of World War II*. New York: W. W. Norton and Co.

Dumit, Joseph. 2004. *Picturing Personhood: Brain Scans and Biomedical Identity*. Princeton, NJ: Princeton University Press.

Edwards, Derek, and David Middleton. 1988. "Conversational Remembering and Family Relationships: How Children Learn to Remember." *Journal of Social and Personal Relationships* 5 (1): 3–25.

Ehrenreich, Barbara, and Janet McIntosh. 1997. "The New Creationism: Biology under Attack." *The Nation*, June 9, 1997.

Eng, David L. 2010. *The Feeling of Kinship: Queer Liberalism and the Racialization of Intimacy*. Durham, NC: Duke University Press.

Farquhar, Judith. 2002. *Appetites: Food and Sex in Post-Socialist China*. Durham, NC: Duke University Press.

Farquhar, Judith, and Margaret Lock. 2007. "Introduction." In *Beyond the Body Proper: Reading the Anthropology of Material Life*, edited by Margaret Lock and Judith Farquhar, 1–18. Durham, NC: Duke University Press.

Ferguson, James. 2009. "Global Disconnect: Abjection and the Aftermath of Modernism." In *Industrial Work and Life: An Anthropological Reader*, edited by Massimiliano Mollona, Geert de Neve, and Jonathan Parry, 311–328. Oxford, UK: Berg.

Fields, Karen. 2001. "Witchcraft and Racecraft: Invisible Ontology in Its Sensible Manifestations." In *Witchcraft Dialogues: Anthropological and Philosophical Exchanges*, edited by Geore Clement Bond and Diane Ciekawy, 283–315. Athens, OH: Ohio University Center for International Studies.

Fivush, Robyn. 2008. "Remembering and Reminiscing: How Individual Lives Are Constructed in Family Narratives." *Memory Studies* 1 (1): 49–58.

FosterClub. 2020. "The Impact of COVID-19 on Youth from Foster Care: A National Poll." Last modified May 13, 2020. https://www.fosterclub.com/sites/default/files/docs/blogs/COVID%20Poll%20Results%20May%2010%202020.pdf.

Foucault, Michel. 1978. *The History of Sexuality, Volume 1*. New York: Pantheon.

Foucault, Michel. 1995. *Discipline & Punish: The Birth of the Prison*. New York: Vintage.

Franklin, Sarah. 1997. *Embodied Progress: A Cultural Account of Assisted Conception*. New York: Routledge.

Franklin, Sarah, and Susan McKinnon. 2001. "Introduction." In *Relative Values: Reconfiguring Kinship Studies*, edited by Sarah Franklin and Susan McKinnon, 1–25. Durham, NC: Duke University Press.

French, Brigittine M. 2012. "The Semiotics of Collective Memories." *Annual Review of Anthropology* 41: 337–53.

Frühstück, Sabine. 2003. *Colonizing Sex: Sexology and Social Control in Modern Japan*. Berkeley: University of California Press.

Fujisawa, Yoko. 2012. "*Jidō jiritsu shien shisetsu ni okeru seikatsu rinshō to shinrishoku no yakuwari*" ("The Role of Lifestyle-Centered Approaches to Clinical Psychiatry in Independent Living Facilities"). In *Shakaiteki yōgo ni okeru seikatsu rinshō to shinri rinshō* (*Lifestyle-Centered Approaches and Clinical Psychology in the Context of Social Protective Care*). Edited by Takashi Masuzawa and Kikuyo Aoki, 131–142. Tokyo, Japan: Fukumura shuppan.

Futaba Flat Home. 2012. *Shakaiteki yōgo shisetsu nado oyobi sato oya shushinsha jittai chōsa gaiyō hōkokusho* (*Report Summary of Survey of Actual Conditions Regarding Alumni of Child Welfare Institutions and Foster Families*). http://jiritsukakehashi.com/wp-content/themes/kakehashi/images/resarch_2015.pdf.

Gal, Susan. 2002. "A Semiotics of the Public/Private Distinction." *Differences: A Journal of Feminist Cultural Studies* 13 (1): 77–95.

Garon, Sheldon. 1997. *Molding Japanese Minds: The State in Everyday Life*. Princeton, NJ: Princeton University Press.

Garon, Sheldon. 2010. "State and Family in Modern Japan: A Historical Perspective." *Economy and Society* 39 (3): 317–336.

Gaskins, Suzanne. 2013. "The Puzzle of Attachment: Unscrambling Maturational and Cultural Contributions to the Development of Early Emotional Bonds." In *Attachment Reconsidered: Cultural Perspectives on a Western Theory*, edited by Naomi Quinn and Jeannette Marie Mageo, 33–64. New York: Palgrave MacMillan.

Gluck, Carol. 1985. *Japan's Modern Myths: Ideology in the Late Meiji Period*. Princeton, NJ: Princeton University Press.

Goffman, Erving. 1961. *Asylums. Essays on the Social Situation of Mental Patients and Other Inmates.* New York: Anchor.

Goffman, Erving. 1963. *Stigma: Notes on the Management of Spoiled Identity.* New York: Simon and Schuster.

Goldfarb, Kathryn E. 2010. "Making the Oral Contraceptive 'for Me' in Japan: Managing the Semiotics of Reproductive Health in Virtual Space." In *Liberalizing, Feminizing and Popularizing Health Communications in Asia,* edited by Liew Kai Khiun, 129–148. Burlington, VT: Ashgate.

Goldfarb, Kathryn E. 2013. "Japan." In *Child Protection and Child Welfare: A Global Appraisal of Cultures, Policy and Practice,* edited by John Dixon and Penelope Wellbourne, 144–169. London: Jessica Kingsley.

Goldfarb, Kathryn E. 2014. "Anne Allison's *Precarious Japan.*" *Somatosphere,* May 29, 2014. http://somatosphere.net/2014/05/anne-allisons-precarious-japan.html.

Goldfarb, Kathryn E. 2015. "Developmental Logics: Brain Science, Child Welfare, and the Ethics of Engagement in Japan." *Social Science & Medicine* 143: 271–278.

Goldfarb, Kathryn E. 2016a. "'Coming to Look Alike': Materializing Affinity in Japanese Foster and Adoptive Care." *Social Analysis* 60 (2): 2016.

Goldfarb, Kathryn E. 2016b. "'Self-Responsibility' and the Politics of Chance: Theorizing the Experience of Japanese Child Welfare." *Japanese Studies* 36 (2): 173–189.

Goldfarb, Kathryn E. 2017. "Food, Affect, and Experiments in Care: Constituting a 'Household-like' Child Welfare Institution in Japan." In *Child's Play: Multi-sensory Histories of Children and Childhood in Japan,* edited by Sabine Frühstück and Anne Walthall, 243–263. Berkeley: University of California Press.

Goldfarb, Kathryn E. 2018. "Beyond Blood Ties: Intimate Kinships in Japanese Foster and Adoptive Care." In *Intimate Japan,* edited by Allison Alexy and Emma Cook, 181–198. Honolulu: University of Hawai'i Press.

Goldfarb, Kathryn E. 2019. "Relationships That Matter: Embodying Absent Kinships in the Japanese Child Welfare System." In *Handbook of Medical Humanities,* edited by Alan Bleakley, 282–289. London: Routledge.

Goldfarb, Kathryn E. 2021. "Parental Rights and the Temporality of Attachment: Law, Kinship, and Child Welfare in Japan." *positions: asia critique* 29 (3): 469–493.

Goldfarb, Kathryn E., and Caroline Schuster. 2016. "Editor's Introduction: (De)materializing Kinship: Holding Together Mutuality and Difference." *Social Analysis* 60 (2): 1–12.

Goldfarb, Kathryn E., and Sandra Bamford, eds. 2024. *Difficult Attachments: Anxieties of Kinship and Care.* New Brunswick, NJ: Rutgers University Press.

Goodman, Nelson. 1972. *Problems and Projects.* Indianapolis, IN: The Bobbs-Merrill Company.

Goodman, Roger. 1998. "The 'Japanese-Style Welfare State' and the Delivery of Personal Social Services." In *The East Asian Welfare Model: Welfare Orientalism and the State,* edited by Roger Goodman, Gordon White, and Huck-Ju Kwon, 139–158. New York: Routledge.

Goodman, Roger. 2000. *Children of the Japanese State: The Changing Role of Child Protection Institutions in Contemporary Japan.* New York: Oxford University Press.

Goodman, Roger. 2002. "Anthropology, Policy and the Study of Japan." In *Family and Social Policy in Japan,* edited by Roger Goodman, 1–28. Cambridge, UK: Cambridge University Press.

Goody, Jack. 1969. "Adoption in Cross-Cultural Perspective." *Comparative Studies in Society and History* 11 (1): 55–78.

Greenhouse, Carol J., ed. 2010. *Ethnographies of Neoliberalism.* Philadelphia: University of Pennsylvania Press.

Gupta, Akhil. 2012. *Red Tape: Bureaucracy, Structural Violence, and Poverty in India.* Durham, NC: Duke University Press.

Gypen, Laura, Johan Vanderfaeillie, Skrallan De Maeyer, Laurence Belenger, and Frank Van Holen. 2017. "Outcomes of Children Who Grew Up in Foster Care: Systematic-Review." *Children and Youth Services Review* 76: 74–83.

Hacking, Ian. 1996. "The Looping Effects of Human Kinds." In *Causal Cognition: A Multidisciplinary Approach*, edited by Dan Sperber, David Premack, and Ann James Premack, 351–383. Oxford, UK: Clarendon Press.

Halbwachs, Maurice. 1992. *On Collective Memory*. Chicago: University of Chicago Press.

Hamada, Tomohiro. 2021. "Life after Foster Care No Bed of Roses for Many." *Asahi Shimbun*, May 1, 2021. http://www.asahi.com/ajw/articles/14341374.

Hankins, Joseph. 2014. *Working Skin: Making Leather, Making a Multicultural Japan*. Berkeley: University of California Press.

Haraway, Donna. 1988. "Situated Knowledges: The Science Question in Feminism and the Privilege of Partial Perspective." *Feminist Studies* 14 (3): 575–599.

Harootunian, Harry D.. 1989. "Visible Discourses/Invisible Ideologies." In *Postmodernism and Japan*, edited by Masao Miyoshi and Harry D. Harootunian, 63–92. Durham, NC: Duke University Press.

Harris, Celia B., Helen M. Paterson, and Richard I. Kemp. 2008. "Collaborative Recall and Collective Memory: What Happens When We Remember Together?" *Memory* 16 (3): 213–230.

Hayes, Peter, and Toshie Habu. 2006. *Adoption in Japan: Comparing Policies for Children in Need*. New York: Routledge.

Hennessy, Sumiko. 2004. *Ko o aisenai haha: haha o kyohi suru ko (Mothers Who Cannot Love Their Children, Children Who Refuse Their Mothers)*. Tokyo, Japan: Gakushū kenkyūsha.

Hennessy, Sumiko. 2006. *Ki ni naru ko: rikai dekiru kea dekiru (Worrisome Children: Being Able to Understand and Care)*. Tokyo, Japan: Gakushyū kenkyūsha.

Hertz, Robert. 1973 [1909]. "The Pre-eminence of the Right Hand." In *Right and Left: Essays on Dual Symbolic Classification*, translated by Rodney Needham and Claudia Needham, edited by Rodney Needham, 3–31. Chicago: University of Chicago Press.

Hinata Bokko. 2009. *Shisetsu de sodatta kodomotachi no ibasho "Hinata Bokko" to shakaiteki yōgo (A Place to Belong for Children Who Were Raised in Institutional Care: "Hinata Bokko" and Social Protective Care)*. Tokyo, Japan: Akashi shoten.

Hirst, William, and David Manier. 2008. "Towards a Psychology of Collective Memory." *Memory* 16 (3): 183–200.

Ho, Michelle H. S. 2020. "Queer and Normal: *Dansō* (Female-to-Male Crossdressing) Lives and Politics in Contemporary Tokyo." *Asian Anthropology* 19 (2): 102–118.

Hook, Glenn D., and Hiroko Takeda. 2007. "'Self-Responsibility' and the Nature of the Postwar Japanese State: Risk through the Looking Glass." *Journal of Japanese Studies* 33 (1): 93–123.

Horiguchi, Sachiko. 2011. "Coping with Hikikomori: Socially Withdrawn Youth and the Japanese Family." In *Home and Family in Japan: Continuity and Transformation*, edited by Richard Ronald and Allison Alexy, 216–235. New York: Routledge.

Howell, Signe. 2006. *The Kinning of Foreigners: Transnational Adoption in a Global Perspective*. New York: Berghahn.

Howell, Signe. 2009. "Adoption of the Unrelated Child: Some Challenges to the Anthropological Study of Kinship." *Annual Review of Anthropology* 38: 149–66.

Hozumi, Baron Nobushige. 2004. *Ancestor-Worship and Japanese Law*. London: Kegan Paul.

Hume, David. 1977. *An Enquiry Concerning Human Understanding*. Indianapolis, IN: Hackett.

Ide, Tomohiro. 2012. *"Jidō fukushi shisetsu ni okeru shinrishoku no genjō"* ("Current Status of Psychologists in Child Welfare Institutions"). In *Shakaiteki yōgo ni okeru seikatsu rinshō to shinri rinshō (Clinical Life and Clinical Psychology in Social Care)*, edited by Takashi Masuzawa and Kikuyo Aoki, 41–57. Tokyo, Japan: Fukumura shuppan.

Ide, Tomohiro. 2021. *"Shakaiteki yōgo ni naizai suru sōshitsu to sore ni tomonaū hitan ni tsuite no hōkatsuteki rikai to shien ni kansuru rironteki kentō"* ("A Theoretical Review about Comprehensive Understanding and Support Pertaining to Grief and Loss in Alternative Care"). *Bulletin of Counselling Room for Developmental and Clinical Needs* 5: 33–47. https://eprints.lib.hokudai.ac.jp/dspace/bitstream/2115/84515/1/04_2434-7639_5_33-47.pdf

Ingold, Tim. 1990. "An Anthropologist Looks at Biology." *Man* 25 (2): 208–229.

Ingold, Tim. 2004. "Beyond Biology and Culture. The Meaning of Evolution in a Relational World." *Social Anthropology* 12 (2): 209–221.

Ingold, Tim. 2013. "Prospect." In *Biosocial Becomings: Integrating Social and Biological Anthropology*, edited by Tim Ingold and Gisli Palsson, 1–21. Cambridge, UK: Cambridge University Press.

International Care Leavers Convention. 2020. "Event Report." https://bettercarenetwork.org/sites/default/files/2021-04/CLC_Report.pdf.

International Foster Care Alliance (IFCA) Project C. 2020. *Shingata korona no kansen kakudai ni yoru anata no seikatsu e no eikyō ni tsuite no kinkyū chōsa (Emergency Survey on the Effect of the Coronavirus Pandemic on Your Life)*. https://www.ifca-projectc.org/%E8%AA%BF%E6%9F%BB%E6%A6%82%E8%A6%81.

Irvine, Judith, and Susan Gal. 2000. "Language Ideology and Linguistic Differentiation." In *Regimes of Language: Ideologies, Polities, and Identities*, edited by Paul V. Kroskrity, 35–84. Santa Fe, NM: School of American Research Press.

Ivry, Tsipy. 2010. *Embodying Culture: Pregnancy in Japan and Israel.* New Brunswick, NJ: Rutgers University Press.

Ivy, Marilyn. 1995. *Discourses of the Vanishing: Modernity, Phantasm, Japan.* Chicago: University of Chicago Press.

Japan Federation of Bar Associations (JFBA). 2009. "The Japan Federation of Bar Associations" Report on the Japanese Government's Third Report on the Convention on the Rights of the Child and the Initial Reports on OPAC & OPSC." https://www.nichibenren.or.jp/library/ja/kokusai/humanrights_library/treaty/data/child_report_3_en.pdf.

Jasanoff, Sheila. 2004. "The Idiom of Co-production." In *States of Knowledge: The Co-production of Science and Social Order*, edited by Sheila Jasanoff, 1–12. New York: Routledge.

Johnson, Rebecca, Kevin Browne, and Catherine Hamilton-Giachritsis. 2006. "Young Children in Institutional Care at Risk of Harm." *Trauma, Violence & Abuse* 7 (1): 34–60.

Kameda, Hideko, Shizuaki Fujieda, and Takashi Nakamura. 2014. *"Jidō yōgo shisetsu ni okeru chokusetsu shogū shokuin no sutoresu ni kansuru kenkyū: kinmu nensū tangun to kinmu nensū nagagun e no hankōzōka mensetsu ni yoru chōsa"* ("Study of Stress on the Direct Care Workers at Child Welfare Institutions: Semi-structured Interviews with Staff of Both Long and Short Years of Service"). *Journal of Kawaguchi Junior College* 28: 149–163. https://saigaku.repo.nii.ac.jp/record/354/files/04_kameda-fujieda-nakamura.pdf.

Kanda, Yukie, Hiromichi Morimoto, and Masafumi Inada. 2009. *"Jidō yōgo shisetsu shokuin no shisetsunai taiken to kanjō jōtai"* ("Workplace Experiences of Employees Working in Children's Care Homes and Their Emotional States"). *Kawasaki Medical Welfare* 19 (1): 35–45.

Keane, Webb. 1997. *Signs of Recognition: Powers and Hazards of Representation in an Indonesian Society*. Berkeley: University of California Press.

Keane, Webb. 2003. "Semiotics and the Social Analysis of Material Things." *Language and Communication* 23: 409–425.

Keller, Evelyn Fox. 2010. *The Mirage of a Space between Nature and Nurture*. Durham, NC: Duke University Press.

Kim, Eleana J. 2010. *Adopted Territory: Transnational Korean Adoptees and the Politics of Belonging*. Durham, NC: Duke University Press.

King, Michael M. 2012. "Who Cares? Exploring the Disparity in Contemporary Japanese Rates of Tertiary Education Progression between Children from Child Welfare Institutions and the General Population." Master's thesis, University of Oxford.

King, Michael Rivera. 2021. *Child Guidance Centres in Japan: Alternative Care, Social Work, and the Family*. London: Routledge.

Kitanaka, Junko. 2012. *Depression in Japan: Psychiatric Cures for a Society in Distress*. Princeton, NJ: Princeton University Press.

Kizuna no kai, ed. 1997. *Kazoku zukuri: Engumi kazoku no shuki* (*Making Family: Notes on Adoptive Family*). Yokohama, Japan: Seorishobō.

Kleinman, Arthur. 1988. *The Illness Narratives: Suffering, Healing, and the Human Condition*. New York: Basic.

Kodomo kateichō shienkyoku kateifukushika (Children and Families Agency). 2024. "*Shakaiteki yōgo no suishin ni mukete*" ("Advances in Social Protective Care"). https://www.cfa.go.jp/assets/contents/node/basic_page/field_ref_resources/8aba23f3-abb8-4f95-8202-f0fd487fbe16/f554b24c/20240216_policies_shakaiteki-yougo_84.pdf.

Kono, Makoto. 2005. "The Welfare Regime in Japan." In *East Asian Welfare Regimes in Transition: From Confucianism to Globalisation*, edited by Alan Walker and Chack-kie Wong, 117–144. Bristol, UK: Policy Press, University of Bristol.

Krieger, Nancy. 2006. "If 'Race' Is the Answer, What Is the Question?—on 'Race,' Racism, and Health: A Social Epidemiologist's Perspective." http://raceandgenomics.ssrc.org/Krieger.

Krogness, Karl Jacob. 2008. "The Koseki System and 'Koseki Consciousness.'" PhD diss., University of Copenhagen.

Krogness, Karl Jacob. 2011. "The Ideal, the Deficient, and the Illogical Family: An Initial Typology of Administrative Household Units." In *Home and Family in Japan: Continuity and Transformation*, edited by Richard Ronald and Allison Alexy, 65–90. London: Routledge.

Kroskrity, Paul V. 2000. *Regimes of Language: Ideologies, Polities, and Identities*. Santa Fe, NM: School of American Research Press.

Kuriyama, Shigehisa. 2002. *The Expressiveness of the Body and the Divergence of Greek and Chinese Medicine*. New York: Zone.

Kuwajima, Kaoru. 2019. "My Husband Is a Good Man When He Doesn't Hit Me: Redefining Intimacy among Victims of Domestic Violence." In *Intimate Japan: Ethnographies of Closeness and Conflict*, edited by Allison Alexy and Emma E. Cook, 112–128. Honolulu: University of Hawai'i Press.

Lebra, Takie Sugiyama. 1993. *Above the Clouds: Status Culture of the Modern Japanese Nobility*. Berkeley: University of California Press.

Levy, Terry M., and Michael Orlans. 2014. *Attachment, Trauma, and Healing: Understanding and Treating Attachment Disorder in Children, Families and Adults*. London: Jessica Kingsley.

lewallen, ann-elise. 2016. *The Fabric of Indigeneity: Ainu Identity, Gender, and Settler Colonialism in Japan*. Santa Fe, NM: School for Advanced Research Press.

Lie, John. 2001. *Multiethnic Japan*. Cambridge, MA: Harvard University Press.

Lipsky, Michael. 2010. *Street-Level Bureaucracy: Dilemmas of the Individual in Public Service*. New York: Russell Sage Foundation.

Lock, Margaret. 1993. *Encounters with Aging: Mythologies of Menopause in Japan and North America*. Berkeley: University of California Press.

Lock, Margaret. 1998. "Perfecting Society: Reproductive Technologies, Genetic Testing, and the Planned Family in Japan." In *Pragmatic Women and Body Politics*, edited by Margaret Lock and Patricia A. Kaufert, 206–239. Cambridge, UK: Cambridge University Press.

Lock, Margaret. 2001. "The Tempering of Medical Anthropology: Troubling Natural Categories." *Medical Anthropology Quarterly* 15 (4): 478–492.

Lock, Margaret. 2002. *Twice Dead: Organ Transplants and the Reinvention of Death*. Berkeley: University of California Press.

Lock, Margaret. 2015. "Comprehending the Body in the Era of the Epigenome." *Current Anthropology* 56 (2): 151–177.

Lock, Margaret. 2018. "Mutable Environments and Permeable Human Bodies." *Journal of the Royal Anthropological Institute* 24: 449–474.

Lock, Margaret, and Gisli Palsson. 2016. *Can Science Resolve the Nature/Nurture Debate?* Cambridge, UK: Polity.

Lock, Margaret, and Vinh-Kim Nguyen. 2010. *An Anthropology of Biomedicine*. Malden, MA: Wiley-Blackwell.

Mainichi Shimbun. 2020. "*Sato oya itaku ritsu 'kikenteki na hikusa' shien dantai, kōrōshō ni jichitai keikaku no yarinaoshi yōsei*" ("Foster Care Placement Rates Are 'Dangerously Low'; Support Groups Call on the Ministry of Health, Labour and Welfare to Revise the Policy Plans of Localities"), March 16, 2020. https://mainichi.jp/articles/20200316/k00/00m/040/239000c.

Malabou, Catherine. 2008. *What Should We Do with Our Brain?* New York: Fordham University Press.

Mattingly, Cheryl. 1991. "The Narrative Nature of Clinical Reasoning." *American Journal of Occupational Therapy* 45 (11): 998–1005.

Mattingly, Cheryl. 1994. "The Concept of Therapeutic 'Emplotment.'" *Social Science and Medicine* 38 (6): 811–822.

Mattingly, Cheryl. 1998. *Healing Dramas and Clinical Plots: The Narrative Structure of Experience*. Cambridge, UK: Cambridge University Press.

Mauss, Marcel. 1973. "Techniques of the Body." *Economy and Society* 2 (1): 70–88.

Mazzarella, William. 2009. "Affect: What Is It Good For?" In *Enchantments of Modernity: Empire, Nation, Globalization*, edited by Saurabh Dube, 291–309. Oxford, UK: Routledge.

McCall, Robert B., and Christina J. Groark. 2015. "Research on Institutionalized Children: Implications for International Child Welfare Practitioners and Policymakers." *International Perspectives in Psychology* 4 (2): 142–159.

McKinnon, Susan, and Fennella Cannell, eds. 2013. *Vital Relations: Modernity and the Persistent Life of Kinship*. Santa Fe, NM: School for American Research Press.

McKinnon, Susan, and Sydel Silverman. 2005. "Introduction." In *Complexities: Beyond Nature & Nurture*, edited by Susan McKinnon and Sydel Silverman, 1–22. Chicago: University of Chicago Press.

McLaughlin, Levi. 2019. *Soka Gakkai's Human Revolution: The Rise of a Mimetic Nation in Modern Japan*. Honolulu: University of Hawai'i Press.

McLelland, Mark. 2009. "The Role of the '*Tōjisha*' in Current Debates about Sexual Minority Rights in Japan." *Japanese Studies* 29 (2): 193–207.

McLelland, Mark. 2011. "Japan's Queer Cultures." In *Routledge Handbook of Japanese Culture and Society*, edited by Victoria Bestor, Theodore C. Bestor, and Akiko Yamagata, 140–149. New York: Routledge.

Meloni, Maurizio. 2014. "How Biology Became Social, and What It Means for Social Theory." *Sociological Review* 62: 593–614.

Meloni, Maurizio. 2019. *Impressionable Biologies: From the Archaeology of Plasticity to the Sociology of Epigenetics*. New York: Routledge.

Merleau-Ponty, Maurice. 1968. *The Visible and the Invisible*. Translated by Alphonso Lingis. Evanston, IL: Northwestern University Press.

Miller, Laura. 2017. "Japan's Trendy Word Grand Prix and Kanji of the Year: Commodified Language Forms in Multiple Contexts." In *Language and Materiality: Ethnographic and Theoretical Explorations*, edited by Jillian R. Cavanaugh and Shalini Shankar, 43–62. Cambridge, UK: Cambridge University Press.

Ministry of Health, Labour and Welfare (MHLW). 2017. "*Atarashii shakaiteki yōgo bijon*" ("New Vision for Social Protective Care"). https://www.mhlw.go.jp/file/05-Shingikai-11901000-Koyoukintoujidoukateikyoku-Soumuka/0000173888.pdf.

Ministry of Health, Labour and Welfare (MHLW). 2019a. "*Shakaiteki yōgo no suishin ni mukete*" ("Advances in Social Protective Care"). https://www.mhlw.go.jp/content/000503210.pdf.

Ministry of Health, Labour and Welfare. 2019b. "*Minpōtō no ichibu o kaisei suru hōritsu an (tokubetsu yōshiengumi seido no minaoshi)*" ("Proposal for the Revision of One Part of the Civil Code [Reconsidering Special Adoption]"). https://www.mhlw.go.jp/content/12601000/000484802.pdf.

Ministry of Health, Labour and Welfare and Head of the Child and Family Division (MHLW). 2011. "*Sato oya itaku gaidorain ni tsuite*" ("About Foster Parent Placement Guidelines"). March 30, 2011. https://www.mhlw.go.jp/stf/shingi/2r98520000018h6g-att/2r98520000018hlp.pdf.

Mitsubishi UFJ Research and Consulting (MUFG). 2021. "*Jidō yōgo shisetsu nado e no nyūsho sochi ya sato oya itaku nado ga kaijō sareta mono no jittai hāku ni kan suru zenkoku chōsa*" ("Survey of Care Leavers from Child Welfare Institutions and Family-Based Foster Care"). https://www.mhlw.go.jp/content/11900000/000863975.pdf.

Miyazaki, Hirokazu. 2006. "Economy of Dreams: Hope in Global Capitalism and Its Critiques." *Cultural Anthropology* 21 (2): 147–172.

Morris, Meaghan. 1997. "Foreword." In *Translation and Subjectivity: On 'Japan' and Cultural Nationalism* by Naoki Sakai, ix–xxii. Minneapolis: University of Minnesota Press.

Müller-Wille, Staffan, and Hans-Jörg Rheinberger. 2012. *A Cultural History of Heredity*. Chicago: University of Chicago Press.

Nagano, Saki. 2017. *Shakaiteki yōgo no moto de sodatsu wakamono no "raifuchansu" (The "Life Chances" of Young People Raised in the Child Welfare System)*. Tokyo, Japan: Akashi shoten.

Nakane, Chie. 1967. *Kinship and Economic Organization in Rural Japan*. New York: Humanities Press.

Narahara, Shinya, and Takashi Masuzawa. 2012. "*Jidō fukushi shisetsu ni okeru shinrishoku no ayumi*" ("History of Psychologists in Child Welfare Institutions"). In *Shakaiteki yōgo ni okeru seikatsu rinshō to shinri rinshō (Clinical Life and Clinical Psychology in Social Care)*, edited by Takashi Masuzawa and Kikuyo Aoki, 27–40. Tokyo, Japan: Fukumura shuppan.

National Society for the Study of Child Protection Issues. 2012. "*Jidō yōgo shisetsu shokuin no shigoto to katei no chōwa (wāku raifu baransu) no arikata ni kansuru chōsa kenkyū*" ("Survey Research on the Balance Between Work and Home [Work-Life Balance] for Child Welfare Institution Staff"). Project Results Report. https://www.nisshasai.jp/fukusijyoseijigyo/download/s25/n37_zenkoku_jidouyougo.pdf.

Needham, Rodney. 1960. "The Left Hand of the Mugwe: An Analytical Note on the Structure of Meru Symbolism." *Africa* 30 (1): 20–33.

Nelson, Charles A. III, Charles H. Zeanah, Nathan A. Fox, Peter J. Marshall, Anna T. Smyke, and Donald Guthrie. 2007. "Cognitive Recovery in Socially Deprived Young Children: The Bucharest Early Intervention Project." *Science* 318 (5858): 1937–1940.

Nelson, Katherine, and Robyn Fivush. 2000. "Socialization of Memory." In *The Oxford Handbook of Memory*, edited by Endel Tulving and Fergus I. M. Craik, 283–295. Oxford, UK: Oxford University Press.

Nelson, Katherine, and Robyn Fivush. 2004. "The Emergence of Autobiographical Memory: A Social Cultural Developmental Theory." *Psychological Review* 111 (2): 486–511.

Nelson, Maggie. 2015. *The Argonauts*. Minneapolis, MN: Graywolf.

NHK *muen shakai purojekuto shuzaihan* (Society without Connections News Team), ed. 2010. *Muen shakai* (*Society without Connections*). Tokyo, Japan: Bungeishunjū.

Nemtzov, Florence Treyvaud. 2019. "Be the Change! Improving Outcomes for Care Leavers." Innsbruck, Austria: SOS Children's Villages International.

Niewöhner, Jörg. 2011. "Epigenetics: Embedded Bodies and the Molecularisation of Biography and Milieu." *BioSocieties* 6 (3): 279–298.

Niewöhner, Jörg, and Margaret Lock. 2018. "Situating Local Biologies: Anthropological Perspectives on Environment/Human Entanglements." *BioSocieties* 13 (4): 681–697.

Nishida, Yoshimasa, ed. 2011. *Jidō yōgo shisetsu to shakaiteki haijō* (*Child Welfare Institutions and Social Exclusion*). Osaka, Japan: Kaiho shuppansha.

Nobe, Yōko. 2018. *Yōshiengumi no shakaigaku: "Nihonjin" ni totte "ketsuen" to wa nani ka* (*The Sociology of Adoption: What Are "Blood Ties" to "Japanese People"?*). Tokyo, Japan: Shinyosha.

Norbeck, Edward, and Harumi Befu. 1958. "Informal Fictive Kinship in Japan." *American Anthropologist* 60 (1): 102–117.

Nozawa, Shunsuke. 2012. "Discourses of the Coming: Ignorance, Forgetting, and Prolepsis in Japanese Life-Historiography." In *The Anthropology of Ignorance: An Ethnographic Approach*, edited by Casey High, Ann H. Kelly, and Jonathan Mair, 55–85. New York: Palgrave Macmillan.

Nozawa, Shunsuke. 2015. "Phatic Traces: Sociality in Contemporary Japan." *Anthropological Quarterly* 88 (2): 373–400.

Ochiai, Emiko. 1997. *The Japanese Family System in Transition*. Tokyo: LTCB International Library Foundation.

Ochs, Elinor, and Lisa Capps. 1996. "Narrating the Self." *Annual Review of Anthropology*. 19–43.

Oguma, Eiji. 2002. *A Genealogy of 'Japanese' Self-Images*. Melbourne, Australia: Trans Pacific.

Oka, Tomofumi. 2013. "Self-Help Groups in Japan: Historical Development and Current Issues." *International Journal of Self-Help and Self Care* 7 (2): 217–232.

Oliphant, Elayne. 2021. *The Privilege of Being Banal: Art, Secularism, and Catholicism in Paris*. Chicago: University of Chicago Press.

Omori, Hisako. 2016. "Creating Families: Tenrikyō Foster Homes in Japan." *Japanese Studies* 36 (2): 213–229.

Onchōen Children's Support Group. 2001. *Jidō shisetsu no jidō gyakutai* (*Abuse within Child Welfare Institutions*). Tokyo, Japan: Akashi shoten.

Ortega, Francisco. 2009. "The Cerebral Subject and the Challenge of Neurodiversity." *BioSocieties* 4: 425–445.

Ortega, Francisco, and Fernando Vidal. 2007. "Mapping the Cerebral Subject in Con- temporary Culture." *Electronic Journal of Communication Information and Inno- vation in Health* 1 (2): 255–259.

Ortner, Sherry B. 1972. "Is Female to Male as Nature Is to Culture?" *Feminist Studies* 1 (2): 5–31.

Oyama, Susan. 2000. *The Ontogeny of Information: Developmental Systems and Evolu- tion.* Durham, NC: Duke University Press.

Pasupathi, Monisha. 2001. "The Social Construction of the Personal Past and Its Impli- cations for Adult Development." *Psychological Bulletin* 127 (5): 651.

Paulson, Joy Larsen. 2010. *Family Law Reform in Postwar Japan.* Bloomington, IN: Xli- bris Corporation.

Povinelli, Elizabeth A. 2002a. *The Cunning of Recognition: Indigenous Alterities and the Making of Australian Multiculturalism.* Durham, NC: Duke University Press.

Povinelli, Elizabeth A. 2002b. "Notes on Gridlock: Genealogy, Intimacy, Sexuality." *Pub- lic Culture* 14 (1): 215–238.

Povinelli, Elizabeth A. 2006. *The Empire of Love: Toward a Theory of Intimacy, Geneal- ogy, and Carnality.* Durham, NC: Duke University Press.

Quinn, Naomi, and Jeannette Marie Mageo. 2013. "Attachment and Culture: An Intro- duction." In *Attachment Reconsidered: Cultural Perspectives on a Western Theory,* edited by Naomi Quinn and Jeannette Marie Mageo, 3–32. New York: Palgrave MacMillan.

Rakugi, Akiko. 2006. "*Kazoku: Ketsuen naki 'ketsuen kankei'*" ("Family: 'Blood Rela- tionship' without a Blood Tie"). In *Komyunitī no gurupu dainamikkusu (Group Dynamics of Community),* edited by Toshio Sugiman, 239–270. Kyoto, Japan: Kyoto University Press.

Rapp, Rayna. 1999. *Testing Women, Testing the Fetus: The Social Impact of Amniocentesis in America.* New York: Routledge.

Rasell, Jennifer. 2020. *Care of the State: Relationships, Kinship and the State in Children's Homes in Late Socialist Hungary.* London: Palgrave Macmillan.

Reavey, Paula, and Steven D. Brown. 2007. "Rethinking Agency in Memory: Space and Embodiment in Memories of Child Sexual Abuse." *Journal of Social Work Practice* 21 (1): 5–21.

Reavey, Paula, and Steven D. Brown. 2009. "The Mediating Role of Objects in Recollec- tions of Adult Women Survivors of Child Sexual Abuse." *Culture & Psychology* 15 (4): 463–484.

Rees, Tobias. 2010. "Being Neurologically Human Today: Life and Science and Adult Cerebral Plasticity (an Ethical Analysis)." *American Ethnologist* 37 (1): 150–166.

Reitan, Richard. 2012. "Narratives of 'Equivalence': Neoliberalism in Contemporary Japan." *Radical History Review* 112: 43–64.

Roberts, Elizabeth F. S., and Camilo Sanz. 2017. "Bioethnography: A How to Guide for the Twenty-First Century." In *The Palgrave Handbook of Biology and Society,* edited by Maurizio Meloni, John Cromby, Des Fitzgerald, and Stephanie Lloyd, 749–775. London: Palgrave Macmillan.

Roberts, Glenda. 2002. "Pinning Hopes on Angels: Reflections from an Aging Japan's Urban Landscape." In *Family and Social Policy in Japan: Anthropological Approaches,* edited by Roger Goodman, 54–91. Cambridge, UK: Cambridge University Press.

Robertson, Jennifer. 1991. *Native and Newcomer: Making and Remaking a Japanese City.* Berkeley: University of California Press.

Robertson, Jennifer. 2002. "Blood Talks: Eugenic Modernity and the Creation of New Japanese." *History and Anthropology* 13 (3): 191–216.

Roebuck, Kristin. 2016. "Orphans by Design: 'Mixed-Blood' Children, Child Welfare, and Racial Nationalism in Postwar Japan." *Japanese Studies* 36 (2): 191–212.

Ronald, Richard, and Allison Alexy. 2011. "Continuity and Change in Japanese Homes and Families." In *Home and Family in Japan: Continuity and Transformation*, edited by Richard Ronald and Allison Alexy, 1–24. London: Routledge.

Rose, Nikolas. 1999. *Governing the Soul: The Shaping of the Private Self*. New York: Free Edition.

Rose, Nikolas, and Abi-Rached, J. M. 2013. *Neuro: The New Brain Sciences and the Management of the Mind*. Princeton, NJ: Princeton University Press.

Rose, Richard. 2012. *Life Story Therapy with Traumatized Children: A Model for Practice*. London: Jessica Kingsley.

Rose, Steven. 1998. *Lifelines: Biology Beyond Determinism*. Oxford, UK: Oxford University Press.

Rowe, Jane, and Lydia Lambert. 1973. *Children Who Wait: A Study of Children Needing Substitute Families*. London: Association of British Adoption Agencies.

Rubin, B. 2009. "Changing Brains: The Emergence of the Field of Adult Neurogenesis." *BioSocieties* 4: 407–424.

Rutherford, Danilyn. 2009. "Sympathy, State Building, and the Experience of Empire." *Cultural Anthropology* 24 (1): 1–32.

Rutherford, Danilyn. 2013. "Kinship and Catastrophe: Global Warming and the Rhetoric of Descent." In *Vital Relations: Modernity and the Persistent Life of Kinship*, edited by Susan McKinnon and Fenella Cannell, 261–282. Santa Fe, NM: School for Advanced Research.

Rutherford, Danilyn. 2015. "About Time." *Anthropological Quarterly* 88 (2): 241–249.

Rutter, Michael, and the English and Romanian Adoptees (ERA) Study Team. 1998. "Developmental Catch-Up, and Deficit, Following Adoption after Severe Global Early Privation." *Journal of Child Psychology and Psychiatry* 39 (4): 465–476.

Sahlins, Marshall D. 2011. "What Kinship Is," Parts I and II. *Journal of the Royal Anthropological Institute* (N.S.) 17: 2–19, 227–242.

Sahlins, Marshall D. 2013. *What Kinship Is—And Is Not*. Chicago: University of Chicago Press.

Saimura, Mari. 2009. *Umareta kazoku kara hanarete kurasu kodomotachi no tame no raifu sutōrī bukku* (*A Life Story Book for Children Living Apart from Their Families of Birth*). Tokyo, Japan: Fukumura shuppan.

Samejima, Kōji. 2006. *Kono ko o, kudasai* (*This Child, Please*). Tokyo, Japan: Aspect.

Samuels, Gina Miranda, and Julia M. Pryce. 2008. "'What Doesn't Kill You Makes You Stronger': Survivalist Self-Reliance as Resilience and Risk among Young Adults Aging Out of Foster Care." *Children and Youth Services Review* 30: 1198–1210.

Sand, Jordan. 2003. *House and Home in Modern Japan: Architecture, Domestic Space, and Bourgeois Culture, 1880–1930*. Cambridge, MA: Harvard University East Asia Center.

Scarry, Elaine. 1985. *The Body in Pain*. Oxford, UK: Oxford University Press.

Schneider, David. 1968. *American Kinship*. Chicago: University of Chicago Press.

Schneider, David. 1984. *Critique of the Study of Kinship*. Ann Arbor: University of Michigan Press.

Schwartz, Richard C. 2001. *Introduction to the Internal Family Systems Model*. Oak Park, IL: Trailheads.

Scott, Joan. 1991. "The Evidence of Experience." *Critical Inquiry* 17 (4): 773–797.

Shirai, Chiaki. 2010. "Reproductive Technologies and Parent-Child Relationships: Japan's Past and Present Examined through the Lens of Donor Insemination." *International Journal of Japanese Sociology* 19 (1): 19–35.

Shirai, Chiaki. 2013. *"Funin josei ga motsu hiketsuenteki oyako ni taisuru senkō ni tsuite"* ("Concerning the Preferences of Infertile Women Regarding Non-Blood-Related Children"). Shakaigaku nenshi 54: 69–84.

Silverberg, Miriam. 2007. "War Responsibility Revisited: Auschwitz in Japan." *Asia-Pacific Journal: Japan Focus*. http://japanfocus.org/-Miriam-Silverberg/2470.

Silverstein, Michael. 1993. "Metapragmatic Discourse and Metapragmatic Function." In *Reflexive Language: Reported Speech and Metapragmatics*, edited by John Lucy, 33–58. Cambridge, UK: Cambridge University Press.

Silverstein, Michael. 2004. "'Cultural' Concepts and the Language-Culture Nexus." *Current Anthropology* 45 (5): 621–652.

Smith, Wendy B. 2011. *Youth Leaving Foster Care: A Developmental, Relationship-Based Approach to Practice*. Oxford, UK: Oxford University Press.

Song, Jesook. 2009. *South Koreans in the Debt Crisis: The Creation of a Neoliberal Welfare State*. Durham, NC: Duke University Press.

Spiro, Melford E. 1972. *Children of the Kibbutz: A Study in Child Training and Personality*. New York: Schocken.

Stasch, Rupert. 2009. *Society of Others: Kinship and Mourning in a West Papuan Place*. Berkeley: University of California Press.

Strathern, Marilyn. 1992. *Reproducing the Future: Essays on Anthropology, Kinship and the New Reproductive Technologies*. New York: Routledge.

Stryker, Rachael. 2010. *The Road to Evergreen: Adoption, Attachment Therapy, and the Promise of Family*. Ithaca, NY: Cornell University Press.

Sugiyama, Toshirō. 2007. *Kodomo no gyakutai to iu daiyon no hattatsu shōgai (Child Abuse, the Fourth Type of Developmental Disability)*. Tokyo, Japan: Gakken Plus.

Supreme Court General Secretariat Family Affairs Bureau (*Saikōsaibansho jimu sōkyoku kateikyoku*). 2020. *"Shinken seigen jiken oyobi jidō fukushi-hō ni kitei suru jiken no gaikyō"* ("Overview of Parental Authority Restriction Cases and Cases Stipulated in the Child Welfare Act"). https://www.courts.go.jp/vc-files/courts/2020/20200515zigyakugaikyou_h31.pdf.

Sutton, John. 2008. "Between Individual and Collective Memory: Coordination, Interaction, Distribution." *Social Research*: 23–48.

Sutton, John, Celia B. Harris, Paul G. Keil, and Amanda J. Barnier. 2010. "The Psychology of Memory, Extended Cognition, and Socially Distributed Remembering." *Phenomenology and the Cognitive Sciences* 9 (4): 521–560.

Takahashi, Mutsuko. 2003. "Care for Children and Older People in Japan: Modernizing the Traditional." In *The Young, the Old and the State: Social Care Systems in Five Industrial Nations*, edited by Anneli Anttonen, John Baldock, and Jorma Sipilä, 81–108. Cheltenham, UK: Edward Elgar.

Takahashi, Mutsuko and Raija Hashimoto. 1997. "Minsei i'in—Between Public and Private: A Local Network for Community Care in Japan." *International Social Work* 40: 303–313.

Taussig, Michael. 1993. *Mimesis and Alterity: A Particular History of the Senses*. New York: Routledge.

Tenrikyo Doyusha. 2010. *"Tamashii no kazoku" no monogatari: Sato oya—kamisama ga musunda kizuna (The Story of the "Spirit Family": Foster Parents, the Bonds Created by God)*. Tenri: Tenrikyo Doyusha.

Thompson, Charis. 2005. *Making Parents: The Ontological Choreography of Reproductive Technology*. Cambridge, MA: The MIT Press.

Tokunaga, Shōko. 2011. *"Hikō rinshō ni okeru raifu sutorī wāku no jissen ni tsuite"* ("Application of Life Story Work for Delinquent Youth: A Case Study"). *Kodomo no gyakutai to negurekuto (Child Abuse and Neglect)* 13 (1): 47–54.

Tokyo Metropolitan Government Social Welfare and Public Health Bureau. 2011. *"Tōkyōto ni okeru jidō yōgo shisetsu nado taishosha e no ankēto chōsa hōkokusho"* ("A Survey of Tokyo Metropolis Careleavers from Institutional and Foster Care"). https://www.fukushi.metro.tokyo.lg.jp/kodomo/katei/taishosha-chosa.files/r4-1.pdf.

Tsuda, Takeyuki (Gaku). 2022. "Racism without Racial Difference? Co-ethnic Racism and National Hierarchies among Nikkeijin Ethnic Return Migrants in Japan." *Ethnic and Racial Studies* 45 (4): 595–615.

Tsuge, Azumi. 1999. *Bunka to shite seishoku gijutsu: Funin chiryo ni tazusawaru ishi no katari.* (*Reproductive Technology as Culture: Narratives of Japanese Doctors Regarding Infertility Treatment*). Kyoto, Japan: Shoraisha.

Tsuzaki, Tetsuo. 2009. *Kono kuni no kodomotachi: Yōhogo jidō shakaiteki yōgo no nihonteki kōchiku; otona no kitoku keneki to kodomo no fukushi* (*This Country's Children: Constructing Social Care for Children in Need of Care; The Vested Interests of Adults and Children's Welfare*). Tokyo, Japan: Nihon Kaijo Shuppan.

Ukai, Natsuko. 2010. *"Jidō yōgo shisetsu ni okeru rinshō shinrishi no katsudō jōkyō no chōsa oyobi kongo no kadai"* ("Survey of the Activities of Clinical Psychologists within Child Welfare Institutions and Future Issues"). *Osaka keidai ronshu* 60 (5): 241–252. https://www.i-repository.net/il/user_contents/02/G0000031Repository/repository/keidaironshu_060_005_241-252.pdf.

United Nations Committee on the Rights of the Child (UNCRC). 2010. Consideration of Reports Submitted by States Parties under Article 44 of the Convention: Convention on the Rights of the Child: Concluding Observations: Japan, 20 June, CRC/C/JPN/CO/3. http://www.unhcr.org/refworld/docid/4c32dea52.html.

Van der Kolk, Bessel A. 1994. "The Body Keeps the Score: Memory and the Evolving Psychobiology of Posttraumatic Stress." *Harvard Review of Psychiatry* 1 (5): 253–265.

Vlastos, Stephen, ed. 1998. *Mirror of Modernity: Invented Traditions of Modern Japan.* Berkeley: University of California Press.

Vorria, Panayiota, Zaira Papaligoura, Jasmin Sarafidou, Maria Kopakaki, Judy Dunn, Marinus H. Van IJzendoorn, and Antigoni Kontopoulou. 2006. "The Development of Adopted Children after Institutional Care: A Follow-Up Study." *Journal of Child Psychology and Psychiatry* 47 (12): 1246–1253.

Walker, Alan, and Chack-kie Wong. 2005. "Introduction: East Asian Welfare Regimes." In *East Asian Welfare Regimes in Transition: From Confucianism to Globalisation,* edited by Alan Walker and Chack-kie Wong, 3–20. Bristol, UK: Policy Press, University of Bristol.

Watanabe, Chika. 2019. *Becoming One: Religion, Development, and Environmentalism in a Japanese NGO in Myanmar.* Honolulu: University of Hawai'i Press.

Watanabe, Yōhei. 2016. *"Jidō yōgo shisetsu ni okeru shinrishoku no senmonsei ni tsuite no bunkenteki kentō"* ("A Literature Examination of Professionalism among Child Welfare Institution Psychologists"). *Hokuseigakuendaigaku daigakuin ronshū* 7: 131–139. https://hokusei.repo.nii.ac.jp/?action=repository_action_common_download&item_id=2122&item_no=1&attribute_id=45&file_no=1.

Weismantel, Mary. 1995. "Making Kin: Kinship Theory and Zumbagua Adoptions." *American Ethnologist* 22 (4): 685–709.

Weiss, Brad. 1996. *The Making and Unmaking of the Haya Lived World.* Durham, NC: Duke University Press.

Weston, Kath. 1991. *Families We Choose: Lesbians, Gays, Kinship.* New York: Columbia University Press.

White, Linda. 2018. *Gender and the Koseki in Contemporary Japan: Surname, Power, and Privilege.* Oxford, UK: Routledge.

White, Merry Isaacs. 2002. *Perfectly Japanese: Making Families in an Era of Upheaval.* Berkeley: University of California Press.

Wilson, Elizabeth. 2004. *Psychosomatic: Feminism and the Neurological Body.* Durham, NC: Duke University Press.

Winnicott, Donald Woods. 1992. *Babies and their Mothers.* Cambridge, MA: Perseus.

Winter, Alison. 2012. *Memory: Fragments of a Modern History.* Chicago: University of Chicago Press.

Wozniak, Danielle F. 2002. *They're All My Children: Foster Mothering in America.* New York: New York University Press.

Yamamoto, Chikao, Shinya Narahara, Shōko Tokunaga, and Shūzō Hirata, eds. 2015. *Raifu sutorī wāku nyumon (Life Story Work Manual).* Tokyo, Japan: Akashi shoten.

Yamanta, Tokuji, and Ikuko Yorozuya. 2015. *'Akachan engumi' de gyakutaishi o nakusu: Aichi hōshiki gatsunaida inochi (Eliminating Deaths from Abuse through Infant Adoption).* Tokyo, Japan: Kōbunsha.

Yanagisako, Sylvia, and Jane Collier. 1987. "Toward a Unified Analysis of Gender and Kinship." In *Gender and Kinship: Essays Toward a Unified Analysis,* edited by Sylvia Yanagisako and Jane Collier, 14–50. Stanford, CA: Stanford University Press.

Yanagisako, Sylvia Junko. 2002. *Producing Culture and Capital: Family Firms in Italy.* Princeton, NJ: Princeton University Press.

Yngvesson, Barbara. 2010. *Belonging in an Adopted World: Race, Identity, and Transnational Adoption.* Chicago: University of Chicago Press.

Yonemoto, Marcia. 2016. *The Problem of Women in Early Modern Japan.* Berkeley: University of California Press.

Yoneyama, Lisa. 1995. "Memory Matters: Hiroshima's Korean Atom Bomb Memorial and the Politics of Ethnicity." *Public Culture* 7: 499–527.

Yoshimura, Miyuki, and Yuzuru Yoshimura. 2022. "*Jidō yōgo shisetsu no shokuba kankyō ni kansuru kenkyū—shussan ikujichū no shokuin ga hataraki tsuzukerareru yōken no kōsatsu*" ("A Study on the Working Conditions of Children's Care Homes— Analysis of the Conditions for Employees Who Are Giving Birth or Child Rearing to Continue Working"). *Annual Report of the Nagoya University of Arts Institute of Human Development* 10: 1–10. https://www.nua.ac.jp/research/files/pdf/00e6a 9e06d2ef2a8d34fb171a34a5315.pdf.

Young, Allan. 1997. *The Harmony of Illusions: Inventing Post-traumatic Stress Disorder.* Princeton, NJ: Princeton University Press.

Zeanah, Charles H., Anna T. Smyke, Sebastian F. Koga, and Elizabeth Carlson. 2005. "Attachment in Institutionalized and Community Children in Romania." *Child Development* 76 (5): 1015–1028.

Zeanah, Charles H., Charles A. Nelson, Nathan A. Fox, Anna T. Smyke, Peter Marshall, Susan W. Parker, and Sebastian Koga. 2003. "Designing Research to Study the Effects of Institutionalization on Brain and Behavioral Development: The Bucharest Early Intervention Project." *Development & Psychopathology* 15: 885–890.

Zelizer, Viviana A. 1985. *Pricing the Priceless Child: The Changing Social Value of Children.* Princeton, NJ: Princeton University Press.

Zelizer, Viviana A. 2000. "The Purchase of Intimacy." *Law & Social Inquiry* 25 (3): 817–884.

Index

abuse: in child welfare institutions, 120, 187n1; and embodiment, 101–2, 167; in family of origin, 139; group care as, 119, 182n10; memory of, 169–70. *See also* neglect; trauma

adoption: attitudes regarding, 31–32, 87, 89, 90, 91, 93; and child welfare institutions, 6, 48–49; and fostering, 30–31; framing of adoptive kinship as obligatory, 40–41; and genealogical continuity, 87–89; in Japanese historical context, 9, 87; and kinship technologies, 28–29; and *kizuna*, 43–45; motivations for, 31; process, 6; "promiscuous," 9, 83–89; refusal of, 156–57; rights of adopted children, 185n14; son-in-law, 9, 85–86, 87, 89, 185n6; special, 31, 87, 88–89, 182n12, 183n20, 185n13; and stigma and secrecy regarding children in state care, 33–36; traditional / "feudal," 31; transnational and transracial, 186n16; and violence of blood ties, 11

adulthood, parenthood and perception of, 90, 91

Ainsworth, Mary, 120, 121

Ainu people, 183n19

Alexy, Allison, 7, 66, 182n15, 183n21

anshin (secure), 109, 115, 117–18, 179

anzen (safe), 179

appearance: and kinship ties, 29, 34, 36–37, 41, 45; and ontology, 46–47

approximation, mimetic, 52–53, 74–75, 180

aspirational normalcy, 74–75, 180

attachment theory / attachment disorder, 46, 112–17, 191n12, 192n24

autobiographical memory, 164

Bamba, Sachiko, 194n14

Barad, Karen, 105, 191n9

Bartlett, Frederic C., 165–66, 196n13

belonging, 174–76, 189n2

Benedict, Ruth, 181n4

bioethnography, 190n3

biology: and fragility of kinship ties, 75–76; intra-action between culture and, 104–5; local biologies, 104, 110, 191n8; social history of culture and, 105–6. *See also* embodiment

biosocial differentiation, 110

birthdays, 61–62

birthrate, decline in, 84, 177

blood ties: and connection, 76, 77, 78, 92–93; contemporary rhetoric concerning, 45, 184n4; intimacy and affect ascribed to, 10, 11, 91; in Japanese historical context, 8–11, 177; and kinship among Ainu people, 183n19; and national and cultural membership, 183n29; violence of, 8, 11

blood type, 34–35, 37, 39

bodily signs and characteristics. *See* embodiment

Bourdieu, Pierre, 125, 154, 164

Bowlby, John, 120, 121–22, 192n24

Brazil, return migrants from, 183n29

Brown, Steven, 172

Browne, Kevin, 192n19

buraku people, 183n29

Burgess, Chris, 196n6

Capps, Lisa, 163, 164, 195n4

Carsten, Janet, 45, 66, 190n4

Caruth, Cathy, 168, 170, 196n18

chance: child welfare system as depending on, 130–31; in leaving state care, 128–30, 131–32; and starting from disadvantage, 136–48; and *tōjisha* communities, 133–36

Chapman, Christopher, 181n8

chewing, 111

Chiaki, Shirai, 8, 20, 92–93

childbearing: and conceptions of life paths, 91–92, 94; and love for others' children, 90–91, 93; remediating familial loss through, 99–100

child development, 110–11, 116–19, 124, 190n1, 191n14

child guidance centers (CGC), 5, 57, 155, 157, 159, 160, 188n10

childhood memory, 153–54

child of a stranger, 90–94

Children's Views and Voices (CVV), 193n1, 194n10

child rights, 119

www.ingramcontent.com/pod-product-compliance
Lightning Source LLC
Chambersburg PA
CBHW030312270326
41926CB00010B/1338